Suffering and Surviving
Finding Sunshine in the Storm

Tom Baca
Melodee Cooper
Rachel Gardner

Brighton Publishing LLC
435 N. Harris Drive
Mesa, AZ 85203

SUFFERING AND SURVIVING

FINDING SUNSHINE IN THE STORM

TOM BACA
MELODEE COOPER
RACHEL GARDNER

BRIGHTON PUBLISHING LLC
435 N. HARRIS DRIVE
MESA, AZ 85203
WWW.BRIGHTONPUBLISHING.COM

ISBN13: 978-1-62183-414-4
ISBN 10:1-62183-414-X

PRINTED IN THE UNITES STATES OF AMERICA

First Edition

COVER DESIGN: TOM RODRIGUEZ

COVER PHOTOGRAPH: AMBER HAGEN

Dedication

To Kathy McGuire, a woman whose veins were filled with the milk of human kindness.

To Stephen, Kyle, Ryan, and Evan, a few of the most important reasons for Melodee's survival.

To all those who have been challenged by the devastating effects of cancer.

Prologue

*"We are all visitors to this time, this place.
We are just passing through. Our purpose here is
to observe, to learn, to grow, to love...and then
we return home."*

~Proverb

The topic of why people suffer has been discussed since the creation of mankind. Adam and Eve were admonished, "...cursed is the ground for thy sake; in sorrow shalt thou eat of it all the days of thy life."

[1] From our first parents, down to the current day, suffering reaches all. No one is untouched by grief or pain. Whether wealthy or poor, bond or free, all will experience tragic circumstances. Each person enters this world with the initial shock of leaving the comfort of a mother's womb, and continues facing tribulation throughout mortality. If a person has never suffered, he has never lived.

Our fears are a manifestation of our suffering. People fear death for many reasons, but when sufferings become unbearable they willingly accept death to end the pain. In most cases death is not the worst thing that can happen to a person. The worst thing that can happen to people is that they never live; that they never take advantage of the tremendous potential in them to make a difference in life. Regardless of an individual's suffering, the best way to prepare for death is to live life with a purpose. There are no excuses for not truly living, no matter what suffering a person may experience. God's gift to us is mortal life; our gift to God is what we do with that life.

Of all the possible trials of mortality, few phrases strike more fear in a person than "you have cancer." One possible reason is that the treatment of cancer itself is barbaric and causes great anguish, misery, and pain. The best hope for a cancer survivor is to remain in remission, because the body can never be completely cured of the disease.

The human body is extremely complex and is made up of more than thirty-seven trillion cells, the building blocks of tissues and organs. There are over 100 different types of cancer, with each being classified by the type of cell that is initially affected. For a cancer to start, certain changes take place within the genes of a cell or a group of cells. Normally the body's control systems ensure that cells grow and reproduce in an orderly and controlled manner. Replacement cells are produced to keep the body healthy, but sometimes things go wrong.

A former doctor explained, "Cancer can be an insidious, almost subtle encroachment upon and within your body, or it can be a blatant, almost consumptive disease that very quickly saps your vitality. The variation of types of cancer is reflected in the variation of treatments. The treatment of choice for many cancers entails a combination of drugs, or chemotherapy, radiation, or radiotherapy, or surgical intervention. Unfortunately, sometimes these are not successful. The very best thing one can do is to be informed. Get information anywhere you can and do not be afraid. Remember the cowardly die a thousand times; the brave, only once. Live your life so that you have no regrets and have a positive attitude. Remember, nothing succeeds like optimism. Yes some people die from cancer, but more live, and that is the optimism of life."[2] This sense of optimism is essential to overcoming the challenge of cancer, as well as any other form of suffering.

Because everyone suffers, Rabbi Harold Kushner's popular book, *"When Bad Things Happen to Good People"* attracted countless readers. Those who feel tragedy is a form of divine punishment have debated Kushner's conclusion, that suffering is not punishment from a cruel God. One such example can be found in the life of Horatio Spafford, a prominent American lawyer, best known for penning the Christian hymn *It Is Well With My Soul*. Spafford had invested in real estate north of an expanding Chicago in the spring of 1871. When the Great Fire of Chicago reduced the city to ashes in October of that same year, it destroyed most of Spafford's sizable investment. Two years later, in 1873, Spafford lost his four daughters in a tragic boat accident. On February 11, 1880 their son, Horatio Goertner Spafford died of scarlet fever at the age of four.[3] The Presbyterian Church his family attended at the time considered these experiences to be a form of punishment from God. Spafford left the church. Spafford had every reason to "curse God and die." Instead, he founded a new sect dubbed, 'The Overcomers,' and dedicated his life to running soup kitchens, hospitals, orphanages and other charitable ventures in Israel during WW1.[4] The interesting thing is that Spafford was not a Jew.

In order to better understand why people suffer, serious questions must be asked. However, as Tad Callister, a prolific writer pointed out, "Not all questions are of equal value." Some questions are of such a deep and soul-searching nature "That, if explored, they not only inform us, but they change

iv

us."[5] The authors hope that in seeking the answers to the questions of why we suffer, the reader might find hope and be changed for the better.

All suffering is shared. God the Father, an omnipotent (all powerful), omniscient (all knowing), and omnipresent (ever present) being, loved his Only Begotten Son in the flesh, yet watched Him take upon Himself all the sufferings of the world. Jesus was humiliated, beaten, slapped, and punched by Roman Soldiers. He was abused by the Sanhedrin, crowned with thorns, spit upon, and scourged with a whip that tore his flesh. He was then made to carry his own cross to his death by crucifixion. God suffered so that we could receive eternal life, and we suffer so that we can show our absolute commitment to follow Him.

This book takes the reader through the lives of a few modern day Jobs - individuals who seem to suffer in the extreme. Heroic figures such as Jesus, Job, the Apostle Paul, Mother Teresa, and others will also be discussed. We invite you to follow the full story of Melodee, a two-time cancer survivor, and gain glimpses of other personal trials throughout the book in the hope of gaining a better understanding of why we suffer. Even though this book was written primarily for the Christian community, it is our hope that there are some things of great value for anyone who has suffered.

It Is Well With My Soul

When peace, like a river, attendeth my way,
When sorrows like sea billows roll;
Whatever my lot, Thou hast taught me to say,
It is well, it is well with my soul.
It is well (it is well),
With my soul (with my soul),
It is well, it is well with my soul.
Though Satan should buffet, though trials
should come,
Let this blest assurance control,
That Christ hath regarded my helpless estate,
And hath shed His own blood for my soul.
My sin, oh the bliss of this glorious thought!
My sin, not in part but the whole,
Is nailed to His cross, and I bear it no more,
Praise the Lord, praise the Lord, O my soul!
For me, be it Christ, be it Christ hence to live:
If Jordan above me shall roll,
No pain shall be mine, for in death as in life
Thou wilt whisper Thy peace to my soul.
And Lord haste the day, when the faith shall be
sight,
The clouds be rolled back as a scroll;
The trump shall resound, and the Lord shall
descend,
Even so, it is well with my soul.

Introduction

THE ORIGINS OF SUFFERING—MORTALITY AND IMPERFECTION

"ULTIMATELY, MAN SHOULD NOT ASK WHAT THE MEANING OF HIS LIFE IS, BUT RATHER MUST RECOGNIZE THAT IT IS HE WHO IS ASKED. IN A WORD, EACH MAN IS QUESTIONED BY LIFE; AND HE CAN ONLY ANSWER TO LIFE BY ANSWERING FOR HIS OWN LIFE; TO LIFE HE CAN ONLY RESPOND BY BEING RESPONSIBLE."

~VIKTOR E. FRANKL

We live in a world where both good and bad things happen to everyone. Women die in childbirth, babies are born with defects, and young and innocent children are kidnapped and killed. People die tragically of cancer, leukemia, and from a variety of genetic diseases over which they have no control. Earthquakes and natural disasters kill thousands of innocent people. Human beings battle depression, loneliness, and all kinds of mental challenges and disorders. Marriages break up, and children are abused in families. All suffer adversity of one kind or another, and there are some individuals who seem to suffer extraordinary trials in mortality. All kinds of tragedies occur all over the world, many unique to a certain people or region, yet the one word most often uttered in response to suffering is simply, "Why?"

Why? This is the question often asked by those in the midst of suffering. For as many individuals as have lived and will live on this earth, there are as many individual types of suffering, as well as variations in the answers to the question of 'why?' The answer that seems to fit for every person and for all types of suffering is simple in its complexity: Because each of us has much to learn, and part of being mortal is to suffer. Both good and bad things happen to all of mankind, so instead of simply asking why bad things happen to good people, one could dig deeper and ask the more basic question, "Why do *things* happen at all?"

There is a plan for mortality. We live in a mortal world of physical, natural, and man-made challenges. We are made in the image of God. However, if God directed our every action, we would be nothing but robots or puppets. We would have no freedom of choice and therefore have no growth. That is not God's plan.

We are here on earth for a mortal experience, one that proves to God that we are worthy to return to Him. C.S. Lewis said, "If we find ourselves with a desire that nothing in this world can satisfy, the most probable explanation is that we were made for another world."[6] Nevertheless, this earth is the only world we have now, so we have to make the most of it. Many people believe that the suffering of this world is detrimental. They cannot fathom why a God, who is both good and great, could allow anyone to suffer. Rabbi Kushner concluded that God wants the best for everyone and does not desire for anyone to suffer. But since men do suffer, God does not stop the suffering. Suffering is necessary for our growth. Suffering, according to Kushner, is an important part of man's progression. [7] This progression lasts all of mortality and follows into the eternities.

From the time we are born, we are on a steep learning curve. We first learn to bond with people, to study the world around us, to cry, to laugh, and to communicate at higher levels. Every person who has ever lived has experienced difficulties directly related to the human, mortal body. From the time of the first breath down to the last, humans feel pain and sorrow. In learning to walk, we stumble and fall; enduring bumps and bruises for the sake of mobility. None among us can escape life without scars of one kind or another. Our imperfect bodies are wired to feel pain, indicating that pain is inevitable. We suffer because we are imperfect, mortal beings.

We were born with imperfections, but God's plan for us is to progress and learn through the challenges of mortality. Mark Twain once said, "The two most important days in your life are the day you are born and the day you find out why." [8] The amount of growth required from conception to birth is pretty much limited to a certain time frame. There is, however, no set duration for that second most important day to occur, the day when each person awakens to the reality that life has a purpose, that he is a part of that purpose, and that the path to discover that purpose is sometimes rocky. This journey is the 'why' of life, and it could take a lifetime to understand! In the meantime, there will most likely be difficult days in that discovery. Are we just to accept that a trial is simply "part of life," especially when accepting that fact does little to make trials less tragic?

The suffering involved in the human condition is universal and connects us. Suffering invites us to be radically human with one another, perhaps doing nothing more than reaching across the table, clasping hands, and weeping together. We are afforded the chance to create a safe place for someone else to mourn. You cannot possibly give a sufficient answer to the reason behind another's suffering, so in the moment, don't try. Nothing is needed but space, proximity, presence, and empathy. Grief cannot be sidestepped; it must be endured, so may we be people who endure with one another rather than constantly mitigating, explaining, or propping up. Let's just hold one another through the dark night and wait for the sun to rise.[9]

In God's Plan, our reason for coming here was to experience great joy, to be tested and to suffer. Mortality and adversity seem to go hand in hand, as this world is filled with countless challenges. It has been said, "Some of our greatest tribulations are the result of our own foolishness and weakness and occur because of our own carelessness or transgression"[10] Other afflictions are the result of disease and weakness of the mortal body. Some adversity is the result of wicked individuals misusing their agency. God's judgments against the wicked can bring famine, pestilence, earthquakes, and other tribulations. Trials and suffering are the norm in this life, not the exception.

According to Dallin H. Oaks, a former College President and religious leader, "Adversity will be a constant or occasional companion for each of us throughout our lives. We cannot avoid it. The only question is how we will react to it. Will our adversities be stumbling blocks or stepping-stones?"[11] The answer to that question in each of our lives will be found in our response to the unique suffering as well as in the entire story of our lives. What will truly matter when the end of mortality is near? Atul Gawande speaking about what matters most in mortal life, stated:

"In the end, people don't view their life as merely the average of all of its moments—which, after all, is mostly nothing much plus some sleep. For human beings, life is meaningful because it is a story. A story has a sense of a whole, and its arc is determined by the significant moments, the ones where something happens. Measurements of people's minute-by-minute levels of pleasure and pain miss this fundamental aspect of human existence. A seemingly happy life may be empty. A seemingly difficult life may be devoted to a great cause. We have purposes larger than ourselves. Unlike your experiencing self—which is absorbed in the moment—your remembering self is attempting to recognize not only the peaks of joy and valleys of misery but also how the story fits as a whole.

"That is profoundly affected by how things ultimately turn out. Why would a football fan let a few flubbed minutes at the end of the game ruin three hours of bliss? Because a football game is a story. And in stories, endings matter. Yet we also recognize that the experiencing self should not be ignored. The peak and the ending are not the only things that count. In favoring the moment of intense joy over steady happiness, the remembering self is hardly always wise.

"An inconsistency is built into the design of our minds. We have strong preferences about the duration of our experiences of pain and pleasure. We want pain to be brief and pleasure to last. But our memory... has evolved to represent the most intense moment of an episode of pain or pleasure (the peaks) and the feelings when the episode was at its end. A memory that neglects duration will not serve our preference for long pleasure and short pains. When our time is limited and we are uncertain about how best to serve our priorities, we are forced to deal with the fact that both the experiencing self and the remembering self-matter. We do not want to endure long pain and short pleasure. Yet certain pleasures can make enduring suffering worthwhile. The peaks are important, and so is the ending."[12]

Although suffering is part of the story of each of our lives, the important memories scripted during the strife give the story greater significance. Through those arcs of both good and bad times, we develop faith that there is always the reward of a new day, the blessing of service from our fellow man, and the promise of hope.

It is said that Abraham Lincoln, the sixteenth President of the United States, was not a churchgoer, but he understood *The King James Bible* (KJB) and read it every day. He suffered through many challenges because of the circumstances of his day. The following was said in his inaugural address:

"Fondly do we hope, fervently do we pray, that this mighty scourge of war may speedily pass away. Yet, if God wills that it continue until all the wealth piled by the bondsman's two hundred and fifty years of unrequited toil shall be sunk, and until every drop of blood drawn with the lash shall be paid by another drawn with the sword, as was said three thousand years ago, so still it must be said "the judgments of the Lord are true and righteous altogether."[13]

Lincoln had come to understand God's plan for mortality. He had found the hope that even when life's challenges seem greater than one can bear - with no end in sight - one can still look to God for comfort and find faith to believe that all will be well in the end.

This faith stems partly from teachings in Genesis that God is in control, and we need not be overly concerned with our current suffering, for it is short lived.[14] When we place trust in that truth, we begin to seek what can be learned from trials, rather than simply suffering needlessly. We begin to see that, as difficult as trials may be, there are great lessons to be learned from them. We see that there can be beneficial effects of adversity.[15] James E. Faust, a religious leader, taught about how adversity fits in with God's plan for mortality when he said, "In the pain, the agony, and the heroic endeavors of life, we pass through a refiner's fire, and the insignificant and the unimportant in our lives can melt away like dross and make our faith bright, intact, and strong. In this way the divine image can be mirrored from the soul. It is part of the purging toll exacted of some to become acquainted with God. In the agonies of life, we seem to listen better to the faint, godly whisperings of the Divine Shepherd."[16] In essence, although suffering is not a desirable thing, there is light at the end of our journey. We often see the cause of adversity first; but it is more important that we learn to recognize how the Lord uses this adversity to perfect us. *There is sunshine in the storm.* It is up to each of us to find it in the midst of our own adversity.

Some of the most profound light during the storm of suffering can be seen through the comforting words of the scriptures, particularly the words of Isaiah. Isaiah spoke frequently of the Messiah's mission and described His humiliation and sufferings. Isaiah prophesied that Jesus Christ would make His soul an offering for our sins, our sorrows, and all the pains we would endure in this life. It was a prophecy that would be fulfilled in the meridian of time. Isaiah's prophecy was written a thousand years before Jesus Christ himself preached about His life and declared that He would bear our suffering.

Isaiah and other prophets wrote eloquently about the Savior's grief and His role in overcoming the sorrow that all of mankind would endure in mortality.

"He is despised and rejected of men; a man of sorrows, and acquainted with grief: and we hid as it were *our* faces from him; he was despised, and we esteemed him not. Surely he hath borne our grief, and carried our sorrows: yet we did esteem him stricken, smitten of God, and afflicted. But he *was* wounded for our transgressions, *he was* bruised for our iniquities: the chastisement of our peace *was* upon him; and with his stripes we are healed. All we like sheep have gone astray; we have turned everyone to his own way; and the Lord hath laid on him the iniquity of us all."[17]

We also read, "[Christ] shall go forth, suffering pains and afflictions and temptations of every kind; and ... he will take upon him the pains and the sicknesses of his people...."[18] Because Christ experienced the feelings associated with all human pains and suffering, He is the most prepared to give aid and supply comfort unique to each individual. He has suffered all, that all may be healed through Him.

Much of Christ's mortal ministry was devoted to blessing and healing the sick with all kinds of maladies—physical, emotional, and spiritual. "And I beheld multitudes of people who were sick, and who were afflicted with all manner of diseases. ... And they were healed by the power of the Lamb of God."[19]

We too can be healed through the power of the Lamb of God, but not all healing comes at once, or even completely during mortality. We must learn humility and patience, as Job did, even while in the midst of great suffering. We should "be patient in afflictions, for we shall have many."[20] Patience is often thought of as a quiet, passive trait. A religious leader,

Dieter F. Uchtdorf said, "Patience is not passive resignation, nor is it failing to act because of our fears. Patience means active waiting and enduring. It means staying with something … even when the desires of our hearts are delayed. Patience is not simply enduring; it is enduring well."[21] When patience in mortality is mastered and we have the hope to "endure to the end," then will the story of our suffering turn to one of surviving.[22]

How can we endure when bad news seems to be endless? Stories of natural disasters, terrorism, and wars fill the nightly newscasts with negativity. Why didn't God create an earth where bad things, misery, and pain simply could not exist? Isn't God perfect? Shouldn't everything He creates be perfect, as well?

God *is* perfect. He has structured a world tailored for our joy, as well as for our individual growth and progression. However, we cannot progress without being tested. Every person on earth is known to God and is unique. Each person has an individual fingerprint that is not duplicated in any other individual. Each person is unique in intelligence and unique in his ability to return to God. Because man is unique, God has an individual plan designed for each of us. God lays out that plan in the book of Moses, *"For behold, this is my work and my glory—to bring to pass the immortality and eternal life of man."* [23] God's work is to help us pass through this mortal life, learning all we need to learn to return back to Him. He wants us to experience great joy, but understands that part of mortality includes great suffering. God's glory comes through helping us learn to navigate life's storms and find the sunshine on the other side. Mortality is the time when we, as imperfect beings, must learn how to survive. We must endure the pain, grief, heartache, and sorrow of life's great storms. We must learn to see the light of hope and trust that God knows each of us. We must strive to discover the source of all light and accept that we can survive through any suffering by seeking out sunshine in the storms. Suffering spans across this mortal existence, but truly surviving means rising above and discovering our unique answers for why each of us suffers. God allows bad things to happen so we can learn the lessons of mortality. Living is suffering, but living is also surviving.

Chapter One

MELODEE'S STORY

*"IF THERE IS A MEANING IN LIFE AT ALL, THEN THERE
MUST BE A MEANING IN SUFFERING. SUFFERING IS A PART
OF LIFE, EVEN AS FATE AND DEATH. WITHOUT SUFFERING
AND DEATH HUMAN LIFE CANNOT BE COMPLETE."*

~VIKTOR FRANKL, MAN'S SEARCH FOR MEANING

THE SCANS

The last thing a thirty-three-year-old mother of three boys should be worrying about is scheduling a mammogram, especially so close to the holidays.

"Yet, here I am," thought Melodee Cooper, as she made the call her OB/GYN had recommended. *"This is such a waste of time!" she told herself. "Even Dr. Smith said the lump was most likely swollen lymph nodes or possibly glandular tissue. I only weaned Evan from breastfeeding a few weeks ago. Maybe I'm just being paranoid."*

Mel thought back to only weeks before when her husband, Stephen, had first discovered the abnormality. "You know you have a lump here, don't you?" Stephen guided her hand to the area deep under her left breast, and she certainly felt something she'd never noticed before. However, the hardened tissue was similar to tissue she'd felt during difficulties with breastfeeding. Even though Stephen had encouraged it, she barely followed through with making an appointment for a breast exam. In fact, even when Dr. Smith's office called to schedule her yearly appointment and informed her there were no openings until the beginning of next year, Mel signed up for the first available time. It was at the last minute when she casually mentioned, "Would it make any difference if I told you I found a lump in my breast?" that the nurse told her to come in the following week. This made Melodee a little more anxious, but during the appointment, Dr. Smith saw no cause for great concern. Surely, a mammogram was excessive.

Mel dialed the number for the center, anyway, "just to be sure," as Dr. Smith had counseled. The kind receptionist took her information, including insurance, and looked at the schedule. "The earliest we can fit you in so close to the end of the year, dearie, is late in December."

"But that is over a month away!"

"I'm sorry, sweetie, but toward the end of the year, we have a large number of appointments, as people squeeze in their yearly exams before their insurance deductibles start over again."

As she had no other choice, Mel scheduled the appointment, annoyed over having to wait four more weeks before she could ease her mind over this nonsense. There was little time to dwell on those thoughts, as she heard crying from upstairs, the signal that her baby was just waking up from his afternoon nap.

A few weeks later, Melodee's phone rang, and she was surprised to see the number from the imaging center on the caller ID. *"Maybe they had a cancelation and can squeeze me in earlier!"* Melodee thought to herself. Instead, she was informed by someone in the billing department that she had not met her insurance deductible for the year and would be responsible for the full amount of $832 at the time of her mammogram.

"Why do I even *have* insurance?" Mel was stunned over that price tag. How would they be able to shell out that kind of money so close to the end of the year? Was this scan "just to be sure," even worth it? There was no point in meeting the deductible in the last few weeks of the year, so Melodee decided to reschedule her appointment for January, when at least the money could be applied to a fresh deductible for the months ahead. The extended time frame also gave Melodee a chance to call around to different centers and locate one that would charge less than half that price. Her new appointment date was set for January 14, 2013, which also meant nearly another month of waiting.

"I'll make it through the holidays now, will save up for the deductible, and I won't have to think about it again until the New Year," Melodee assured herself and her mother, when Mom questioned Melodee's decision to postpone the exam.

The holidays flew by as usual, and January 14 soon approached. In the days leading up to the scan, Mel kept asking Stephen if the lump was still there. She was convinced she was imagining things now, and the technicians and doctors would laugh when the mammogram revealed nothing at all. The 'big day' was on a Monday, one of Stephen's scheduled days off from work. Since he was able to stay at home with their boys, Mel could arrive at her appointment without the added stress of making child care arrangements.

The imaging center was not far from their home, a miracle in the busy traffic of Houston, Texas. Melodee was the only patient in the waiting area. After completing the required paperwork, she was escorted to the dressing room and instructed to remove only her clothes from the waist-up and place the provided robe on, with the opening to the front. Once properly dressed, Melodee followed the technician, who introduced herself as Nancy, into a room with the mammography equipment.

The corner suite, surrounded with windows, let in plenty of light and provided a bright and comfortable ambience. Calming images of the ocean and mountain streams were framed and hung around the room, and soothing music was playing. Like many women, Melodee had heard horror stories of the pain and discomfort of mammograms and how unpleasant they were, but the atmosphere of this room and the company of the friendly and funny technician began to put her at ease.

Nancy then demonstrated how she wanted Melodee to stand and where she should place her arms. She placed Melodee's left breast on the machine's lower plate and guided an upper plate until it pressed down on the breast in order to capture the required images at the proper angles. The plate was only compressed for a few seconds before the technician repeated the process with the right breast. After reviewing the images from the screen, Nancy excused herself, advising Melodee to have a seat in one of the chairs while she went to talk to the doctor.

Alone with her thoughts, Melodee reflected on the procedure. *"That's it?"* she thought. *"What was everyone warning me about? That whole process took less than twenty*

minutes and was only a bit uncomfortable for a few seconds at a time! If this is all there is, I was worried over nothing!"

Nancy returned a few minutes later and stated, "The doctor feels that the initial results from your mammogram require me to conduct a more thorough test with an ultrasound, as you have dense breasts, with a high amount of calcification. The lump in your left breast also looks suspicious."

Two thoughts went through Mel's mind: *"Well, I'm not crazy; there is truly a lump"* and *"Where have I heard about 'dense breast' before?"* As if suddenly reminded, Melodee responded, "That makes sense! My mom had a biopsy a few years ago of some calcifications in her breast, but the results were benign. She's been told she has dense breast tissue, too." Perhaps all of this was all just a result of dense breast tissue.

At this point, Melodee still had no reason to worry; an ultrasound was harmless. An ultrasound (diagnostic sonography) uses high frequency sound waves to create an image of some part of the inside of the body, such as the stomach, liver, heart, tendons, muscles, joints and blood vessels.

Melodee followed Nancy into another room, darker and more closed off, with no windows or soothing portraits. Melodee was asked to lie down on her back, keeping her left arm above her head. She then placed a wedged pillow under Melodee's shoulder and helped her turn on her side, providing a more effective angle for the ultrasound. Warmed gel was squeezed out and applied to Melodee's breast and onto the tip of a probe, which was placed on her skin and gently moved around to examine the suspicious tissue. While Melodee thought the mammogram had gone by more quickly than she had expected, she was starting to feel like the ultrasound would never end.

Nancy was being quite thorough and taking more than a handful of images. She stopped and informed Melodee to stay in position, as she was going to consult with the radiologist and have him check the images. Unexpectedly, the radiologist came into the exam room and introduced himself as Dr. Adlo. "After reviewing your photos with Nancy," he explained, "I want to examine you myself." For several more minutes, Dr. Adlo glided the transducer across Melodee's skin and examined the screen where the images were displayed. Finally, he spoke.

"We're done. Nancy will get you cleaned off, and I want to speak with you in my office."

Nancy's cleaning off was not effective, and Melodee asked for extra towels to wipe the now chilled and sticky gel off the skin from under arms and across her chest. She couldn't wait to get home and take a hot shower and put this day behind her!

Melodee got dressed and was led to a corner room, where she waited, as instructed, in a comfortable armchair across from a large, mahogany desk, in what she could only assume was Dr. Adlo's office. She admired the smiling faces of what must be his family—children and grandchildren. She also noted the honors from schools and other organizations hanging prominently on his walls. "He's been doing this for a very long time," she guessed.

Just then, Dr. Adlo walked in, carrying a laptop, and closed the door behind him.

"I've been reviewing your images, both the ones Nancy took and my own," Dr. Adlo began. "There is calcification all over your breast tissue. In addition, the lump in your left breast is in an area we need to look at more closely. In my 30 years as a radiologist, I have never seen a mammogram or ultrasound like yours, and I would like to discuss your case with some colleagues for second opinions. I also recommend scheduling a biopsy of the lump, and I have an opening on Wednesday, two days from today. How does that work?"

"What, exactly, will happen during this biopsy?" Mel still wasn't sure anyone needed to go to all of this trouble.

"A breast biopsy," Dr. Adlo explained, "is a procedure to remove a small sample of breast tissue for laboratory testing. This allows us to evaluate any suspicious areas of breast tissue that show up in scans to determine if there is breast cancer or simply a benign mass. During the biopsy, I will remove samples of breast tissue to send to a lab, where a pathologist will examine and evaluate the sample under a microscope to identify non-cancerous (benign) or cancerous (malignant) tissue in the areas of concern. The lab report from the breast biopsy can help determine whether or not you need additional surgery or other treatment."

Melodee's mind was racing in a million different directions.

"What does he mean, 'he's never seen a mammogram like mine'? Is it because of my age? Are the images abnormal? He's never seen that amount of calcifications in one breast, but what could that mean? With Stephen's schedule on Wednesday, who will I get to watch the boys and who will be able to do preschool pick-up?"

Her thoughts were suddenly interrupted. "Will Wednesday work for you, Mrs. Cooper?"

Brought back to the present, Melodee finally answered in the affirmative. "Yes, I think Wednesday will work."

"Great. Follow me to the front desk, and Amanda will get you scheduled and give you more information."

For the next two days whenever Melodee's mind started to turn to the negative, Stephen, a medical professional himself, reassured her: "They just want to be sure." Melodee also was comforted by remembering her mother's story of her own biopsy of dense and calcified breast tissue that all turned out to be benign and normal. "Genetics must play a role, and my tissue is probably similar to my mom's," she reasoned.

Everyone had warned Melodee about the pains of a mammogram; no one prepared her for what she would encounter with a biopsy.

THE BIOPSY

Having dropped the boys off at school and with friends, Melodee made the short drive back to the hospital. She again dressed in the stylish gown and had her vitals taken. She followed Nancy back to a different room, one that was not calming, but sterile. An ultrasound technician, Angelica, was waiting to assist the doctor. As instructed, she eased onto the table where the nurses adjusted her body to the correct position and opened the gown, exposing only the left side. A large area was prepped and disinfected, and Dr. Adlo entered.

"I will use a needle to numb the area with a local anesthetic," he explained. "This needle will probably be the most painful of the entire procedure."

With that reassurance, Melodee figured this was going to be nothing to worry about. *"I'll finish up here and still be able to keep a lunch date with friends,"* she thought. Just then, Dr. Adlo used a towel to cover Melodee's eyes, explaining,

"You probably don't want to see the actual collection. It's better if you just close your eyes and try to relax." Melodee then felt pressure from the ultrasound probe, which Angelica used to guide the needle placement. Next came the prick of a needle, almost like a bee sting, and a slight discomfort and burning. After a few seconds, the process was repeated, and Melodee wasn't able to feel the third. It was time to collect the samples.

Because the suspicious area from the ultrasound covered such a large mass of breast tissue, it was necessary to collect several samples to be analyzed. Guided by ultrasound, Dr. Adlo used a small, hollow needle to withdraw small samples, or cores, of breast tissue. Each time a needle was inserted, Melodee felt pressure, a pushing and pulling sensation, and a loud 'snap!' as the sample was withdrawn. The first needle release startled Melodee so much; she jumped, as if her body was instinctively trying to pull away from danger. After three or four samples, she was hoping for a break. It had been wise to cover her eyes, to remove any possibility that she might witness the needles digging in and snapping back out.

Thankfully, Dr. Adlo left the room with the first group of samples, explaining that he needed to review them under the microscope to confirm he had truly collected the calcium of the questionable mass. He instructed Melodee to apply pressure to the sample sites while he was gone to stop the bleeding. It was then that Melodee figured the lidocaine must have worn off because this small amount of pressure was causing a great deal of pain. Not one to complain about pain, she finally expressed her concerns when Dr. Adlo returned to the room. He promptly administered more local anesthetic to alleviate the pain while he collected more samples to send to the pathologist.

Melodee had not been prepared for the extent of this biopsy. She had expected something closer to getting a few flu shots at once. She was shocked at the need to remove such a large number of cores. There had been seven core sample needles, the maneuvering and digging of each inserted needle to collect from the correct spots, and seven pops of the mechanisms retracting, along with a tensing of muscles in expectation. With each needle insertion and the following snapping, clicking, shocking closure, Melodee prayed it would be over. The emotional stress was building, and her mind was racing:

"Why does he need so many samples?
Why is this so painful?
Will these tests discover something terrible?
It's bad enough to hear the needle snapping, now the pain is becoming almost unbearable!
How many more jolting clicks can I take?"

Melodee was anything but relaxed; the anxiety and worry began to be overwhelming. The longer this procedure went on, the less able she became to keep her emotions hidden. Silent tears began to spill from the corners of her eyes. She was not able to wipe them away because she had been instructed to remain still during the biopsy, but that only made the situation worse. Before long, streams of burning tears and streaks of mascara were running down her cheeks and onto the back of her neck. She kept thinking, *"It's got to be almost done. If I can just keep it together and they don't talk to me or notice the tears, I'll be fine."*

But Nancy and Angelica had noticed.

One of them asked if Melodee was in pain. "Are you alright? Do we need to take a break? We are almost done, only the marker left. Maybe you should just think about your boys."

Melodee was able to remain strong and stoic for the last needle, which placed a small, metal clip in the lump, to mark the area for future tests or surgeries. When she followed the advice of the nurses and did think of her boys, it only led to thinking about the worst and what might happen to them if this test revealed bad news. That only made the emotional toll worse! The floodgates opened, and tears quickly became sobs. She could no longer hold still for any more sample collections. Melodee was overwhelmed and weeping, then felt alone and embarrassed for becoming so emotional in front of practically strangers.

Thankfully, both the nurse and doctor acted as true caregivers by staying by Melodee, holding her hands, and offering words of affirmation like, "This *is* overwhelming. It's a lot to deal with so soon into a new year. You're an amazing patient." They cleaned and bandaged the sample sights and assured her that the procedure was over.

Once she could finally sit up and clean her face, Melodee was able to compose herself. She was cleared to drive home, as long as she promised to rest and follow the instructions of no heavy lifting or exercising and no baths for seven days. Dr. Adlo had also given her a prescription for something to ease the pain, which was stronger than she guessed it would be. She was not completely surprised to notice the amount of bruising in her left breast, which highlighted the areas where the cores were taken. She was concerned that the entire breast looked a bit deflated from the large amount of tissue that had been removed from its center.

Before Melodee left his office, Dr. Adlo had explained that results of these tests could usually be expected within 48-72 hours. Since it was Wednesday, he guessed she *might* hear something by Friday, but more likely by Monday of the following week. Imagine the shock when Melodee's phone rang the following afternoon, displaying the phone number of her OB/GYN and referring physician, as the caller.

"Hello?"

"May I speak with Melodee?"

"Speaking."

"Hi, Melodee. This is Kris Smith. How are you?"

"I'll be better when I'm able to put all of this behind me. How are you?"

"Fine, thank you. So, I've received only an initial verbal report back from the radiologist. I requested the earliest reports because I will be having my baby tomorrow and will be out on maternity leave after that. I need you to come to my office today, as soon as possible, to discuss these initial reports and to set you up with a specialist before my leave."

No longer could Mel's attempt at positivity outweigh the realist inside. This was not good news.

"Maybe she just wants to tie up loose ends before she has her baby," Melodee wondered aloud. "No doctor is going to call you personally and ask you to come to their office the same day to tell you the tests came back negative. This probably isn't going to be good," was Stephen's response.

Securing last minute babysitting, Stephen and Melodee hurried to Dr. Smith's office, the same office where only a year before they were making preparations for the birth of their last baby. Stephen donned his pink polo shirt "to ward off evil spirits," but it wasn't enough. The couple was ushered back to the nearest exam room and, without having them wait more than two minutes, the doctor entered, sat at the desk, opened a file, and without making direct eye contact with either Mel or Stephen, said:

"The initial reports from the radiologist indicate that you have breast cancer."

Stephen bent down, placing his head on his hands and began to cry. Melodee stared forward, stunned, shocked, and defeated. The room was spinning. She couldn't breathe. *This couldn't be happening! Perhaps it was just a nightmare, one from which she needed to wake up. Deep down she knew it was too real to be made-up in her head. "How bad could this be?"* she thought silently.

As if reading her patient's thoughts, Dr. Smith continued. "I do not even have the final pathology report, but Dr. Adlo has confirmed with me that there are cancer cells present in the samples, and we should move on to the next step immediately. I can set you up with a team of breast specialists here in this building, if you would like. You are free to look around for another doctor as well, if that would make you more comfortable."

Stephen spoke up first, "Who would you recommend?"

"If I was diagnosed with breast cancer, the pair of doctors I would trust with my treatment plan actually work in this building. Dr. Nabhi is the oncologist in the team, and Dr. Plack is the breast surgeon. I think they are each outstanding in their fields, and I like that they are women," Dr. Smith counseled.

Melodee was easily convinced. "That's good enough for me. I want the best doctors possible. I want to get rid of this. The best way to begin the fight is with the best people on your team."

The Specialists

It was cancer. This small lump that so many people had assured them was 'nothing' was indeed 'something.' There was little time to process all of the emotions, as only minutes after hearing Dr. Smith's cancer diagnosis, Melodee and Stephen found themselves on the elevator heading downstairs for an initial consultation with Dr. Plack, the breast surgeon Dr. Smith had recommended. Thanks to an emergency referral, the couple was able to schedule the last appointment of the day. At 4:00 p.m., Stephen and Mel were the only patients in the waiting room, so it did not take long for a nurse to call Melodee's name and lead the couple back to an exam room. Dr. Plack entered soon after. As she introduced herself and her philosophy, Melodee could sense a calm, peaceful, almost spiritual demeanor, which eased some apprehension.

"You have been referred because we have only an initial report of 'invasive ductal carcinoma.' We can begin to make plans based on that and will adjust them as we receive further information. Let me be clear with you: based on your age alone, most of these tumors are very aggressive. They can double in size in a month and will require chemotherapy. You will lose your hair, and it will be rough."

Mel had not yet cried over her diagnosis, but this was the statement that made it truly real. That image of the stereotypical cancer patient: bald, frail, and failing, was soon to be her reality. She could feel the tears welling up and allowed her head to droop, as any remaining walls around her heart could no longer hide the hopelessness. She was now a cancer patient; the nightmare was real.

Dr. Plack continued explaining the tentative treatment plan, obviously prepared for these kinds of emotional breakdowns. "Assuming your pathology reports come back as we predict they will, in cases like yours our plan includes both chemotherapy and surgery. You might be familiar with breast cancer treatment plans that include an immediate lumpectomy and radiation to eradicate the cancer from your body as soon as possible. Our treatment takes a different route. We start with chemotherapy. The theory behind this timing is that leaving the cancerous cells of the tumor in place while fighting them with specific drugs allows us to monitor your progress. We will scan you before, during, and after chemotherapy, in order to measure the tumor shrinking. If we remove the tumor before chemo, we are only able to speculate on the strength and success of chemotherapy. You will meet your oncologist tomorrow, and we will schedule your surgery for port placement and a lymph node biopsy for the middle of next week."

At this point, all the information was starting to saturate Melodee's mind. Plans were happening so quickly! She first heard the cancer diagnosis, one that had never entered her list of fears, forty minutes earlier. Already, she was a new patient of one cancer specialist, was on the calendar to meet another, and had a window for surgery!

The drive home was a long, mostly silent one. It's quite possible both Melodee and Stephen were in a state of shock and had reached their word quota for the day, so they sat in silence, both privately processing. It was difficult to put any kind of positive spin on this situation, and from the plan Dr. Plack presented, there seemed to be no easy fix. Melodee was only going to survive after a long, difficult battle, and they both started to grasp the realization that life, as they knew it, would never be the same again.

Stephen and Melodee began to split up the task of telling their family and friends. Emails flooded in with more questions than they had answers. That familiar 'ding,' Melodee's signal for text messages, became demoralizing. Normally, hearing Bono's voice belting out, "It's a beautiful day!" when friends and family called would bring a smile to her face. For now, she just couldn't find any truth in those words of one of her favorite U2 songs.

What can be beautiful about the day you discover a deadly disease is about to steal a year of your life away? She let the first few calls go to voicemail and then turned her phone off completely. Stephen and Mel each passed on the limited information to one set of parents and asked them to pass it along to the rest of the families. Repeating bad news only makes it more overwhelming, so they were grateful to not have to continue to retell the story.

Stephen had to work the next day, Friday, so Melodee asked his brother, Jordan, to attend her doctor appointment as moral support and to help her ask the right questions, as he also worked in the medical field. Her oncologist was Dr. Nabhi, pronounced "knob-ee." The office in which Melodee would normally visit Dr. Nabhi was conveniently located down the hall from Dr. Plack's office, but Nabhi had Friday office hours in another building downtown. This was not so convenient, but could be arranged in order to continue making plans to begin treatment as soon as possible.

After signing in and filling out stacks of paperwork, Melodee was called back up to the front desk. "You are responsible for the entire cost of a doctor visit today, as you have not met your deductible for the year. You don't have a co-pay, which means you pay all costs until you have met that amount, which for you is $3,000 per person, plus $6,000 total out-of-pocket. For today's exam, you owe $173.66."

"Really! Can't you bill me?"

"Unfortunately, no. This is the negotiated rate, and we must ask for it up front. If you can't pay today, you will have to reschedule."

The appointment was not starting well. Melodee handed the office manager, Bonnie, her credit card. "Oh, I'm sorry. We don't take American Express."

Melodee's inner anger was starting to take over. "Are you KIDDING ME!" she fumed to herself, as she searched for a card that would be acceptable. Was it not enough that her life was crashing down around her, thanks to cancer? Now she had the financial burden to face, as well.

It's amazing how Bonnie's demeanor softened, once the money had cleared. As if the swish of the credit card through the scanner somehow signaled the office door to open and to allow one of Dr. Nabhi's nurses to escort Melodee and Jordan to the back.

"Hi, there. My name is Lila."

"I'm Melodee Cooper, and this is my brother-in-law, Jordan."

Lila nodded to Jordan, saying, "Nice to meet you," and turned back to Melodee. "I need to take your vitals first. Sit down here," she said, extending her arm to offer a chair next to the machine. "I'll just put this cuff on your arm to take your blood pressure. Put this under your tongue," she explained, clicking the thermometer into a box of plastic protectors and sliding it into Mel's mouth.

Lila made small talk as the blood pressure cuff tightened around Mel's arm, tighter, even tighter, and then slowly began to release, a little more, once again, and then completely, revealing the stats: "Your temperature is 97.6 and BP is 106 over 64. Wow. I cannot believe how low your blood pressure is, especially just after a cancer diagnosis!"

With the most basic of assessments complete, Lila led their newest patient and her guest back to a corner room at the back of the hall, one with no desk in sight. It was comforting to wait in what felt more like a friend's formal living room than a cold, sterile doctor's office. There was no table, covered with the typical white protective paper. No counter with a sink and containers of cotton balls and swabs. This room was for meeting and chatting, not examining, and there had been plenty of that already this week. Melodee chose the couch and Jordan claimed the nearest side chair, reminding Melodee of the most important questions to ask while they waited for the doctor to join them. He didn't get far into the conversation before the door opened again.

A woman in a white coat walked in. She was younger than Mel had expected, with long, black hair, beautifully shaped eyebrows, and deep brown eyes. She wore simple make-up, except lipstick in a dark shade of plum, which complimented the tone of her medium-brown skin and her smart and classy business casual outfit. She walked closer to the couch, extending her hand and smiling. "Hello. I'm Dr. Nabhi. Thank you for coming in today on short notice." Melodee couldn't place her accent, but guessed she was of Middle Eastern or Indian descent, based mostly on her last name.

Taking a seat on the couch directly across from Melodee, Dr. Nabhi got straight to business.

"When we have a cancer diagnosis, we first discuss the biology of the cancer, the stage of the cancer, and how we will treat this cancer. I still do not have the full pathology reports, as you only had a biopsy performed on Wednesday of this week, but let's start with what we do know about the biology of your tumor. It is an invasive ductal carcinoma. Let me break things down so you can understand. There is a grade given, based on the rate at which it grows, which can be seen as the cells divide under a microscope. I am guessing your grade is somewhere between 2 and 3, 3 being the worst."

Thankfully, Jordan was taking notes, so Melodee could just focus on what her oncologist was saying. She was already feeling information overload, but she tried to take it all in, knowing Stephen and her mom would both expect a full report.

"The next part of the biology is the results for the receptors. The receptors we recognize are ER, Estrogen; PR, Progesterone; and one called HER2. These results indicate the types of substances that are feeding the tumor, causing it to grow. Again, we don't have the report for these results yet. Let's just hope for the best-case scenario, which would be ER positive, PR positive, and HER2 negative." She wrote it out on paper for Melodee like ER+, PR+, HER2- and used the tip or her pencil to point to the list. "If these first 2, the hormonal receptors, are both positive, it is easy to treat, by simply blocking these hormones. If you are HER2 positive, we have a special drug to combat that, as well. The worst result is 'triple negative.' This means all the receptors come back negative, but something else is still causing your tumor to grow. It is not as easy to fight if we don't know exactly what we are fighting.

Let's just pray that the results come back with anything but triple negative."

Because of her previous research, Melodee knew about the hormones, but had never heard of HER2. She knew there would be additional Internet searches in her future, but she didn't have time to ponder all the unknowns, for Dr. Nabhi continued her explanations.

"Cancer is also given a stage." Finally, something Melodee was familiar with! "All I can do is guess at your stage, but I would say you are somewhere between Stages 2 and 3. This means that your tumor is large and has traveled into your lymph nodes, but there will not be tumors in the rest of your body. I will order a CT scan and bone scan for next week to confirm the stage. You will also need genetic testing. You might have heard of this. It's called BRCA1 and BRCA2. Because of your age and the lack of family history of breast cancer, there might be a genetic mutation that could be contributing to the tumor's growth. If this comes back positive, we can basically be sure that you will develop cancer again in the future, so a double mastectomy along with an oophorectomy (removal of ovaries) would be recommended. Also, with a positive result, your siblings and children are encouraged to be tested and become aware of their possible risks."

"What if this genetic testing comes back negative? Where will we go from there?" Jordan was helpful in the questioning.

"That is the next part of our discussion, your treatment. You have choices to make in this area. Chemotherapy is a must, however. It will last for six months, but we will wait on the pathology results to determine the order. Chemo is designed to kill any cells in the body that are dividing rapidly, and at this point, it cannot differentiate between 'good cells' and 'evil cells.' It will kill them all in order to kill the cancerous ones. Your chemo will be split into two main 'cocktails'. First, is FEC, which will be administered every three weeks for four doses. The side effects will include nausea and vomiting, fatigue, immune suppression, hair loss, mucositis, constipation, and gray nails. However, for each side effect, there are treatments and developments to alleviate the suffering. If you follow my drug prescriptions religiously, you will most likely not ever vomit but may just be a little queasy. We can give you Ritalin to help with the fatigue, and you're going to need all the help you can get with those three boys you have! For your immune system, we will give a growth factor to replenish white blood cells. This is to stimulate your bones to mass-produce white blood cells in defense of the chemo. Even though chemo will kill off most of your supply, with the growth factor, you should be left with enough to keep you healthy. For mucositis, you will need to keep your mouth cold with ice and popsicles during the infusion of FEC.

"And now for the really bad news. As for the hair loss— well, there's really nothing we can do about that. You will lose your hair. You will lose it in three weeks, and it will be dramatic. I suggest that once you lose that initial clump at around two weeks, you should cut your hair very short to make it less shocking. You'll most likely just want to shave it off completely before too long, and be aware that you might experience pain at the follicles until all of your hair is gone."

"So there's no way around it? My hair will all be gone?" Perhaps, Mel thought, there was a glimmer of hope.

"I'm afraid so."

Then came more tears. Why was the issue of hair loss the thing that hit so close to her heart?

Dr. Nabhi continued, "I suggest you get a wig right away. I will write a prescription for one, as insurance companies usually cover the cost of your first wig. The nurses can give you a list of the places we recommend. You should get a wig as soon as possible, especially for the sake of your boys. They are too young to understand, and you want to look normal to them and not scare them."

Great, Mel thought. *Not only am I thinking about losing all of my hair, now she's got me focusing on my children and how they will react.* Melodee reached over to the side table to grab some tissues, as the tears were flowing now. She should have come prepared with waterproof mascara! Up to this point, Melodee listened to everything Dr. Nabhi had been explaining and believed she was the expert.

When it came to her sons, however, Melodee knew better than this doctor. She was planning on being upfront and honest with her boys about cancer, even the ugly and hard parts. It was not realistic for her to only let the boys see her as "normal" by covering up with a wig. Was she supposed to keep it under her pillow to throw on if one of them came to her in the middle of the night if they were sick or after a bad dream? What about the days when it was hot and humid, as Texas summers often are, and a wig was too uncomfortable? She couldn't possibly wear a wig while swimming, so what then? No, her boys needed to be part of this battle. They needed to be there for the good and the terrible.

Melodee's thoughts were quickly brought back to the doctor's explanations. "The second chemotherapy drug is called Paclitaxel."

There's more? Indeed, there was more to the treatment of cancer than Melodee had ever imagined. She was only hitting the tip of the iceberg with this initial consultation and already she felt as if she should have studied medicine to keep up.

"Paclitaxel will be given once a week for twelve weeks. Fortunately, there is a shorter list of side effects with this drug. The nausea and vomiting can still be an issue, and many people experience nail changes and neuropathy. The nerves in your hands and feet can become damaged, and you might feel weakness, numbness, or pain. It could take several treatments before this becomes an issue, if at all, and the condition will most likely reverse itself after time."

"That will be the treatment plan for chemo, unless your results come back as HER2 positive. In that case, there is a specific drug, called Herceptin that we add to the chemotherapy, but it cannot be given in conjunction with FEC, as that combination can lead to cardiomyopathy. If it is shown that you are HER2 positive, we will switch the order of your chemotherapy. Paclitaxel first, along with Herceptin, then FEC, without Herceptin. After FEC is completed, we would continue Herceptin for a total of 52 doses. So, let's hope you are not HER2 positive, as the treatment time will be much longer in that case."

All the acronyms were enough to put alphabet soup to shame. Mel's head was spinning with all of this foreign information. It was easy to feel overwhelmed, so Melodee decided that she would take things one-step at a time, learning more about the individual chemotherapies as they were administered. There was still more to take in.

"After chemo, we will evaluate your surgical options. If your genetic testing comes back positive, you will have a bilateral mastectomy. If not, you could opt for a lumpectomy plus radiation, or a complete mastectomy. We will cross that bridge when we get there. The good news is that 90% of my patients continue to work while receiving chemotherapy. We will work around your schedule to find the best day and time for your treatments. Chemo is much more improved than it once was."

Melodee was once again so thankful that Jordan had come along, for he had been keeping great notes. He asked clarifying questions every now and then and recorded the answers. She knew his notes would come in handy, as she would need to explain the treatment plan to Stephen and everyone else.

The last part of this initial meeting was a physical exam. Dr. Nabhi led Melodee across the hall and out of the comfortable sitting room into a typical exam room and, once again, instructed her to undress from the waist up and don the provided robe, with the opening to the front. Then came the soft knocking on the door before the doctor reentered the room. Dr. Nabhi performed a breast exam, similar to the original one that started this whole process. She examined both breasts carefully, paying close attention to the surrounding areas, around and up under each arm.

"Your tumor is large. It is measuring around 4.5 to 5 cm, larger than a golf ball, but smaller than a tennis ball. At this size of a tumor, the best option will probably be a full mastectomy. Having measured your tumor, I might put you closer to Stage 3 than Stage 2, but it does not appear to have migrated to your lymph nodes as they do not seem to be enlarged, thank God."

She believes in God, Melodee thought to herself. Finally, some good news! It was as if God had given a small sign that she was not alone in this. That was a welcome blessing, a tender mercy at the end of a very long week.

"So, that's it for today," announced the doctor. "Head to the front, and the nurses will set you up for scans and a follow-up appointment. I will see you soon!" Melodee dressed and met back up with Jordan. At the front desk Jan slid an appointment card across the desk, which displayed the times for her bone and CT scans for the following Wednesday. She also included a map of the location.

"You'll have a follow-up with Dr. Nabhi next Thursday, the day after your scans, and Dr. Plack has tentatively scheduled the surgery for your port placement for Friday. Dr. Nabhi likes that operation to heal for a few days before starting chemo, so you will most likely begin treatment a week from Tuesday. We will let you know for sure at your follow-up appointment next week. See you then!"

With that, Mel gathered her things and walked through a door that would become more familiar than she would ever want it to, past faces she would see again and again over the course of the next fifteen months. Her mind was filled to capacity with more information than she could process, and she was sure that both Dr. Plack and Dr. Nabhi had only reviewed the highlights of what was to come. It was time to visit another doctor. There seemed to be healing powers, at least emotionally, in Mexican food and Dr. Pepper.

TELLING THE BOYS

After what seemed like the longest week of their lives, Melodee and Stephen felt like they had been through a crash course on cancer. Just days earlier, life had been predictable. 'Normal' as they knew it was over. Their new 'normal' included fighting cancer. They had no experience from which to gauge the effects of cancer on their daily life. Would Stephen be able to keep his strenuous work schedule? How much help would Melodee need during the day? How would their relationship be tested? Would the boys be at a disadvantage developmentally based on their exposure to the effects of this hardship on their mother? How would Stephen and Mel find the energy to battle this disease, while already juggling so much? Only time would tell.

Doctors had given Stephen and Melodee all the available information up to this point, although they still had not yet received full reports from pathology. An exact treatment plan or start date was still to be determined. Dr. Nabhi strongly suggested they try to keep as much normalcy for their young boys as possible, to keep as much of the details of treatment from the children as they could. Mel was also aware of another woman in their group of acquaintances, recently diagnosed with cancer, who decided not to tell her young children. Instead, she set up play dates during treatments and asked all who took care of her young ones to never utter the "C-word." Melodee and Stephen felt strongly about being upfront and honest with their children. They decided to try to explain as much as they could and to keep the lines of communication open during the process.

Their three boys stayed with Stephen's parents over the weekend following Melodee's cancer diagnosis. This gave the couple some private time to try to wrap their heads around this cancer diagnosis, which was somewhat easier without the natural interruptions that parenting assumes.

There were so many unknowns in Mel's case. How did the cancer develop? Cancer did not run in her family, yet she had it. She was so young. She had breastfed all three of her babies. She exercised three to five times a week. Still, cancer found its path to her. How would she respond to treatment? Surely, she would not fall into that ten percent of patients whose cancer is resistant to chemotherapy. Also, if she had been trying to live a healthy lifestyle and still ended up with cancer, how could she trust that sticking to current medical recommendations would allow her to achieve and remain in remission? So many of these concerns had no answer at this time.

Friday night they went out to eat, but this date turned into a mostly silent dinner, with a husband and wife each reflecting on how this trial would change life as they knew it.

"Why is this happening?" Stephen asked over and over again. "What have we done to deserve this? Have we not been through enough in life already?" It was not an easy question to answer. The doctors did not yet have enough information to fully diagnose her cancer, let alone discover the causes of its origin. Still, Stephen's heart ached for Melodee, as he knew there was little he could do to protect her from the pain he knew she would endure. Anger and fear crept in, as well. Who was he angry with? God? Doctors? It was hard to tell. Mostly, the whole thing just made his soul ache.

"Melodee does not deserve this! *We* do not deserve this! We are good people, so why do all of these bad things keep happening?" He kept most of the thoughts inside, as Melodee was already dealing with enough anguish; he did not want to add to her pain.

When Melodee looked up at him in the middle of dinner, she could tell he was deep in thought. She even saw tears in his eyes. Or were they left over from tears they had both cried earlier? Again, it was hard to know, as neither could yet formulate their own thoughts enough to carry on a full discussion.

"What are you thinking?" Mel finally asked.

"I don't know." (He was not one to share his feelings often.) "It's almost like I feel nothing, I've felt so much that now I'm numb."

"I know what you mean. This is so overwhelming, and it hasn't even begun!" She was starting to be past tears as well. "How do we tell the boys?"

"What do you think?" He was good about letting her lead the way.

"I know for sure that I don't want to keep this a secret or try to hide it from our children. Dr. Nabhi felt I should always have a wig, so they wouldn't be scared. I don't think that's practical. This will affect them, so they should know about each step as we come to it. How can we pretend nothing is wrong when *everything* is wrong? They need to be a part of this, too, as much as they can."

"I agree," he answered. They won't understand everything, but they should at least be able to know what is going on.

"Not that I think this is going to happen," she began, "but if I die, I want them to be prepared for it. I cannot imagine stringing them along, only to find out the day before I'm gone that I've been ill."

"I don't even want to think about that now!" Stephen could not imagine his life without his wife and knew it was too early to dwell on those thoughts.

One thing they did agree upon was to include the boys in the fight against cancer. First, Stephen and Melodee would need to plan a time when they could sit down as a family and explain what they had been told about Mel's diagnosis, how they were going to fight it, what changes the boys might expect to see, and how they could all help each other as a family. For the remainder of the weekend, Stephen and Mel spent quality time together, trying to soak in every moment they could before cancer would steal their life away for a time. They also planned the best way to talk to their children about the disease.

That Sunday night the boys returned home. The parents had missed the craziness of their young family, which might have distracted from the despair they were feeling. After dinner, the time had finally come; they had to explain the bad news to their boys. This was hard! The children were too young to be dealing with something like this! Melodee was too young to be going through this! Wasn't this a disease for the later years, once you've raised children and lived a full life? No one with young kids should have to suffer through cancer. Life, however, is not perfect. If it weren't cancer they were dealing with, it would be something else. So, here they were, seated around the dinner table, eating some dessert, thinking life was as sweet as the ice cream and chocolate sauce in the bowls before them.

Both Stephen and Melodee figured their boys, (Kyle-5, Ryan-2, Evan-1), were not old enough to understand cancer or the complexities of what would be taking place over the coming year. Instead of trying to tell everything all at once, Stephen and Mel decided to simply be upfront, to explain cancer from a child's point of view, and to leave the lines of communication open to allow each boy to ask any questions they might have at any time in the process.

After all were happily enjoying their sweet treat of the evening, Mel's eyes glanced in Stephen's direction, her head softly nodding, giving the signal that it was time to begin the conversation.

"Boys," they all turned to face him. "I need you all to listen to me very carefully." Stephen was rarely this serious, so this change of tone caught the boys' attention immediately.

Melodee was not sure she was going to remain emotionally strong for this. Stephen's mind was racing, searching for the best words. "You know how Mommy has been going to lots of doctors this week?" He started with a question he was sure they could understand.

Three sets of big, brown eyes shifted focus quickly from their Dad over to Melodee.

Stephen continued, "Well, we found out that Mommy is sick. She is very sick! She has some BIG boo-boos. She'll be going to lots of doctor appointments. She will also need some very strong medicine, the kind that is very yucky."

Melodee tried to pay attention to any slight changes in the boys' expressions that might indicate a level of understanding. So far, they remained unchanged. Maybe it was time for her to start explaining.

"Can you remember a time when you got a boo-boo?" Kyle nodded. The others just stared her way. "Well, I'm sure you can remember a time when you were hurt or sad or crying. Mommy is also going to be sad sometimes and she might be crying a lot, too," she explained. That got them. They said nothing, but there was sadness (or was it shock?) in their eyes, a look of concern.

Mel continued, "My hair is even going to all fall out, and I might wear a wig or just look kind of funny and different soon."

"What's a wig?" Kyle spoke up for the first time.

"It's like dress up, pretend hair. I might wear hair of all kinds of colors and styles."

"Ha. Ha. That would be really funny!" There was at least one smile to come out of this conversation.

Stephen went on to explain, "There will be lots of people who will be coming over to help out. They might stay for many days, and Kyle will have to give up his bedroom. You might have to go to other people's houses so Mommy can go to the doctor or rest when she is really sick. Mommy might be very, very tired or so sick that she is throwing up."

The throwing up part got a response from the two older boys.

"YUCK!"

"Ew!"

Kyle and Ryan knew about throwing up from the time Kyle vomited on the stairs and Ryan crawled in it, smashing the bits of food and liquid further into the carpet. Mom had not been very happy that day, and the smell lingered. That experience came to mind now.

"When Mom is sick, she will not be able to do as much as she has been able to do for you up until now. We will need your help and for you to make really good choices. We also need to say lots of prayers that Mommy will feel better and get all better soon."

At this point, Melodee could tell the attention span of their three little ones was waning. She and Stephen had given as much information as the boys were ready to take in. To sum up, they asked Kyle if he had any questions. (Ryan was a late bloomer and did not speak much yet.) After a few seconds of thought, he shook his head, "No." Then, he turned to Mel and simply asked, "Mommy, why are you sick?"

There was no answer that made logical sense, especially on a child's level. Trying to explain that cancer developed when cells mutated or grew at an uncontrollable rate would be above the level of their children's understanding. Cancer had not even been on the radar of something for which their family needed to be on the lookout.

Melodee looked to Stephen for help as she felt a lump growing in her throat and knew she would not be able to look at Kyle and answer him without crying uncontrollably. She wanted to be strong and to not scare her boys; crying at this point would do more harm than good. Plus, Kyle was inquisitive and would continue this line of questioning until he received an answer that would pacify his curiosity.

Stephen started with the only answer he could give. "Well, Kyle, sometimes in this life, bad things happen."

"Why?" This was the line of questioning Mel had feared. Would they ever be able to give an acceptable answer? This could go on forever!

Stephen wasn't sure how to answer, but he started explaining what he knew about life and the challenges that come along with it. "Well, Kyle…we came to this earth to learn, and sometimes the only way we learn is to see how we will act when we have to go through hard things."

"But, *why?*"

"We don't always know exactly why hard times happen, Kyle. All we know is that this world can be hard. Sometimes, life is hard, and some of the hardest things in life are when we feel hurt or sad or sick. We are going through one of those hard times now. Mom is sick and will be hurt and sad. We all are going to feel sad while she is going through this hard time. There might be times when we don't really know the answers of 'why,' and we might not really know what to do to make things better. We just need to pray that Mommy will get better and her boo-boos will go away."

"Okay, Daddy. I will. I don't want Mommy to be sick."

"Me neither, Kyle."

"I'm going to pray lots and lots!"

"That will help Mommy so much."

The family finished dessert in near silence until someone accidentally spilled a drink and, while Mel was trying to clean up that mess, the baby started screaming and threw his spoon to the floor, splattering chocolate syrup in its path. What an honest reminder of how the craziness of daily life continues to roll forward, in spite of cancer or any other trial. At that moment, 'new normal' felt a lot like old normal.

After baths and prayers, Mel put the boys to bed that night. Kyle whispered, "Mommy, I love you. I'm going to say a prayer right now. I'm going to thank God that you'll be better soon. I'm going to pray every day."

Her mothering heart wanted to comfort Kyle and tell him that his prayers would be answered just how he wanted. That precious seed of faith needed to be nurtured. What impression would this trial have on her sweet baby's testimony in God if she were not to get better soon? Would he continue to question, "why"? Would his unanswered questions cause him to be angry with God? Melodee wanted more than anything to comfort her son with the news that it would all be over in a few months, but she knew there was a possibility that would not come true. Instead, she just kissed her precious oldest son, silently thanking God for his sweet spirit, and hugged him a little tighter and a little longer than she had in quite a while.

Relating the conversation to Stephen, Melodee finally let the tears come.

His eyes glistened, too. How he loved this woman! She made his life complete. He wanted more than anything for her to be happy and to have a long and comfortable life, full of all the blessings she deserved. He would take this pain from her if he could. She should not have to suffer through this. No one should. He had no words to express his concerns and fears, but just pulled her close to him, wrapping his arms around her as they stood just inside their bedroom and cried together.

THE FIRST SURGERY

In the following week, Melodee began to discover more and more about her cancer and the exact treatment she would undergo. The pathology report finally arrived, uncovering the biology of her tumor: ER+, PR-, HER2+. As Dr. Nabhi put things, "Not the best, but not the worst." Melodee was honestly not surprised at the results. She guessed Progesterone would not be a culprit; her pregnancies had discovered that her body was low on the production of that substance. She wasn't happy about the aggressiveness of the HER2, but was grateful to have some answers, versus a result of 'triple negative.' Some news was good news, in this case. Although answers about the origin of Melodee's cancer came in slowly, they most often learned what it *wasn't* more than what it *was*. Both a bone scan and a CT scan revealed no other signs of cancer in her body; the cancer was confined to only her breasts. The size and position of Mel's tumor meant that Dr. Nabhi gave her a stage of 2B. All of this was not great news, but it was all something they could deal with.

Before Mel could begin chemotherapy, she would have surgery to place a port in her chest, and before that surgery could be scheduled, she would need to meet with Dr. Plack once again. At this appointment, Mel actually had a few minutes of wait time in the front room of Dr. Plack's office and paused to take in her surroundings. The office had an obvious Asian motif, a calm atmosphere of soothing, blue tones, complimented by the strong reds and crisp black of the painted bamboo edges on the furniture. This was no sterile waiting room; it had been designed.

"Melodee?" a nurse called her name and she followed.

The theme and *Feng Shui* continued down the halls and into the exam rooms inside. Instead of entering one of these, the nurse led Melodee to the end of the hall and into a back office with one large, darkly stained desk flanking the back wall and couches and comfortable chairs framing the sides, similar to the room at Dr. Nabhi's office from the Friday before. Had it only been a few days? That felt like another lifetime.

"Wait here," the nurse instructed. "Dr. Plack will join you shortly."

Melodee made herself at home, choosing the couch and picking up one of the available magazines to catch up on the latest Hollywood gossip. A few articles later, Dr. Plack knocked softly before opening the door and strolling in, smiling and wearing brightly colored scrubs covered in Japanese cherry blossoms and women in kimonos, holding fans.

"I like her, and someday I'll ask her to explain the significance of all this Asian influence," Mel thought to herself.

"It's good to see you again." Dr. Plack's smile and warm demeanor set Mel at ease. "I won't ask how you are because I can only imagine what you've been going through over the last week. I'm sure you're worried and anxious, among other emotions." Melodee laughed at the understatement!

"I see we finally received the pathology reports. You are ER positive, PR negative, and HER2 positive. You will start chemo next week, correct?"

Mel nodded yes.

"We need to get your port in as soon as possible so you can get going on treatment according to plan. Let me go over the procedure with you."

Mel tried to follow everything, but so much information had been flooding her way, and it was difficult to keep it straight. She should be taking notes but had no paper and felt foolish asking.

Dr. Plack continued her explanations.

"You will arrive at the hospital early Friday morning, and we will try to get you in first thing. Someone should be calling tomorrow to pre-register you, and you'll need to bring your ID and insurance to the hospital. Don't eat or drink anything after midnight the night before. You will get an IV and be under general anesthesia for this surgery, but it is very quick. I will place a port under the skin. Because your tumor is in your left breast, the port will be placed on the right side of your chest. The port is a small device," she reached for a pamphlet behind her desk containing a sample port and illustrations. "As you can see, the port you will get is a triangular, quarter-sized device that is sealed with this silicone top, called a septum."

She paused to allow Melodee a few seconds to inspect the model of her first surgical implant. It was made of a dark pink colored plastic base with a squishy, opaque silicone top with three distinct bumps, in a triangular pattern, one that reminded Melodee of braille. The entire port was only slightly larger than Melodee had expected.

Dr. Plack continued her explanations. "The port contains a catheter, that tube coming off the base, that is placed inside the vena cava, the large central vein that takes blood to your heart. This way the chemo can have the best direct access to your bloodstream. Believe me, your port will be your best friend in the process because you won't have to get an IV with every treatment of chemotherapy."

That sounded wonderful to Melodee, who hated IVs. She'd had plenty of experiences with terrible IV sticks. During every former surgery or baby delivery, the IVs had been the worst part, with the misses and painful digging to reposition the needles. She always felt like a pincushion when it came to IVs. Her veins couldn't handle an IV for every chemo treatment for the next year, so she was grateful for the port already.

"For each chemotherapy treatment," Dr. Plack went on, "a curved, hollow needle, called a Huber needle, will be inserted through the port's septum to create access for the drugs, as shown here." She referred to the pamphlet, which showed an example of the specialty needle. "It has a beveled tip that won't hurt or scar like other needles can."

This was all sounding like an easy procedure that would bring great benefits.

"The port placement surgery only takes 30-45 minutes, and you'll be in the recovery room until you wake up and are able to eat and drink. After that, you'll be discharged and should be back home to rest by early afternoon. Any questions?"

Melodee had a million but not specifically about this surgery. It had all been explained in sufficient detail. Before this meeting with Dr. Plack, Mel was experiencing anxiety, due to all of the unknowns about this surgery. Now she was put at ease and actually felt gratitude for this amazing invention that would save her from the constant IVs that would be necessary without it.

Before she left the office, Melodee had to finish up the paperwork that pre-qualified her for the procedure. She also met with Dr. Plack's nurse, Stephanie, who calmed any remaining fears Melodee might have had. "Dr. Plack is incredible," Stephanie testified. "I've been here with her from the beginning and there is something special about her. She cares. She's a woman of great faith. Before every surgery, she prays with her patients, and even if you don't want her to pray with you, she prays for herself."

"Wow," Melodee thought. *"In this day and age, it's a small miracle to be paired with a surgeon with that philosophy and to have them talk about it openly."* Suddenly, an overwhelming feeling of warmth and love enveloped Melodee's entire body. She felt at that moment the confirmation that she had chosen health care professionals that had her best interest at heart and who were sensitive to Melodee's specific needs.

"And, one more thing!" Stephanie seemed excited about this last surprise. "We've had some wigs donated for our patients, so you get to pick one. Sorry that the selection has been picked through."

She wasn't kidding. There were only three wigs left—a short, curly gray one, a pixie blonde, and a medium length auburn. She went with the red, and decided then and there to begin a tradition of naming each of her wigs. This one would be known as "Ginger"

Prayers and a free wig: Melodee couldn't think of a better way to end the appointment.

The morning of surgery came quickly. Melodee, not usually a morning person, was wide-awake, packed and ready before Stephen's alarm went off. They drove to the hospital, and got set up in pre-op. Miraculously, the nurse who put in the IV actually did a great job. For the first time in history, Melodee didn't have to be stuck more than once! What a tender mercy!

Shortly after, a nurse anesthetist pulled back the drape, entered the room, and introduced himself. "I'm going to be your best friend today. I will be giving you the good stuff! Let's get started." He made a few preparations and then explained, "This will calm you before the procedure." As the drugs pulsed through her veins, she felt relaxed and carefree. It was time to say goodbye to Stephen and move to the operating room.

The nurses rolled Melodee through a labyrinth of hallways and swinging doors back to the OR, where Dr. Plack was waiting. There were others in the room to help Melodee move from the stretcher to the OR bed, and then she felt Dr. Plack hold her hand and lean in close to pray. She was only aware of the sounds and the calming, peaceful feeling; the words began to slur together as she drifted off into darkness.

The next thing she remembered was hearing someone calling, "Melodee? Melodee? It's time to wake up!" She didn't want to open her eyes! She had been having the most restful, deep sleep and didn't want it to end. The voices wouldn't stop calling her name, and she started to recognize one of them as Stephen's. It was time to follow their directions and awake.

Melodee was in a recovery area, and Stephen was there talking with the nurses. Melodee usually came out of anesthesia well, and was soon eating ice chips and asking for something more substantive to eat. She quickly scarfed down graham crackers and three cups of cranberry juice. It had been over twelve hours since she'd had anything to eat or drink, and she was hungry. She peeked under her gown to observe what the surgeon had done to her. She saw only a 4-inch-square dressing taped in place, covering the top of her right breast.

The pain was minimal, and she was directed to not lift anything over ten pounds for fourteen days, to not shower for twenty-four hours, and to stay out of baths, hot tubs, or swimming pools for two weeks. She was discharged and able to go home and rest.

All that was left to do was wait for chemotherapy to begin the following Tuesday. Time was a strange thing. It had not even been two weeks since Melodee had learned that the lump in her breast was a malignant tumor, and now she had to simply wait around for days until she could begin to do anything about it. The anticipation to start fighting was becoming nearly as challenging as the trial itself! Over the weekend, the boys were passed around between Stephen's parents, his brother and their sister-in-law, and Melodee's mom, who had flown in to help.

Even with all this extra help, the morning before chemo was tough. Stephen was at work, and the boys were at the park with Mel's mom. For the first time in the busiest two weeks of her life, Melodee was alone, not with any member of her family or a healthcare professional. The house was much too quiet, and reading through the cards and messages that had poured in wasn't enough to ward off the overwhelming heartache. Up until that moment she had been able to remain relatively put together, despite her world crashing down around her. Not that morning.

Suddenly, a wave of emotions hit her all at once, and she was overcome. She sat on the floor of her bedroom, feeling completely alone and in total darkness. She was enveloped with a gripping despair.

"I can't do this!

I don't want to do this!

This can't be happening!"

Fear, anger, sadness, confusion, frustration, anxiety, hate, loneliness, fatigue, hopelessness, and grief all at once seemed to cloud her thinking, as if an actual mist of darkness had descended upon her, choking her.

"This is too much! I haven't even begun and already I hate everything about this. I've done many hard things in the last thirty years, but I do not want to do this one! It's not fair, and it's nothing I've ever thought I even needed to be worried about! I'm already tired."

Her heart ached in sorrow, and it became difficult to breathe. She thought she was a strong person, but fighting the unknown and scary cancer foe was too much.

This internal agony was all in her head until she finally caught her breath again. It was mostly a reflex of emotion, but she cried out, screaming, as she was alone, and no one would hear. She screamed, again, louder and longer, as if it was the last sound she'd ever make. Grabbing a pillow to smother the noise, she finally called out, "WHY?" after coming up for air. This one word spilled out between deep sobs.

"Why, WHY, *why?*"

Her shoulders shook as she cried heavy, ugly tears, and her entire body began to tremble in response.

She had never before felt this way. Maybe once, when her group of friends suddenly turned on her in 7th grade causing her to spend most of a month hiding in the bathroom during lunch, came close. The worst imaginable of all human feelings, loneliness, seized her entire soul. This lack of companionship was more terrifying than cancer. It was as if she were totally alone, the loneliest she had ever been, and no one could possibly hear or understand.

At that moment, Melodee prayed for comfort like never before. She prayed that she might be strong enough, with help from above, to endure the pains of this trial. She prayed for peace. Suddenly, she did not feel so alone in that empty house. She was not forced to suffer alone for long; her plea had not gone unheard. Shortly after the question had escaped her lips, she sensed a peace, even lightness. She was able to breathe again and felt the heaviness begin to lift. The tears slowed, and her fear dispersed. She was reminded of that feeling of her physician holding her hand and leaning in close to pray before surgery. She had not ever been alone, and God would continue to bless her as she pressed on. She felt love from above; light replaced the darkness of despair

Nothing about this process would be easy. Melodee would suffer through pain, sickness, and many unknowns, but she would never be alone.

CHEMO AND HAIR LOSS

The first day of chemo felt a lot like the first day of school. Melodee woke up early that morning with a combination of anxiety and excitement. She put on a new outfit and packed her new bag full of books to keep her busy and a few snacks, including chocolate! Her mom, who had flown in from out of town, wanted to take Mel's picture by the front door and even got to drive her on that first day.

Melodee signed in at the front desk of Dr. Nabhi's office, paid her $108 co-pay, and waited to be called. This office was much more convenient to Melodee's home, only 30 minutes away versus an hour, and it was just down the hall from Dr. Plack. She was not alone in the waiting area, but was by far the youngest person there. Once, again, Mel thought, *"I'm too young for this!"* as she noticed one patient after another arriving in a wheelchair, with help from a child who was older than she. She tried to keep calm by focusing on the

TV and whatever mindless show was playing, but she still had no idea what to expect and was getting more and more anxious.

Finally, her name was called, and she followed Amanda, one of Dr. Nabhi's nurses, through the door and into the main infusion room. A row of Tiffany Blue reclining chairs faced a wall of windows. Each station had a television, complete with headphones, a visitor chair, and a curtain for privacy. Mel was somewhat shocked that the area was so open to other patients and their guests.

"Pick your chair," Amanda instructed.

For some reason, Melodee didn't feel comfortable picking a chair in the middle of the group; she felt those were too exposed, with little privacy. Melodee asked her mom to place her bag in the chair at the far end of the room, the one in the corner and closest to the restroom. There seemed to be some safety in having at least one real wall to close off her space. Instead of being immediately seated, Melodee then followed Amanda into a small side room to take her weight, temperature, and blood pressure before beginning the actual treatment. Melodee's vitals were still normal, although her blood pressure was higher than a week before. "You must be nervous," Amanda guessed, and Melodee just smiled and nodded. There was no hiding it from the machines. "Nervous is an understatement!"

Amanda recorded Melodee's weight and instructed, "Wait in your chair while I gather your medicines."

A few moments later, Amanda returned to Melodee's chair and pulled a privacy curtain behind them to make a private room.

"Did you use the cream this morning?" Amanda asked, as she placed a mountain of fluids, cased in clear plastic bags, on the side table and pulled a rolling chair close by. She was referring to EMLA, a prescription strength cream with the active ingredients of Lidocaine and Prilocaine, which Melodee had been instructed to spread on her skin in the area over her port a few hours prior to her appointment time to numb her skin and make the needle insertion less painful.

As Melodee pulled her shirt collar down to expose her covered port, Amanda could easily see the answer was yes. "Good. You'll be grateful for that pain control."

Amanda prepared the station to get started. She unwrapped the sterile gloves and special needle. She cleaned the port site, first wiping away the excess EMLA, and then using prepared iodine swabs to disinfect. Then came the fun part.

"Sit up straight and take a deep breath," Amanda instructed.

Mel looked away, as she was not a fan of watching needles penetrate her skin. Thankfully, before she could fully exhale, it was in, and the plastic "wings" on each side of the needle were clicked down to hold everything in place. Amanda flushed the port with a Heparin solution to prevent blood clots and connected the tubing from the needle to the one hanging down from the first bag of medicine.

"First, you'll get some fluids, then a steroid and nausea mixture, and then Benadryl. That should make you very sleepy. Ring the bell if you need anything, and try to relax." Amanda pointed to the silver bell that each patient had at his/her station. "Can you think of anything I can get you now?" Mel shook her head "no" and, in response to another bell ringing down the row, Amanda was off to help another patient.

44

Melodee and her mom were able to talk and catch up, and after an hour into the process, the machine that was pumping her drugs started beeping, indicating the first medicine had finished its infusion. After a few seconds of the alarm sounding, Amanda opened the curtain and changed the bag.

With all the extra fluids being added to her system, soon enough Mel had to use the restroom, and rang the bell at her station, calling to the nurses. Amanda demonstrated how Melodee could simply unplug the pump from the outlet in the floor behind her chair, roll the whole machine into the restroom with her, and then plug it back in at her station, not missing a minute of chemo, as the pump had battery power, as well. Melodee was becoming a pro in no time at all.

With the completion of each bag of fluid, the familiar beeping alarm signaled the nurses to start the next set. Melodee felt nothing at all until the Benadryl was about halfway through. The effects were unmistakable; her body began to feel heavy, her head difficult to hold up. This was a drug-induced sleepiness close to the feeling of being put under anesthesia. The dose was so much higher than an over-the-counter administration of Benadryl that Melodee was not prepared for how strongly the side effects hit her. She tried to fight against the drowsiness, but it was too strong. She wanted to keep reading and chatting with her mom, but instead fell into a deep, drooling sleep and didn't want to wake! In fact, the next drug, Herceptin, was started and completed while she was dreaming. Although Melodee would have happily slept through the entire process, it was necessary that she be awake for observation for the last drug. Both Melodee's mother and Amanda had to shake Melodee for several minutes before they were able to bring her out of her deep sleep.

The next instructions seemed to be the most important of the day. Amanda was hanging the last bag—the actual chemo, Paclitaxel--on the hook and making the preparations to start its administration. "We will run this slowly to pay attention to any signs of allergic reaction." Melodee was still very drowsy from the Benadryl but could sense the seriousness of what Amanda was explaining. "We must pay close attention to any possible signs of a serious allergic reaction to this chemo. Very few patients actually have severe allergies to this drug, but it has been known to happen. We will just monitor you closely for the first treatment. Please alert one of us nurses if you feel extremely nauseous, have any kind of breakout or a terrible itchy feeling throughout your body. If none of these reactions occur, there shouldn't be any risk of allergies."

As the tubing was clicked open and the liquid entered her port, Melodee could feel warmth moving through her chest. It wasn't painful or burning, but she could tell something foreign was pulsing through her veins. She was able to follow her circulatory pathway as it transported the chemo throughout her body, feeling the heat spread across her chest, through her heart, down her core, and out to each limb. Although Melodee could feel her body's response to this unfamiliar substance, she thankfully had no signs of an allergic reaction.

Dr. Nabhi soon made her rounds, stopping by Melodee's area to announce the best news of the day. "We have great news," she began, after the introductions were made between Mel's mother and her oncologist. "The results of your genetic testing have all come back negative." This was good news! "Thankfully, this means that your siblings and children are much less likely to need to be tested early for cancer. It also means you have a wider range of surgical options, and we can wait to make those decisions until after you complete chemotherapy. You seem to have responded well to all of the drugs today, with no complications. That's good. Do you have any questions now that you've completed your first round?"

"Will I need to come back throughout the week before the next round?"

"Yes, you will. You will receive an immunity boosting shot as well as have blood work collected in order to check for any major problems. Make sure you rest as much as possible and try to eat healthy. You need all the strength you can maintain. Call us if you have any problems or a high fever."

Melodee put great trust in Dr. Nabhi and felt confident in her abilities. Mel's mom later confessed how comforting it had been to get to meet Dr. Nabhi and know who was treating her 'baby' from miles and miles away. It put her mind at ease to have been able to attend Mel's first session.

About six hours after the chemo began, it was finally time to go home. All the bags were drained, and the final alarm sounded on Melodee's pump. Amanda returned to Mel's station for the last time of the day, instructed her to take another deep breath, and carefully removed the needle. "Hold pressure here," Amanda instructed, placing a square of gauze over the needle's entry site and allowing Melodee to take hold of the bandage while she disposed of the needle and the tubing. She grabbed a packet of alcohol wipes to clear the remaining iodine from Melodee's port site and covered the needle's entry point with a small, round bandage. Before Melodee could leave, Amanda gave her some clear instructions. "Rest when you can. Drink plenty of fluids. Be sure to take your nausea medicine as prescribed, and stay on top of it, even if you don't feel nauseous; that's the purpose of the drugs you've been given, and if you wait too long to take them, it will be harder for them to work." She handed Melodee two pieces of paper with printed instructions. "This one is your next appointment time. You'll return next Tuesday at around the same time. However, we will need to see you tomorrow morning to give you a shot to boost your immunity and hopefully prevent infections. The next paper is the order for blood work, which will need to be done on Friday."

All of this was news to Mel. Another drive to the hospital tomorrow? Oh, and blood work on Friday? "I might as well move in, as often as I'm going to be a visitor," she thought to herself.

That evening, Melodee was able to rest. She didn't want to overdo things, and she was grateful her mom was in town to help with the boys. She didn't feel sick, thanks to the nausea medication she'd been instructed to take, but did feel more fatigued than usual.

Chemo had not been as bad as she had expected, but the shot the following day was terrible. Melodee followed Lila back to the area where her required stats were recorded. Then Lila began to prepare for the shot. Melodee was shocked at the size of the applicator. Melodee had imagined this would be much like a flu shot and was slightly terrified by the huge needle she saw before her. Lila prepared an injection site about two inches below Melodee's belly button by using a few alcohol swabs to disinfect the skin. She placed the needle near the site, and Mel looked away as the large needle was practically shoved into her gut, which was unbelievably unpleasant. Shortly thereafter, Melodee felt a burning and aching at the entry point.

Melodee did this every week and began to see a pattern in the side effects she experienced. For the next few days, she had bruising and soreness around the area of the shot. Through what was probably a combination of her steroids and nausea medicines wearing off, as well as the side effects from the shot itself, Mel felt terrible for a few days after receiving the shot. She had trouble sleeping and often woke up with a sore jaw from clenching her teeth in the overnight pain and discomfort.

In fact, one Wednesday night after receiving the shot earlier that day, Melodee could not fall asleep. In the early hours of the morning, Melodee's insomnia led her to experience the pain for which she most often was asleep, the same pain that would contribute to those regularly scheduled Thursday morning body aches and clenched jaw pains. The process of her shot doing its work as it moved through her body was excruciating to experience, especially while still awake. A throbbing burn radiated from the shots' entry point in her abdomen, up into her ribcage, and down and around to her hips and spine. She ached all over. Her heart felt as if hundreds of tiny needles were being poked through her chest as well. To describe the side effects she experienced from the shot, Melodee would explain, "It feels like a combination of labor pains, upset stomach, bowel issues, pulled muscles, heartburn, and cramps." This small amount of suffering was nothing life threatening. Certainly, people have endured worse. However, Mel was grateful for the Xanax, which Dr. Nabhi prescribed for anxiety and as a sleep aid. Melodee made sure to follow her doctor's advice and take this on Wednesday evenings to avoid being awake during the hours when her weekly shot forced her bones to work overtime.

From the chemo itself, Mel also experienced a few unpleasant side effects. Food didn't sound appetizing; thanks to the metallic taste in her mouth, and sometimes certain smells made her feel queasy. She was exhausted and in pain for four to five days after chemo. On the sixth day, there was a turnaround, and Mel began to feel better. Unfortunately, this recovery was short lived because as soon as Melodee felt improvement, it would be time to begin the cycle again.

Her calendar for the next three months looked a lot like this:

Tuesday: CHEMO (find someone to watch the boys.)

Wednesday: SHOT (find someone to watch the boys.)

Friday: BLOOD WORK (find someone to watch the boys.)

Before Melodee began her treatment for breast cancer, Dr. Nabhi had given her the glimmer of hope that her hair would merely thin for the first three months because she would begin with the milder of her prescribed chemotherapies. It would not be until the latter half of the process that Mel would experience the drastic and complete hair loss so characteristic of cancer patients. Since Melodee's hair before cancer was just longer than shoulder-length and fairly thick, Dr. Nabhi did advise her to cut it much shorter, which would make the hair loss seem less drastic. Mel's next-door neighbor, Gloria, was also her stylist and was able to cut Melodee's hair into an attractive and trendy short bob. She loved this new look, which suited her bone structure, and it was a small miracle to feel attractive even while undergoing chemotherapy treatments. Her new style was short-lived, however.

A few days after her haircut, Melodee was relaxing in a hot bath, one of her nightly rituals to ease sore muscles and calm her mind. This night, she was also testing a new facial mask, one specifically developed for those with sensitive skin, especially from chemotherapy treatments. As she rinsed her face and ran her hands through her hair to catch any remaining bits, her fingers came out with more than just remaining mask. Looking down in total surprise, she gasped at the sight of a dark nest of hair entangled in her hands. Melodee had experienced hair loss after each of her three pregnancies, but this was a shocking amount of hair, especially for applying almost no pressure to her follicles and after feeling no pain. It took no more than a few days of losing large hair clumps in the shower or while running a brush or her hands through her hair for Melodee to realize that Dr. Nabhi's idea of thinning hair was much different from her own. She had not been adequately prepared for this! She had been promised more time before she would have to accept complete baldness!

One morning while getting ready, Mel brushed her hair and looked down into the bathroom sink. There was hair everywhere: the counter, the floor, her bathroom rug, the shoulder of her bathrobe, and falling from the bristles of her brush. This disturbing and unexpected preview of what was to come triggered a sudden wave of tears. Although she understood that hair loss would be a side effect of her chemotherapy, she just didn't seem to have the tools necessary to be completely prepared for the day the concept of hair loss became her reality. It seemed so superficial that Mel could be so dramatically emotional over something as trivial as hair, but here she was, having another meltdown! This was happening too quickly! It wasn't fair! She was supposed to have more time to adjust to this loss! What was the point of asking Gloria to cut and style hair that was going to fall out anyway? She might as well have had her neighbor shave it off, saving time and energy. As Mel cleaned up the mountain of hair, she noticed the thinning areas on her head, and a new wave of tears began.

When Melodee had gotten her emotions under control, she made a decision. Kristen, a friend from church had offered to host a hat and scarf shower when the time came that Melodee would need those options to cover her balding head. They had both planned a date for later in the year. That day, Mel called Kristen to suggest an impromptu head shaving party/wig and hat shower for the following weekend.

"Are you up to hosting this, or should I just do it alone?"

Kristen responded immediately, "You are NOT going to do this alone! I don't care if I am the only other person there, but you are going to have people to support you in this step of your journey!"

"You're right. I don't need to do this alone. It will be better to have those I love there to buoy me up for something so hard."

"Exactly. I'll call around, and we will make this happen. This is one thing you don't need to worry about putting together. Leave it all to me. I can't wait!"

The party was scheduled for the Friday after Mel's sixth Paclitaxel treatment, the halfway point for her first type of chemo. Much sooner than expected, Melodee was forced to let go of a large part of her identity; the dreaded day of head shaving had arrived too quickly. Melodee insisted that Stephen and the boys attend her party. There was also a great turnout of friends who Mel lovingly named her "Pink Warriors," as they had banded together to support her for one of the most emotional points in her battle. The guests were required to wrap their heads in scarves or cover up with hats, so Mel would not be alone in her new fashion.

When the razor started to buzz, Stephen stepped up and volunteered to have his head shaved first! He broke the ice, taking the spotlight off his nervous and anxious wife. The tension was lifted because Gloria, whom Mel had invited to do the actual shaving, suggested that Melodee take over. The couple laughed and joked as the pile of Stephen's hair on the ground grew and grew.

"I'll be able to sleep fifteen minutes longer each morning, since I won't have to wash or comb my hair," Stephen exclaimed. "Just think of all the money we'll save on hair care products! Neither of us will need them for months!"

It had been a stroke of genius that Gloria convinced Melodee to be the one to shave Stephen's head. Having a role to play shifted Mel's attention from her fears onto the job at hand, and when it was time to switch places, Mel handed the razor over to Stephen.

"Are you *sure?*" he couldn't believe she was trusting him.

"What choice do I have? It's gotta come off somehow!"

That first run of the razor from the back of her neck to the front of her head was the hardest. Mel sat for a few seconds with her head bent down so Stephen could reach the back. As she looked to the ground, tears formed in her eyes, beading up and dropping down onto the pile of hair below. The only sound was the buzz of the clippers. To stop the waterfall of tears, Mel raised her head and smiled, and there was a collective sigh of relief from the entire room. The tears soon dissipated as the entire crowd began to grin, clap, and cheer Mel on. Suddenly the focus shifted. This was no longer a burden, but a blessing. No more would she have that daily reminder of clumps of hair washing down into the shower. Total hair loss was happening whether she wanted it or not, so the sooner she embraced it, the happier she'd be. Mel smiled through the tears and turned this obstacle into an event. There were happy tears, as she was on her way to surviving! Her hair would someday grow back and, until then, she would smile and let her light shine all the way through the top of her baldhead!

This was the moment Melodee first felt like a survivor. She was truly like a soldier preparing for war. Mel was ready for the battle of her life!

The pattern for chemotherapy became more and more like clockwork: chemo, shot, blood work, repeat. Before she knew it, Melodee had reached the first checkpoint of her cancer marathon. She had completed the twelve rounds of Paclitaxel, and it was time for another set of scans to measure the drugs' effectiveness. As Melodee reflected on the process up to this point, she recorded in her journal:

"I have felt tired, run-down, in pain, sad, frustrated, afraid, confused, and upset. However, in all of this, I have felt so blessed, so uplifted, and have felt almost a lightness, whether by the chemo made easier for me to bear, my body being able to withstand it better than some, or having my path made a little easier. I cannot believe how quickly twelve weeks has passed and how much easier--in many ways--this time has been than I originally expected. In the lightness of this trial, I can feel the light of Christ."

MORE CHEMO

There was a required ten-day resting period in between the end of Paclitaxel and the beginning of the next round of chemotherapy. Just as she was getting used to not having to make her weekly trips to the hospital, the day arrived, and Melodee reluctantly traveled back to Dr. Nabhi's office. As usual, she waited for her name to be called, chose her favorite chair, and followed Lila into the side room to record her vitals. Things were starting out exactly as they had before, but today would be different. This was the day chemo began to get more difficult. Melodee was about to begin the first of four rounds of the hard chemo, FEC.

Amanda wasn't working that day, so Melodee received her instructions from a different nurse, Jeremiah, whom she had never before seen in the office. "Your chart says today you'll begin with the same drugs you have become used to: a nausea medicine, a steroid, and Benadryl. However, today you will begin a new chemo treatment, FEC, which stands for Fluorouracil, Epirubicin, and Cyclophosphamide. It's actually administered in scrambled order: C, F, E. Cyclophosphamide can make you feel unusually bad in 10-15 minutes, so let the staff know if you begin to have severely different side effects than you are used to. With Fluorouracil, which is also known as 5FU, you must keep your mouth cold with ice or smoothies.

The cold will close down the blood vessels in your mouth to help prevent the mouth sores the drug can cause. Epirubicin is the drug also called the "red devil." It takes a long time to administer, could leave a bad taste in your mouth, and can cause many of the undesired side effects of chemo. Also, as you will be given more drugs with each round, the time you're here will increase to between six and eight hours, depending on the speed of the drip." With that explanation, Jeremiah finished preparations to begin. He sterilized the port site, unwrapped the needle, and declared, "Alright, let's get started!"

The great thing about FEC was that Melodee only needed four rounds, given once every three weeks. At least she would get a break from the feeling of constantly being at the hospital! She was still required to return the day after chemo for a shot to stimulate the growth of white blood cells, this time one strong enough to last for the three weeks in between rounds. The weekly blood tests had not changed, but she was looking forward to at least four fewer hospital visits within the three-week period.

While the first few bags of medicine were flowing, Dr. Nabhi came to check in on Melodee and review the reports from her most recent scans. It was very good news. Melodee's tumor had shrunk from 5cm down to 2-2 ½ cm, more than halfway!

"This is why we give chemo before surgery. We are able to have concrete results to let us see if you are responding well to chemotherapy. As you can see, the chemo is working! This is a wonderful result. I am very encouraged."

Hearing this small piece of good news gave Melodee even more ammunition for continuing her fight. These results were only the first of many small miracles in her journey.

Instead of the break Mel thought she would have in between rounds of FEC, the few weeks following the first round were almost unbearable. Dr. Nabhi claimed that about 90% of her patients are able to undergo chemotherapy without having it interrupt their daily life or work schedules.

Melodee was beginning to believe that she was one of the unlucky 10% or she just wasn't as strong as she once believed. Even while taking her prescribed doses of Ondansetron and Promethazine, anti-nausea medications, she was still nauseous every day and began to develop abhorrence for nearly all foods. The smell of most food cooking, especially eggs, made her stomach turn. One evening, the aroma of a baking chicken pot pie, something she once regarded as comfort food, sent her running, barely making it to the toilet before vomiting.

The last straw was on the morning of her second round of FEC. On the way to Dr. Nabhi's office, Melodee's breakfast consisted of a fruit smoothie, one of the only foods that had been sustaining her in the previous three unsettling weeks. She drank half and saved the rest to keep her mouth cold during the treatment. However, on the walk from the parking garage to the office, Melodee's stomach began to rumble. The nausea hit her out of nowhere, and she rushed to the nearest trashcan where she vomited her breakfast smoothie. The cold, smooth, burning liquid, acidic from the citrus it contained, had come back up so fast that liquid even spewed from her nose. Her stomach also kept retching, long after its contents had fully emptied. She had been so sick for so long that her reflexes had trouble restoring her body to normal. Frustrated, messy, and embarrassed, she was now crying, weak, and feeling sick before the treatment even started! *"What a sad and pathetic site this must be,"* she thought!

After getting cleaned up and tossing the rest of the smoothie, (who could finish the rest after having it come back up?), Mel marched straight to the front desk of Dr. Nabhi's office and asked to speak with a nurse immediately. When Lila called Melodee back to assess her vitals and answer her concerns, Melodee explained the urgency.

"It isn't just this morning's drama. I have been so sick, much sicker than you or Dr. Nabhi claimed I should be. It doesn't seem fair that you didn't warn me for this."

Lila tried to reassure her. "I'll get Dr. Nabhi and check with her about something stronger we might be able to prescribe for you."

There was no need to wait for an appointment with the doctor before beginning the second round of treatments, as Melodee was not experiencing allergic reactions and would need to complete the three remaining rounds, even if she was nauseous.

Shortly into the infusion, Lila approached Melodee's chair, apologetic. "I checked your charts and only noticed one of the prescriptions you are supposed to be taking. Did you not receive the other?"

Melodee wasn't aware that there was something stronger she could be taking. "Okay, let me check on this," Lila answered.

A few minutes went by before the nurse reappeared. "On the last day of your Paclitaxel, Amanda wasn't here, was she?"

"No. She was on vacation."

"Well...." There was a longer than usual pause. "...there are no notes in your chart about you starting FEC and needing a new prescription. Amanda didn't record it on the day of your last Paclitaxel, and the nurse you had on the day of your FEC must not have made the connection that you hadn't received the prescription, either. Unfortunately, both of those nurses no longer work here, so we can't ask them what happened. We can only get you going from here."

Mel was speechless and a little upset, but listened, hoping there was something positive in this mix-up.

"You should have been taking a drug that comes in a three-pill set. You take one pill the day before starting chemo, one pill the morning of, and the last pill on the day after. This is the 'miracle drug' that keeps people from being nauseous or vomiting while on FEC. I'm really sorry! No wonder you've been so sick!"

Not only had Melodee missed out on the miracle drug for her first round of FEC, she wouldn't feel the full effects of this drug for the second round, as she wouldn't have two-thirds of the pills in her before chemo began.

Dr. Nabhi made her rounds and arrived at Melodee's station. The first thing out of her mouth was, "Why didn't you call us when you were so sick? We could've gotten you something stronger!" Dr. Nabhi inquired.

It was not Mel's job to research which medications they were supposed to prescribe her and call the office when something was missing. "I didn't know there *was* something stronger to take!"

"Well, make sure you pick up the prescription today and take the first two pills right away. You won't have the full effect, but you should see a great improvement over the reaction from the first FEC."

Dr. Nabhi had been correct on that much. It was amazing what having the extra medication did for Melodee's well-being! She was able to make it through the next three weeks without vomiting and with very little nausea. This truly was "better living through science," something her mom would often say.

By mid-June, Melodee had completed her third round of FEC; there was only one more round to go. Although the added medications helped with nausea, this chemo indeed lived up to its name, the "Red Devil." Mel was becoming worn down and weak. She felt worthless, unattractive, exposed, and almost alien. All of her hair was now gone. She no longer had eyebrows or eyelashes, and the top of her head was perfectly bald. She hated this look.

Summer had always been her favorite season, but this was not the summer for which her family had planned; Mom was just too sick. In addition, summertime in Texas was too hot for wigs, and she was too sensitive to being out in the sun for any length of time. She was in pain or some form of discomfort at all times of day and night.

Her last treatment was scheduled for July 4th, and the family had a getaway trip to the beach planned in celebration. The fireworks this year would not only be in remembrance of her country's independence; they would be a celebration of freedom from the bonds of chemotherapy. Her body had different plans.

Melodee could not remember a time in her life when she felt worse. In the week before her last scheduled treatment, she had no energy, experienced cold sweats, fever, chills, aches, fatigue, no appetite, and began to wonder if she had the flu. When Mel finally called Dr. Nabhi, the results of the latest blood test explained the symptoms.

"I was planning on calling you later today," Dr. Nabhi explained, when she came to the phone. "Your white blood cell count from last week came back very low. I am going to call in an antibiotic for you and will send orders to the lab for additional blood tomorrow."

"Does this mean I won't be able to have chemo on schedule?" Melodee probed.

"You can only receive chemo if your numbers are high enough. We can't risk further infection, so if you are not healthy enough for chemo, we will have to reschedule."

Mel expected this answer, but it was not what she wanted to hear. She did not want her treatment to be postponed. "What else can I do to help bring my numbers up?"

Nabhi replied, "Do not eat any fresh fruits or vegetables, get lots of rest, stay hydrated, make sure you get iron, whether from vitamins or from meat, wash your hands, and stay away from other people as much as possible."

Most of these suggestions made sense, but no fresh fruit or vegetables? Melodee could think of no time in the history of history when a doctor would advise *against* fresh produce. Wasn't she supposed to be eating healthy foods to stay healthy? It didn't make sense, but Mel was willing to follow orders exactly if it meant there was a chance for her to stay on schedule.

Unfortunately, when Melodee woke up the next day, the day of her ordered CBC (complete blood count), she hit rock bottom. Her body was showing all the signs of being broken down from months of chemotherapy. When her eyes opened that morning, it took incredible effort to sit up in bed. As if gravity had suddenly changed, every movement felt like wading through molasses. Faint, feeble, feverish, and in a great deal of pain, she knew driving was a bad idea and called around to find someone to chauffeur her to the hospital. Loved ones rallied to step in and take over duties that Melodee just did not have strength to carry out.

A neighbor rushed over to climb stairs and rescue Mel's screaming toddler from his crib. Other friends and family stepped up to care for her children at all hours of the day, to cook meals, and even to help Melodee walk back to bed. She slept most of the day and still did not feel rested. She ate and drank only to stay alive, because nothing sounded appetizing. The best way to describe her state was one of feeling "mostly dead," and the CBC results confirmed what her body was already telling her: WBC (white blood count) was at 0.9, lower than the week before and much lower than the minimum level of 4.0 required to receive another dose of chemo. In addition, her ANC (absolute neutrophil count), which would need to be at least 1.0, came back at 0.2. Melodee wondered if she would ever feel better again.

The worst of the latest side effects Melodee felt just before her final round of FEC began to subside. On the Friday before July 4th, the original scheduled date for her final round, Dr. Nabhi called in STAT blood work, and everyone was relieved to hear that Mel's WBC had come up to 2.7 and her ANC was up to 1.0. This was promising, and Mel received another shot to boost her numbers even higher. She despised these shots, but held out hope that this one would make her well enough to complete the last dose of chemo on schedule and be able to celebrate at the beach.

Sadly, all of Melodee's efforts to remain healthy had been in vain. The discomfort and hassle from the extra shot, staying at home and away from the germs of others, frequent hand washing, taking an iron supplement, eating the right foods, and resting still was not enough to raise her numbers to the minimum requirements for chemotherapy. She would now be forced to wait at least another week before repeating the tests. This disappointing news meant that staying on schedule for chemo was out of the question, and Dr. Nabhi would not clear her to travel to the beach, as planned. Stephen and the boys took the trip with several members of their extended family, leaving Mel at home to rest and recuperate.

With Stephen and the boys gone for the week, the house was quiet...too quiet. Mel had nowhere to go and no energy to leave her bed. Everything she had been holding inside, all the fears and frustrations came pouring out. This was a new low in life. She had never suffered quite as much physically as she was at this moment, and that day she had an emotional breakdown to match her physical one. In her anger and frustration, she began to feel sorry for herself, almost angry. Angry with whom? It was hard to say. Herself? Dr. Nabhi? Anyone who did not have cancer? God?

The whole situation and this level of suffering were beyond frustrating. She cried and questioned the reasons for her hardships. Why couldn't this treatment plan run more smoothly? Why did such a hard trial have to keep getting harder? Wasn't chemo itself adequately difficult? Had she not endured enough? Couldn't she skip all of the waiting and just get this over with? She had been such a fighter for so long, so why couldn't she catch a break? Why was God punishing her with so much intensity?

Suddenly, the only possible answer to her questions came to her mind:

Cancer was finally the one trial that Melodee could not overcome on her own. She could not talk her way out of it or work her way out of it or fake her way out of it or simply remain patient enough for it to pass. She would only survive by finally letting go of stubborn control, humbling herself, and realizing that at times like these she had to strengthen her faith and do her best to press forward, believing God would carry her the rest of the way. Cancer had taught her that on her own, she truly was nothing. Her body was broken down and tired.

If she continued to attempt to battle cancer completely on her own strength, she would not overcome. She needed her doctors, she needed family and friends, she needed prayers from her support system, and most importantly, she needed God. Instead of fighting alone, it was time to develop humility in the midst of suffering and ask for and accept the strengthening power that can come from on high. She had been told her whole life "you are never alone," but it wasn't until this moment that she understood the truthfulness of this promise.

Even though there would be times when she would be frustrated and have questions, like: "Why can't I just be at the beach with my family, listening to the sound of waves crashing on the shore and feeling the sand beneath my toes?" Even then, God would be listening. And, even if the answer was "no, I can't make cancer go away" or, "not now," it was okay to ask, as long as she was willing to accept His will. Through the grace of God, Melodee was able to overcome the pain and the suffering chemotherapy was causing. Relying on her belief in God helped pull her out of despair. With Him, she could overcome.

PREPARING FOR MORE SURGERY

Sometimes, just sometimes, the answers you think you will never understand are actually revealed. It turned out that the family vacation Melodee so desperately wanted to attend became a comedy of errors. Between jellyfish attacks, several waves of food poisoning, and record heat, the beach was anything but a safe environment for a compromised immune system. If Melodee had refused to follow Dr. Nabhi's orders, her "vacation" would have quite possibly landed her in the emergency room, and potentially something worse. In addition, further illness would have easily pushed back her final treatment even further. What she considered to be the last straw of what she was able to bear was actually a blessing in disguise.

If Melodee had not been at the height of physical suffering, she would not have learned this lesson that God truly has her best interests in mind at all times. She was in great pain and extremely weak and exhausted, but she was alive and not confined to a hospital bed. This was a lesson in learning to trust the Lord that she could not have learned another way.

For the next full week, Melodee rested and kept mostly quarantine-like precautions. Her sister, Emmalee, flew in to help catch up on household projects that had been piling up for months. They also stayed up watching movies and laughing, which reset Mel's outlook and attitude on life. When Em had to return home, one of Mel's dear friends, Michele, flew in as a reliever. Michele picked up a variety of meats to build up Mel's iron. Anything on the list of acceptable food that also sounded appetizing, she prepared. She also played with the boys when they returned from the beach. Thanks to Michele, Melodee was well fed and well rested for another week.

The next Friday, Melodee received her latest CBC reports. Her blood counts had finally met the minimum requirements for the last round of chemo! She jumped when she got the news, calling out, "I get to have chemo next week! HOORAY!" (Who knew anyone would be so excited to put "the red devil" in his or her body!) She had learned to be grateful for the silver linings in even the worst and most difficult trials of life.

She approached her last day of FEC with some anxiety, but with a renewed faith. The extra healing time and her trust in God truly made her stronger, and the last round was actually the easiest. She finally had the correct nausea medications, was better prepared to endure the side effects, had been given additional recovery time beforehand, and was humble enough to seek strength through prayer. As the last of the "red devil" drained into her veins, she breathed a sigh of relief!

Melodee's faith had been strengthened through experiencing a trial that caused true suffering. Her faith preceded a miracle, as well. Exactly six months from the day she had been diagnosed with breast cancer, the final ultrasound results came back: no definable mass or lesion with discernible margins could be identified by the scan! This meant chemotherapy had done its job; there was no longer any evidence of disease! It also meant she would now face the next battle in the war against cancer: surgery.

Melodee's doctors had been so focused on helping her body survive chemotherapy that they had not thoroughly explained her surgery options beforehand. In addition, the final choice could not have been made until she had scans done following chemo. Mel's latest tests had shown no evidence of disease, and now she had to decide whether she wanted a lumpectomy paired with radiation, a mastectomy of her left breast only, or a full mastectomy and reconstruction. It was a decision that could affect her entire life, so she consulted with both her oncologist and her breast surgeon to gather information.

Dr. Nabhi got right to the point, as she was only able to squeeze Melodee into her very tight schedule for a few minutes. She was also reluctant to give an exact surgical recommendation, explaining that she deals on a cellular and chemical level and wanted to know the pathology of Melodee's tissue before moving forward with her best opinion.

"Because your initial mammogram and ultrasound showed so many calcifications that are still there," she explained, "it is difficult to know if those areas are precancerous or not. There is a possibility that these areas could later transform into cancer, but we cannot know for sure without looking at the pathology of that tissue."

That was scary.

"Some patients elect for a mastectomy, to be completely done with the whole thing, but you could have a lumpectomy to remove the entire area of the original mass, plus extra tissue for study. After the pathology reports come back, we would have scientific proof of whether or not your calcifications are precancerous. Then, I could give you my final recommendation, based on the percent of possible recurrence of cancer. It might be that your entire breast tissue was precancerous, and you would need to move forward with a mastectomy, anyway. Or, the results might show that all those calcifications just represent your normal tissue, are benign, and the lumpectomy plus radiation would suffice."

That sounded like a lot of extra surgical recoveries, only to still have to go through with the full mastectomy.

"If your tissue came back benign and you chose radiation," Nabhi further explained, "one week after your lumpectomy, you would start that six-week process, five days a week!"

Melodee was shocked at the commitment required for that treatment plan. It also didn't make a lot of sense to have surgery just to discover the pathology of her tissue, which could end up proving that the other surgery was necessary, anyway. She needed the advice of a surgeon and walked down the hall to have her consultation with Dr. Plack, whom she had not seen in six months.

Dr. Plack immediately noticed a difference in Melodee's appearance. Mel was now on the other side of the chemo; her hair was just starting to grow in, and she had gained fifteen pounds in the process.

"You look like a different woman than the one who came to me in January," Dr. Plack commented.

Melodee wasn't sure if that was meant as a compliment or a complaint until her follow-up statement: "You are now a true survivor!"

Melodee expressed concerns about her physical appearance, especially her frustration with the weight gain; she had assumed chemotherapy would cause her to lose weight, not gain it.

"It used to be that way, before advances in both chemo and the corresponding nausea medications," Dr. Plack explained. "Now, we expect patients to gain weight, and we actually prefer it. That helps so much when we get to the surgical part of your journey."

"Speaking of surgeries, I have so many questions!" Melodee got out her notebook to go over the list of questions she had prepared.

"Well, which surgery are you planning to have?" was Dr. Plack's first question.

"I need you to explain all of my options, complete with the pros and cons of each choice. Pretend that I know nothing, and include what you would recommend for me personally," answered Mel.

"Get ready; it's a lot to take in."

Dr. Plack then started off with her recommendation: based on Melodee's age and the aggressive nature of her cancer, she suggested a bilateral mastectomy (removal of both breasts) and reconstruction.

"You have a lot of life left to live, which means decades of time for a possible recurrence. If you choose this option, I will be able to remove approximately 97-98% of breast tissue. This also means there is about a 97-98% chance that cancer won't return. Plus, you will never need another mammogram!"

Mel put a star next to that last point, noticing that the majority of information about this option seemed to fall in the 'pro' column.

Dr. Plack continued, "At the same time of the mastectomy, you would have immediate reconstruction. It is one long surgery, about eight hours combined, and I will be able to keep most of your existing breast skin. A plastic surgeon will then reconstruct breasts by removing abdominal tissue and reattaching it on a micro level, reconnecting the blood vessels."

Dr. Plack did a quick exam of Melodee's midsection, and said, "This is where that extra fifteen pounds comes in handy. Your plastic surgeon will have a lot of tissue to make some nice, big boobies for you!"

"Thanks, I think?" Mel laughed to herself, *"So, I get a boob job and tummy tuck in one! What's wrong with that?"* Who knew she would be able to find a silver lining in her muffin top? She was learning unusual lessons as each chapter unfolded. So far, Melodee had not heard any negatives for this option.

Dr. Plack continued, "This type of reconstruction looks natural, is made from your natural tissue, and lasts forever. After a short healing process, three months or so, you will have another surgery for touch-up work and the reconstruction of your nipples, including tattoos."

Again, this all felt very doable. Dr. Plack had saved the negatives for last.

"The cons of this procedure are the length of surgery, the five-day hospital stay to drain the sites and watch for complications, and a six to eight week post-op recovery time. You will also have quite a bit of pain, a difficult time being able to get up and stand up straight, and will not be able to lift anything over 5 pounds for several weeks."

The first thought that came to Mel's mind over the list of negatives was: *"This is NOT a disease for mothers of young children!"*

Mel had already been leaning toward this surgery but listened to the information about the other option, which was a lumpectomy and radiation. Dr. Plack explained, "The pros to this, in my opinion, are basically just easier surgery and recovery."

Mel could tell this surgeon was not pushing for this route because the cons of radiation seemed to outweigh the pros.

"The area of tissue we would need to remove for your lumpectomy would be quite large, based on the original size of your tumor. After recovery from this surgery, you would follow up with radiation, which can cause skin color changes, skin toughening, and scar tissue. In addition, your breast tissue would shrink even more from radiation. This would probably result in you needing a reduction on your right breast to even everything out."

Even though Mel had heard a few horror stories of radiation, she had never thought about possibly needing plastic surgery just to compensate for the loss of tissue in her infected breast.

"Plus," the doctor went on, "if you chose this treatment and cancer came back, you would require a bilateral mastectomy anyway, and then the doctors would be working with scarred and radiation-damaged skin instead of healthy tissue."

Dr. Plack was, not surprisingly, anti-radiation and pro-surgery. She is a surgeon, after all! With this information, Melodee now felt about 90% sure that the mastectomy and reconstruction was the best option for her. She just needed to meet with the plastic surgeon to ask a few more questions. The surgeon Dr. Plack worked with most often, one of the best in Houston, had an office downtown in the Med Center. He was willing to meet with Melodee at Dr. Plack's office, so an appointment was set for the following week, directly after her next infusion of Herceptin.

One week later, Melodee completed her thirteenth dose of Herceptin and walked down the hall to Dr. Plack's office. She was led back to the conference room and told to "make herself at home" until the plastic surgeon arrived. To keep busy while she waited, Mel went over her notes and recorded a few questions she would ask to help make an informed decision.

About twenty minutes later, Dr. Plack's nurse knocked and entered the room, followed by an attractive man with dark hair and eyes, wearing a white coat and a smile.

"Hello!" he exclaimed, shaking Melodee's hand firmly. "I'm Dr. Sean Boone."

"Melodee Cooper." She smiled back, liking this man already.

"Tell me about yourself, Melodee."

This caught her off guard, as she was expecting to learn about him and the surgery first. "Well, I'm 33. I'm the mother of three boys. I'm an Aggie."

The doctor immediately stopped her.

"I'm an Aggie! Did you know that already?"

She didn't, but the connection from both being former students of Texas A&M pretty much sealed the deal. She knew there was something she liked about him! Instead of discussing breast surgery, they began to share stories of football games and other college memories. He then asked where she was from, how she ended up in Houston and about her work history before sharing a little about his history in education and his practice. Eventually the conversation moved to cancer.

"Okay, let's get down to business. Do you have a family history of breast cancer?"

"No."

"Do you smoke?"

"Never."

"Never? Interesting."

She wondered if he really believed her, but he changed the subject.

"What has been the hardest part of your cancer journey up to this point?"

After a few moments of thinking, she explained that the most difficult thing has been all of the unknowns and extra challenges that have crept in during the process.

"All of the unexpected surprises have been difficult to deal with, on top of the regular physically challenging stuff."

"I can see how you feel that way," he stated, "but I believe our challenges in life can often be blessings. Most of my patients have such a love for life and such a happy outlook, now that cancer is all in hindsight. I haven't had to overcome anything so challenging in my life, so I don't even fully understand it, but I can see the changes in my patients; it's inspiring."

Dr. Boone then went on to explain that his office and Dr. Plack's are both very faith-based. "God has a way of using challenges to build you up and make you stronger, if you have the faith to see the miracles."

Melodee started tearing up as he spoke, reaching for a tissue from the box on the desk. She was a little embarrassed at this reaction and about crying in front of a total stranger. She knew nothing about this doctor's background prior to this initial consultation and had never met him before, but she felt that his testimony of his faith began to form a connection between them. This was just another tender mercy in the process, that God had led her to doctors with a strong belief in God.

"What do you know about reconstruction?" he asked, changing the subject.

"Only what Dr. Plack told me last week. Before that, my only information had been from friends who have told me about their own breast augmentations."

"Good," he replied. "You don't have too many preconceived notions."

He then began to explain the procedure.

"What we will do on you is called DIEP flap surgery. There is an incision made in the abdomen from hip to hip." He pointed one finger to the side of his abdomen, starting at his left hip, and traced an imaginary line all the way across to the other side, as a demonstration.

"That tissue is used to reconstruct breasts. The old way to do this type of surgery was to use some of the entire abdominal muscles to rebuild the breasts, but this resulted in the loss of core strength. Now, we are able to leave the AB muscles intact, by using the blood vessels to reconnect and reconstruct. Plus, most patients, especially those who have had children, don't mind having extra tissue removed from their abdomen. It's not a true "tummy tuck" because there is no liposuction, however." Connecting blood vessels and building new breasts? Melodee's head was spinning, and she just couldn't wrap her head around the specifics, with her limited knowledge.

Dr. Boone continued, "Dr. Plack only refers patients who she thinks are good candidates for this procedure because it's intricate, lengthy, and state-of-the-art. If you just want a mastectomy or an augmentation, there are many doctors in this area who can do it. If you want a good reconstruction, however, it takes a little more experience and skill. This is my specialty. I've done a lot of them, and I'm very good at what I do."

Was this confidence or cockiness? Mel wasn't yet sure. She needed to hear more.

"The pros of the procedure are the natural look and feel. Implants would have to be replaced every ten or so years, but reconstructed breasts will last forever, will always look good, and will grow with you. They'll look good at 40. They'll look good at 60. They'll look good at 90--well, as good as they can look at that age!"

How funny to think about her ninety-year-old self with "natural" breasts! She chuckled at that image. "You said I would need to have implants replaced every ten years, but I have friends with implants older than that. Why would my case be so different?"

"Good question! In a regular breast augmentation, the implant is placed behind fatty tissue or muscle. Even someone with small breasts has a few inches of something to work with." He then pulled out one tissue from the box on the desk. "Pretend this tissue is your skin after Dr. Plack finished your mastectomy. All that would remain of your breast is skin. It is a thin layer, and trying to put implants behind that doesn't look natural at all." He made a fist with hand, and draped the tissue carefully over the top. "Now pretend that my hand is taking the place of an implant. Do you see how the pattern of my hand is easily seen under this thin layer?"

Mel nodded, paying careful attention.

The doctor continued, "You would have a similar look with only a thin layer of skin directly over an implant. The breasts wouldn't look full. They wouldn't last. Scar tissue would build up between the implant and the skin as you healed, especially without any other tissue to hold onto. I've seen patients who have so much scar tissue that they get to a point where it's difficult to lift their arm at the shoulder. With reconstruction, it's natural tissue and they last forever.

Dr. Boone's explanation was complete. "Can I take a look at what we're working with? Follow me over to this open exam room. Remove your top and put on this robe, with the opening to the front." He left to let Melodee follow instructions and knocked a few minutes later before returning. In one of the most awkward doctor/patient experiences of her life, she stood there, embarrassed, as her future plastic surgeon began tugging and gathering all the extra skin and fat out and over the top of her jeans.

"Oh, you're a GREAT candidate for this surgery!" he said, jiggling all of her extra abdominal skin. "I can tell you carried your babies really low and they *really* stretched you out. That's great because I have *lots* of tissue to work with. You are going to be so happy. In fact, you'll probably tell me to make them smaller when we come back for touch-ups!"

When she saw how pleased he was with the possibilities for great results, Mel couldn't be embarrassed for long. She realized that she liked this doctor, even though he had just told her how stretched out and large her muffin top was. She was confident in his abilities and convinced that the pros of reconstruction far outweighed the cons. She did take her notes home to talk with Stephen, but he agreed with her decision: she was going ahead with the Plack/Boone plan.

Melodee could not have surgery for six weeks, which would allow her body to heal sufficiently after her last round of chemotherapy. She continued her weekly doses of Herceptin but felt a newfound freedom, as she now had seven full days before returning to the hospital, where for the last six months she had been coming for both booster shots and lab work in addition to treatments. Who knew that having a whole week hospital-free would make her feel so blessed? Cancer was determined to teach her to be an optimist! Oh, the lessons she was learning through suffering and what growth was being achieved though her discomfort!

THE BIG SURGERY

The date for surgery was set. As Melodee turned over the calendar, she suddenly realized that she would spend her 34th birthday in the hospital. She would still be recovering when her oldest son started Kindergarten. This was not how she had pictured either of these major events six months earlier, but her health was more important than walking Kyle through the doors of his first public school and taking hundreds of pictures. She spent the last of her "normal" weeks making arrangements for childcare, pressuring her son's school to allow her to meet his teacher early, and setting up all other necessities the family would need in the days surrounding her procedure and recovery.

For five weeks, Melodee was too busy to think much about the major changes that would soon take place in her life. However, one week before her surgery, as she sat in those familiar, Tiffany blue chairs in Dr. Nabhi's office, there was little else on which to ponder.

"Will I ever look attractive again? Will I feel attractive? Will my new appearance cause others to feel uncomfortable?"

"Will Stephen want to leave me?"

"Will my children be afraid of my scars?"

"Will I ever fully recover?"

"Is this truly the best decision?"

These were just some of the many questions that plagued her that afternoon. She had been so confident in this choice when she first made it weeks ago, but fear and doubt were starting to set in as the surgery date drew closer. She was terrified of the countless unknowns and afraid of the pain and scars, both physical and emotional. She felt ugly and broken down from chemotherapy. How could she cope with even more? It was a good thing she was alone in the chemo chair that afternoon and that Lila had completely shut the curtain behind her. She needed the solitude to avoid embarrassment. She was usually happy and smiling at her chemo appointments. Today, she was utilizing the standard box of tissues more than ever before.

Melodee needed to get her mind on something more uplifting because no amount of tears could cancel her upcoming hospital stay. She was suddenly reminded of another unwanted surgical procedure from years before.

Melodee had just passed into the second trimester of her second pregnancy. The first had ended in an early miscarriage, but she and Stephen both felt confident that they would finally become parents, as the "danger zone" for miscarriage had come and gone. At her regular monthly appointment, the nurse was having a difficult time finding the heartbeat. "This is normal if the placenta had attached lower on your uterus, especially this early into your pregnancy. I'll call the doctor in to help." When the doctor had trouble, as well, and moved the couple into an ultrasound, Melodee knew. She knew that this would be another miscarriage, a more difficult one, as she had already begun to know this baby, had already made plans, had already heard a heartbeat. What had she done wrong? Why did this greatest desire of her heart always seem just beyond her reach? Did God not want her to become a mother?

Just as she had imagined, the ultrasound proved her greatest fear. Her baby's heartbeat had stopped just days before, "The fetus," as the doctor described, "Was no longer viable." No wonder medical professionals used these generic, impersonal terms when discussing the early stages of pregnancy. This discovery might have been easier to accept if she and Stephen, along with extended family and friends, had not already made plans for her unborn child and already felt love for the baby who would soon join their family. "We will need to perform a D&C because your body has not yet begun a natural miscarriage," her doctor explained. "Can you be at the hospital tomorrow morning?" He went on to explain that a D&C, or dilation and curettage, is a procedure to remove the tissue from inside the uterus, which was necessary to prevent infection or uncontrolled bleeding after a spontaneous miscarriage. As the explanations went on and on, Mel began to cry. Her tears continued throughout the afternoon and evening while she made preparations for this unplanned procedure and continued to mourn the loss of yet another pregnancy. Early the next morning, the tears continued and blended into the flow of water from the shower. All of the pre-op procedures and required questions continued to fuel her misery.

When the OR nurse approached Melodee's bed and witnessed her distress she asked, "Are you sure you want to have surgery today?" Obviously, this nurse had not yet read Mel's chart.

"Of course I don't want to have surgery today!" she practically shouted between sobs. "But I have no choice!"

The grief and hopelessness had been suffocating at the time but seemed less tragic now, especially because Melodee was the mother of three, healthy boys today. However, a similar melancholy plagued her heart, as again, she had little choice in a procedure that would change her forever. Dwelling on the misery and hopelessness of loss was not improving her state-of-mind.

She felt a range of emotions concerning her surgery: excited, positive, nervous, anxious, worried, hopeful, full of anticipation, gratitude, and mostly prepared. Her mastectomy was simply the next big step in her cancer journey, one she would surely survive.

She knew there were many prayers being said concerning her upcoming surgery. She was already feeling some of the blessings. Her body had already endured a great amount of pain and suffering, and now it would be cut apart and sewn back together to completely remove any remaining cancer, nearly eliminating the chance that it would return.

AFTER SURGERY

It had been a full eight hours since Mel had been rolled back to the operating room, but that last kiss from Stephen only felt like twenty minutes before. All she wanted to do was to stay asleep because she could already feel the pain and devastation of a total body reconstruction. Wishing to be left alone to sleep through the pain, she began to become more and more aware of a voice that kept calling to her, almost yelling, interrupting her dreams.

"Melodee?"

"Melodee, it's time to wake up!"

"Open your eyes, Melodee!"

Her eyelids were so heavy, and she started speaking while they were still closed.

"No," she uttered weakly, pleading with the voice to leave her alone and let her remain in her dreams.

Mel continued muttering nonsense words and meaningless phrases while she remained in that strange state of not being fully awake. She did not feel at all in control of her senses, thanks to the effects of eight hours of anesthesia, plus the high doses of narcotics she had been given to ease her pain. Before finally waking up, she had been dreaming about being inflated, like a big red balloon with arms, legs, and a head. Finally she spoke something the nurses could understand. "I'm all red!"

"You're not red, don't worry," came the answer from a different voice.

In fact, Melodee seemed to hear one nurse say to the other, "Her skin is actually quite pale, due to the amount of blood she's lost."

Melodee finally forced her eyelids open to prove she was okay.

The lights in that large space, called the PACU (post anesthesia care unit) were especially bright, and it took some time for her eyes to adjust. She noticed several "rooms," which were just beds separated by curtains, and stark whiteness everywhere. She was propped up in one of those adjustable hospital beds and was suddenly so cold, even with piles of freshly warmed hospital blankets covering her. She wished Stephen were there.

Thankfully, both surgeons soon made their rounds and explained that the surgery had been a complete success. Dr. Plack came by first, pleased that all of Melodee's lymph nodes had been negative for cancer and did not need to be removed. Dr. Boone made a brief visit, confident about the results of the reconstruction, convincing his patient that she would recover well and be happy with her new breasts. Mel still had her doubts but figured they were the experts! Finally, Stephen was able to come back and say hello. She soon fell back asleep, and everything else from that time was a blur.

Melodee remained under observation for a few hours. Her skin had begun to return to a normal coloring, she was coming out of the sleepiness, and her vitals were normal. She still was not allowed to eat or drink anything but was finally released from PACU and wheeled back to her recovery room at seven o'clock that evening.

Stephen was in the room waiting, and she reached out her hand for his. Suddenly, she felt a familiar uneasiness in her stomach. Nausea was one of her least favorite feelings. She took deep breaths and willed herself to keep it inside, but natural forces were too strong. There was no time to warn anyone, and suddenly her body took over, forcefully expelling what she later learned was bile mixed with a blue dye that had been used during surgery. This vibrant blue liquid shot out of her mouth and nose and all over her gown and onto the bed of freshly changed sheets.

Her entire body ached each time her stomach heaved, and Mel was sure that some of her sutures were coming loose. She had not had anything to eat or drink since before midnight the night before, but her stomach pulsed again, and her entire body heaved uncontrollably, again and again. The pain was unbearable! Now, in addition to being covered in a gross, slimy, blue solution, she was sobbing, which only contributed to her pain.

To make this experience even worse, the nurses insisted that she was still not allowed to eat or drink anything, so the lovely aftertaste of the acidic vomit remained in Melodee's mouth all night long.

After helping clean up and getting Mel settled, Stephen had to leave in order to be rested for his early workday the following morning. He'd been waiting anxiously at the hospital for over fifteen hours and was exhausted. Thankfully, Mel's dear friend, Michele, had flown in to keep Mel company in the hospital.

There was no resting that first night, as one nurse after another entered Melodee's room every thirty minutes to check and monitor vitals. They paid special attention to the areas around her reconstruction, explaining the importance of monitoring blood flow in her breast flaps, the circular grafts of skin that had been sewn over the areas where each nipple had been removed. The test involved pressing the chest piece of a stethoscope carefully onto each flap and listening for the sound of blood moving through the reconnected vessels. If blood was not flowing, it meant the vessels had not been connected correctly or had not taken to the surgery. Without proper blood flow, the reconstructed tissue would eventually die.

Blood flow in the flap on Mel's left side was strong, but the evidence in her right breast seemed difficult to locate. For each of the countless tests, the nurse would remain on her right side for what felt like ages. During these observations, Mel would hold her breath anxiously until the pulse was found, thankful that her tissue was still alive. She again had flashbacks to that second pregnancy, when her nurse was unable to find the baby's heartbeat. Thankfully, as the week went on, the blood flow on both sides became much stronger.

Mel was finally cleared to drink and eat on the morning after her surgery. After thirty-six hours of fasting, oatmeal and ice chips never tasted so good! Brushing her teeth and finally ridding her mouth of the taste of bile was heavenly.

Her days at the hospital followed a consistent cycle of sleeping, checking vitals, taking meds, and eating. She was on strict bed rest for five days, which became challenging and monotonous. She was required to wear a gown with a built-in flow of warm air for two full days, to facilitate the blood flow in her reconstructed tissue. It was so hot and uncomfortable, and although she had never before experienced a hot flash,

Mel suspected that was close to her current condition. Although she was uncomfortable and tired, she did have a Dilaudid pump for the pain, one that she could control.

Melodee had always had a high pain tolerance, but she had not been adequately prepared for this level of suffering. The areas of reconstruction constantly ached and her required breathing treatments only proved to add to her pain. Every hour, a nurse would force Melodee to breathe as deeply as she could into an inspirometer, a light-weight, hand-held instrument with a mouthpiece for breathing and a piston that raised and lowered depending on the force Mel was able to use against it. Inside the chamber were numbered levels, and each day Melodee's required level of force from breath would be increased, as the nurses would point out by moving a coaching indicator higher and higher up the scale. It had never before been physically painful to breathe, but Mel's newly cut body was rebelling against her. The deep breathing would also stir up phlegm to cough up, and each cough became more and more excruciating. A nurse taught Mel to keep a pillow handy, holding it against her chest to cushion the force of each cough.

Melodee had also always had incredible core strength, easily passing sit-up tests throughout school and needing only one push to deliver each of her babies. It was now foreign having no core strength to move, as her entire abdominal area had been cut out and stitched back together. In addition, she had no arm strength, due to the amount of reconstruction that had been done to her chest area. It was nearly impossible to adjust herself in bed. Thankfully, Michele or the nurses would help her move around so that she did not develop bedsores.

Day three was a bad one. First, Melodee was pulled off the pain pump. She was not prepared for that major switch, from a constant narcotic drip down to only receiving one pill every six hours! The same amount of tests and breathing checks were required, now without the same level of pain management. Melodee was soon brought to tears! She felt as if her entire body was being sliced by thousands of tiny blades, clear down to the bone. Soon after changing pain medication, she suddenly began to feel an incredible heat that radiated from her core out to her entire body. Blood vessels pulsed in her head, causing aches like she had never before experienced. She began to sweat, wondering if she were suffering from intense fever! Between pain and heat, she was completely miserable, not even being able to sleep away the discomfort.

Finally, Michele had reached her limit. Even though Mel was not one to complain, Michele had assessed the situation and did not like what she saw. She marched down to the nurses' station, and Mel could hear the conversation from down the hall.

"Someone has got to do something for my friend! She cannot keep feeling this way! Can you not contact her doctor and explain her pain level? When is enough, enough?"

Thank goodness for Michele's assertiveness because the nurses responded, "Why hasn't she told us about this? The doctor's notes say she is allowed to have more pain medication, if she asks for it!"

Michele was furious. "She did not know she could ask for more pain medication, but WE ARE ASKING FOR IT NOW!"

In no time at all, Melodee was given a Dilaudid boost to help her transition from the constant drip to lower doses of pain medication, and she was finally feeling more normal, if you could call a body being cut up, put back together, and forced to stay in bed for days, "normal."

The morning of the fifth day started off early. The nurses were required to remove Mel's catheter and to get her up and out of bed and using the restroom before their seven a.m. shift change. After being in bed for nearly five full days, this all seemed to be happening too quickly. Her nurses also removed the I.V. from Melodee's right arm, informing her that it was a bit overdue.

"Do you see how the fluid has infiltrated your surrounding tissue?" one of the nurses explained.

Mel's whole arm had puffed up and was difficult to lift or control.

"It's a good thing I've become used to doing everything with my left hand this week because my right arm is useless!" she thought, trying to carefully massage some feeling back into her swollen arm.

Just then, Stephen showed up at the hospital with some surprise gifts and balloons.

"Happy Birthday!" he cried. Before that, she had been so consumed in her morning tasks that she had completely forgotten that she was now thirty-four!

Dr. Boone cleared her for release, which was another birthday gift. After that great news, Melodee was finally able to shower and get dressed, although she needed help for both tasks. Mel had been covered and confined for days. When she finally looked at her body in the bathroom mirror, Melodee saw that her body was stitched up and swollen. She couldn't yet see the complete scope of surgery, as the bandages over her breasts had not been removed. Having witnessed countless operations in his career, Stephen was not surprised by Mel's appearance, but he was not pleased in discovering bed ulcers on her back and backside. Thankfully, Mel's bed rest was over, and she was glad to finally be going home.

Returning home, however, was not without its challenges. For nearly a week, Mel had become used to having nurses take care of her needs; suddenly she was independent, but she felt rather worthless. She was not cleared to drive, lift anything, lift her arms above her head, wear a bra, climb stairs, or do anything that could compromise the healing process. Walking was slow, and she needed assistance, either holding onto another person or the wall for support. The pain was still intense, but bearable with medication. She needed lots of help—to shower, to get dressed, to tend to the needs of her children, and to do almost everything but move from her bed to the toilet.

Mel's least favorite task of her recovery involved the care of four surgical drains, which had been attached for the purpose of removing blood, pus, and other fluids from her wounds. They consisted of clear tubing inserted into four holes in her body, one from each breast and from either side of her abdomen. At the end of each tube was a clear collection reservoir, which held the fluid until it was time to drain, one duty Mel had been used to the nurses handling. Now, several times a day, Melodee had the task of untangling the mess of tubing, opening each collection reservoir, squeezing out the bloody, sometimes clotted substance, and recording the amount of drainage. She hated the drains and called them her "tentacles." This was the least avoidable evidence of her pain, as they could not easily be covered. In addition, the drains were ugly, a gross reminder of the suffering her body was enduring, and made Mel's boys scared to look her direction.

The boys were not the only ones who were affected. Stephen's mother, Timee, came to stay with Melodee for that first week she returned home. The first morning, Mel asked Timee to help her with showering. The process involved moving a folding chair into the shower, something Melodee could not carry. Next, Mel would need help undressing and climbing into the shower to sit with her back facing the stream of water, so as to not allow the water to have direct contact with any of the wounds. Her limited range of motion meant that she could also not dry off alone. Then, Mel would also need help dressing, in only robes or dresses which buttoned in the front, to accommodate the tubing from the drains, which would be gathered together and pinned to the front of the dress.

Mel had been somewhat hesitant for anyone to see what was under the bandages, embarrassed about requiring so much help with such a personal task, and tried to keep her back to Timee for as long as possible. Timee stepped out of the room while Mel finished her shower. There was no hiding, though, when it was time to step out of the shower and dry off.

"Timee, I'm ready!" she called to the other room.

Mel would never forget the look on Timee's face, as she turned the corner into the bathroom and saw Melodee standing there, coming face-to-face with the effects of this surgery. Mel had not closely examined herself in the mirror up to this point, and she did not need to; the sight of it was reflected in Timee's pale gaze. Mel could feel the frightened glimpse over her unsightly appearance, the utter shock and disbelief, the astonishment at the severity of her scars, fear for her recovery, and shame of not understanding the complexity and invasiveness of the procedure beforehand.

Timee gasped and cried out, "Oh, Mel! I had no idea that you were going to be going through *this*! I thought it was going to be like a C-section. I'm so sorry! How are you even alive and walking?"

Although it was difficult to require so much help with basic needs, Mel was forced into humility, and it helped that her appearance seemed to validate her need for assistance. Timee's full understanding of the level of Mel's suffering suddenly made the trial real. It truly was one of the most difficult and painful times of her entire life.

She spent much of her time in bed, walking around the house only as required and resting back in bed. It was a lonely and frustrating time, and she wondered if this was something she truly could overcome. How could anyone make it through something like this? She just wanted to be healed and be back to normal!

Melodee was seeing her weakness like never before. Literally, her body was broken and weak--cut apart and sewn back together in different places, with jarring scars and obvious challenges. She no longer had feeling in her breasts or in the areas around her abdominal scar. She had a surgically created belly button, one that had to be placed too high up on her body, due to the massive amount of scarring below. She felt much older than her 34 years.

Three weeks after her mastectomy and reconstruction, which was proving to be the most difficult experience of her life, Melodee returned to Dr. Nabhi's office to continue receiving her weekly treatments of Herceptin. Following the first post-surgical treatment, she also had an appointment with Dr. Plack to discuss the pathology reports from the breast tissue samples that were tested after her mastectomy. When the last of Herceptin was drained, Melodee hurried down the hall, a few minutes late to her surgeon's office, but was at once calmed by the now-too-familiar *Feng Shui* of the waiting room.

Once called back to an exam room, Melodee glanced toward a small print hanging on the back wall, one she had never before noticed. She recognized the backdrop as a famous piece of Japanese art, one depicting a treacherous, towering wave washing over small boats, with Mt. Fuji in the distance. A stirring quote had been printed in the lighter background of the piece, in the shadows of the deep blue of the crushing swells. It read, "We can't direct the wind, but we can adjust the sails." Melodee read this sentence over and over again, feeling the significance to her life now. She had been greatly changing the direction of her sails for nearly a year and was sure she would continue to change course throughout her life.

Just then came the familiar knock on the door of Dr. Plack. After the typical greeting, the surgeon pulled up some reports on her laptop. "I want to give you an idea of the aggressiveness of your type of tumor," Dr. Plack began, bluntly. "Do you remember that your breast exam as well as your ultrasound from the week after you completed chemotherapy both reported no signs of a tumor?"

"Yes," Melodee replied, smiling. "It was a much needed miracle."

"We performed your surgery exactly six weeks after your last dose of aggressive chemo, and that short amount of time gave your tumor the opportunity to start growing back."

Mel's mouth hung open wide, but she had no words. What a scary thought!

Dr. Plack continued, "The pathology reports describe a small, residual tumor, which was found to be forming in the tissue that was removed during your mastectomy, meaning that your tumor began to grow back in as little as five to six weeks! Aren't you glad that you opted for a mastectomy?"

Having doubted herself from the moment she woke up in the PACU, due to her terrible recovery experience, Melodee was again confident that her choice to move forward with a bilateral mastectomy had been the right one. If her cancer could begin to grow back in as little as six weeks after aggressive chemotherapy, what could that have meant for the remainder of her life if she had opted to not completely remove her breast tissue? Melodee's type of tumor was obviously aggressive, and she was confident she had chosen the surgical option that matched the strength of her cancer.

Dr. Plack was now smiling. "The miraculous news is that the cancerous breast tissue has been removed, all the samples of lymph nodes are negative, and I can officially report that your body is free of cancer!"

These were the words Melodee had been waiting to hear since January! All of the most difficult battles of the war were over. Now, she just had to complete the fifty-two weekly doses of Herceptin, continue taking an estrogen-blocking drug for five-ten years, and visit Dr. Plack for yearly breast exams for the rest of her life, which would, hopefully, be a very long time. (Dr. Nabhi would not officially proclaim Melodee as "cancer-free" and in remission until the last dose of Herceptin had been completed, which would not be until May of 2014.)

Melodee's recovery was on-going, but every day was a little better. By the third week after surgery, she actually climbed up the stairs in her home. Her range of motion was improving, which meant she was soon able to put on clothes over her head, a momentous occasion. She still felt a great deal of pain, but it was decreasing with each passing day. She was beginning to feel more and more like herself.

Melodee often reflected back to the print she noticed at Dr. Plack's office. She later researched that it was a replica of the famous, "The Great Wave off Kanagawa," by Japanese ukiyo-e artist Hokusai. That ominous dark wave, threatening to destroy all in its path was also an accurate representation of cancer in her life. There had been countless times during this battle when Melodee had wondered if all hope was lost, if she had no choice but to submit to the waves and accept her fate. However, the quote accompanying that print seemed to have made a deeper impression. Mel researched its origin and found that Dolly Parton, among others, had been quoted as expressing similar thoughts, but Melodee was most touched by the version from Thomas S. Monson, which expanded upon the idea of how to change course. He said, "We can't direct the wind, but we can adjust the sails. For maximum happiness, peace, and contentment, may we choose a positive attitude."[24] Choice. It was often the last ability in the midst of suffering. Melodee began to see that when it seemed she had no other option but to submit to the devastating impact of her storms, she always had the power of choice. She might not always be able to choose her experiences, but she could control her reactions to them.

As 2013 came to an end, Melodee's weekly visits to chemo began to drag on and on, as if they would never stop! Technically, there was no longer cancer in her body, and Melodee was growing tired of the never-ending treatments. Nearly a full year had passed since they had begun! Surely, all of these extra drugs were unnecessary. These weekly trips were becoming more difficult, especially as the help from others began to fade. After weighing her options---including just being done altogether---Melodee decided to make a change. She did have the gift of choice, after all. On the last chemo of the year, Melodee started a serious conversation with Dr. Nabhi.

"What's the big deal if I just call this my last chemo?" she asked the doctor.

"Not an option," her oncologist replied immediately, even a bit harshly.

"But, I've finished more than half, and I don't even have breasts anymore. Do I REALLY need to finish Herceptin?"

"Quitting is not an option. Patients who don't complete the entire cycle have a much higher risk of cancer returning. It almost always does. And, it's always Stage 4. And, it's usually in the brain. So, you can see that quitting is just not an option. In fact, now there is actually an additional drug we give patients with your type of chemo. If I had my way, I would add even *more* onto your treatment plan, but there hasn't been enough testing done for cases like yours when the drugs are not administered at the same initial start time. So, be glad you *only* have Herceptin to finish."

"Oh, alright. I'll be here next week."

CANCER FREE!

In order to make the last doses of Herceptin easier to bear, Melodee's nurse, Lila, offered a solution. Instead of weekly, single doses of Herceptin, Dr. Nabhi had been known to combine doses, with longer wait periods between. Melodee jumped on that idea and soon began receiving a double dose of the cancer drugs, once every two weeks. She could hardly believe the blessing of time that this choice created. She now gained one treatment-free week in between doses, and she was able to cut her total visits down from sixteen to eight! This newly found freedom became both a mental and emotional boost to complete the treatments.

Those sixteen weeks flew by, and Melodee's battle with cancer was officially at an end. At her last treatment of Herceptin, Dr. Nabhi and her remaining nurses, Lila and Jan, congratulated her. A bouquet of balloons, in all shades of pink greeted her, tied to the back of her chair. She rang the famous bell, signaling a completion of chemo, and documented the day with pictures taken with the doctor and nurses who had cared so deeply and helped to make her triumph over cancer possible.

"You're going to miss this place," Lila promised. "You won't miss the chair or the treatment, but you'll miss us."

It was true. Melodee had gotten used to her support system and the routine of treatments. But, she had done it! She had beaten cancer! The hard part was over. It's been said, "What doesn't kill you makes you stronger," and that is the bright side of suffering. When she looked back on her experiences, Melodee could start to answer some of those "why" questions, the ones she thought she would never know the answers to. Often, the reason we suffer is to learn things we could learn in no other way.

Chapter Two

COMPASSION AND CHARITY

WE SUFFER TO LEARN COMPASSION AND CHARITY

"WHAT DO WE LIVE FOR, IF IT IS NOT TO MAKE LIFE LESS DIFFICULT FOR EACH OTHER?"

~GEORGE ELIOT

Cancer is a difficult trial, but it is not the only challenge in the world. As each of us experiences suffering of one kind or another, we begin to become more humble and more aware of those around us. We begin to understand that there are countless hard things people must endure, and each challenge is difficult for the individual experiencing that trial. Everyone has been or will be in the midst of a great trial from time to time. When we begin to understand this truth, we learn compassion and charity, or true love for our fellow man.

Without realizing it at the time, Melodee started to become a light for others as she suffered through cancer. She began to understand how to comfort those that stood in need of comfort and how to treat others with the pure love of Christ. She had been so greatly blessed with the ability to withstand her physical suffering, that she was compelled to share her experiences with others and to stand as a witness of the blessings she had received. Serving others became of greater importance to her than it ever had been before. Even though it was a simple thing, she felt impressed to record her thoughts, feelings, and experiences during her cancer journey. Sharing this record of her treatment became a source of light for others in conquering their own darkness and suffering.

Melodee also began to understand that each person is only given trials that they can overcome. She learned to not judge others in their trials because none of us is at the same point in this great journey of life. Through her suffering she was beginning to have more patience and love for those around her. Without the experiences she gained through her own trials, she would have been less likely to understand the trials of others.

Before cancer, Melodee, a strong and independent person by nature, would often look down on those she considered to be weak. She would judge them unfairly, wondering why certain people couldn't deal with *this* or *that*, as she figured *this* or *that* would be something she could easily overcome. Then Melodee was given a trial for which she was not prepared, one that brought her to her knees, pouring out her soul in anguish, wondering how she would ever make it through. Did she understand that everyone is in need of saving? No one could make it through this life without the Savior and without the help of others.

In addition to gaining compassion, personal suffering can create reasons to see others with greater charity, the pure love of Christ, rather than in prideful judgment. Christ took upon himself our pains and afflictions in order to succor his people and so his bowels would be filled with mercy and charity toward us.[25] Melodee learned from experience that, in some small way, through the pains and afflictions of this life, her own heart could be filled with charity. She could begin learning to use the pure love of Christ to comfort others in their afflictions. In that understanding, she began to see her fellowmen with a new love and with more charity.

One Sunday, an acquaintance approached Melodee at church. "I hope I don't embarrass you by saying this, but I think you are just remarkable. The way you have handled this trial is inspiring! Whenever I start to get sad or down about my own challenges, I just think of you and realize I have nothing to complain about."

Instead of simply responding "thank-you" and moving on, Melodee felt compelled to answer, "Yes, cancer is difficult, but it is not the only difficult trial in this life. This is just one form of suffering. The challenge of cancer for me may be equal to the challenges of infertility, loneliness, abuse, poor living conditions, unemployment, death of loved ones, addiction, struggle for identity, unfulfilled desire for marriage, and so on, for another. What you are going through is just as much a trial for you as cancer is for me; your suffering is for your learning and growth, so it is tailored to you."

Melodee learned not to compare herself to others, whether to make herself feel better or worse. With this revelation, her ability to truly love others without negative judgment and to have compassion for their suffering magnified. She could more easily see that each person is given trials for which they must plead to God for help. Although not able to fully imagine or grasp the exact feeling and pains of others in their personal suffering, she could understand true suffering and have empathy for the suffering of others. This level of compassion can only truly develop through enduring affliction.

Melodee began to see how important it was for her to simply have charity and compassion for others who might be suffering in ways only God could see. She was suffering to gain a witness of charity. As the scriptures teach, if you have not charity, you are nothing.[26] If suffering helps us to learn charity, perhaps the darkest storms in life can create in us the brightest light.

Mother Teresa, one of the greatest examples of charity and a source of great light for others, did not have a life free from suffering. She was born on August 26, 1910, in Skopje, the current capital of the Republic of Macedonia. As is the Catholic tradition the following day she was baptized as Agnes Gonxha Bojaxhiu. Her parents, Nikola and Dranafile Bojaxhiu, were of Albanian descent; her father was an entrepreneur who worked as a construction contractor and a trader of medicines and other goods. The Bojaxhius were a devoutly Catholic family, and Nikola was deeply involved in the local church as well as in city politics as a vocal proponent of Albanian independence.[27]

In 1919, when Agnes was only 8 years old, her father suddenly fell ill and died. While the cause of his death remains unknown, many have speculated that political enemies poisoned him. In the aftermath of her father's death, Agnes became extraordinarily close to her mother, a pious and compassionate woman who instilled in her daughter a deep commitment to charity.[28] Even though the family had little money, Agnes' mother frequently offered food and shelter to those in need. This was a lesson Agnes would never forget and would be the seed for her charitable work.

She was riding in a train from Calcutta to the Himalayan foothills for a retreat when she said Christ spoke to her and told her to abandon teaching to work in the slums of Calcutta aiding the city's poorest and sickest people.[29]

Since Mother Teresa had taken a vow of obedience, she could not leave her convent without official permission. After nearly a year and a half of lobbying, in January 1948 she finally received approval to pursue this new calling. That August, donning the blue-and-white sari that she would wear in public for the rest of her life, she left the Loreto convent and wandered out into the city. After six months of basic medical training, she voyaged for the first time into Calcutta's slums with no more specific a goal than to aid "the unwanted, the unloved, the uncared for."

Mother Teresa, a Roman Catholic nun, spent time among the poor, the unpopular, and the burdened of India. She knew that it was the sick, not the whole, who needed a physician. She reached out to those who sorrowed and suffered. This *pattern* of charity, said President Uchtdorf, defines the *path* one must walk to please God. "We are called to follow the example of the Savior, and it is impossible to do so if we set aside our compassion and refuse to care for our fellowmen."[30]

Like all of us who suffer, Mother Teresa had moments of doubt. She revealed the crisis of faith she suffered for most of the last 50 years of her life. In one despairing letter to a confidant, she wrote, "Where is my Faith—even deep down right in there is nothing, but emptiness and darkness—My God—how painful is this unknown pain—I have no Faith—I dare not utter the words and thoughts that crowd in my heart— and make me suffer untold agony." While such revelations are shocking considering her public image, they have also made Mother Teresa a more relatable and human figure to all those who experience doubt in their beliefs.

Part of the reason we suffer is to learn to understand the pain that other people might experience in their most difficult times. Part of our journey through mortality is to transition from being selfish, self-centered beings into those who are selfless and seek to better the lives of those around them. To some, service and charity come naturally. For others, this is a skill that must be learned, a talent that must be practiced. Personal suffering enhances the individual understanding. Through our own experiences, we learn to be more forgiving, more compassionate, and more likely to help our fellowmen ease their pains.

A well-respected religious leader, Dieter Uchtdorf, has maintained that, "Without this transformational work of caring for our fellowmen, the Church is but a facade of the organization God intends for His people.....Without charity and compassion we are a mere shadow of who we are meant to be—both as individuals and as a church. Without charity and compassion, we are neglecting our heritage and endangering our promise as children of God." Jesus Christ—who loved the sick, broken, and rejected—exemplified this pattern of charity.

Despite her efforts to remain ordinary, Mother Teresa carries one of the most recognizable names in history. Mother Teresa was the recipient of numerous honors, including the 1979 Nobel Peace Prize. In 2003, she was beatified as "Blessed Teresa of Calcutta." A second miracle was credited to her intercession by Pope Francis in December 2015, paving the way for her to be recognized as a saint by the Roman Catholic Church.

Upon reading Mother Teresa's story, the authors reflected that if there is a waiting line into heaven, we all want to be behind Mother Teresa, for she was truly a righteous person who followed the Savior's example.

Though we all need to learn to have more compassion and show more love to those around us, there are times we need to learn to more humbly receive charity from others. Some of us are stubborn, strong-willed, and less likely to humbly accept charity. Suffering, such as with Melodee's cancer battle, can lead to the miracle of a change of heart.

Before being diagnosed with cancer, Melodee's life experiences had shaped her into a strong and independent person. Being an oldest child and being married to an oldest child meant she and Stephen had both become used to leading the way and making things work without waiting around for others to help them. This trait, a great talent, could be twisted to a point of pride at times. Even after her diagnosis, Melodee was slow to allow others the opportunity to serve her. She would turn away offers of meals or help in other forms because she didn't feel she was in need of charity. Things began to change as chemotherapy continued. There came a point in her treatments that her suffering became so great that Melodee had no choice but to learn to ask for and accept help from family and friends.

Here was yet another lesson to be learned. There are times when it is better to ask for help than to try to suffer in silence. Before cancer, Melodee was usually the one to offer help. Suffering taught her how to ask for and accept it from others, as well as what a blessing it can be for all involved when people have the opportunity to serve.

As her body became weaker and weaker, Melodee was compelled to a deeper sense of humility toward being the recipient of the charity from her fellowman. After understanding this purpose in her suffering, Melodee later recorded, "before cancer, I thought I could do it all. If I didn't know how to do something, I could usually figure it out or make something work. Then, cancer came along and was a thing that I could not fix on my own. I had to completely trust my physicians and surgeons, who held my life in their hands. In addition, I had to rely on family, friends and neighbors to help with tasks for which I never imagined needing assistance.

"Before actually living through the difficulties of my cancer battle, I expected needing help with childcare, meal preparation, and housekeeping duties. However, the intense suffering involved with the worst days of chemo and difficult surgeries required that I learn to rely on others to assist with even the most simple tasks such as getting out of bed, walking, reaching up to turn on the shower, bending to grab shoes, or lifting anything over five pounds. Before cancer, I was usually the one to offer help. Suffering taught me how to ask for and accept it from others."

Albert Einstein said, "A human being is a part of the whole called by us universe, a part limited in time and space. He experiences himself, his thoughts and feeling as something separated from the rest, a kind of optical delusion of his consciousness. This delusion is a kind of prison for us, restricting us to our personal desires and to affection for a few persons nearest to us. Our task must be to free ourselves from this prison by widening our circle of compassion to embrace all living creatures and the whole of nature in its beauty."[31] Often, the humility gained from experiencing the storms of life can teach us to reach out and be more loving and accepting of others.

Richard Paul Evans [32] shared his experience with adversity. "Lately I've been pondering why it is that when we set out to do something good, we face such difficult adversity. Sometimes it even feels like we're being punished for doing the right thing. Last week I attended a board meeting for the Christmas Box International, a charitable organization I founded about fifteen years ago to help abused and neglected children. As our director read the list of the year's accomplishments, my mind went back to one of our first board meetings–a painful, agonizing one.

"Back then, it seemed *nothing* was going right. Community donations were a fraction of what we'd hoped for, while our first shelter, which was still under construction, was a money pit - six months behind schedule and more than a half million dollars over budget. I had used up nearly all my personal savings building the shelter and now I couldn't even qualify for a loan to finish it. *And we still hadn't helped a single child.* We had no shelter, no money, and no community support and abused children with no place to go. *Surely there couldn't be a more worthy cause than helping abused children,* I reasoned. Then why did it seem that the universe was against us? I remember during those years feeling frustrated and angry that everything seemed to go wrong. Many times I felt abandoned by God.

"Since then I've come to believe that there are two reasons our good deeds are met with opposition. First, is to allow us the opportunity to prove to ourselves the level of our commitment. It's been said that adversity introduces a man to himself. This is true. If all worthy endeavors were easy, there would be no greatness or nobility in the world. Just expediency.

"The second reason is more pragmatic. More times than not we do not succeed *in spite* of our challenges and obstacles, but precisely *because* of them. It is the struggle itself that gives a thing life." Trials and difficulties can lead to progress. God's charity comes through challenges and obstacles.

We can only make it through this world with the help of God and with the totality of mankind who are willing to serve one another. The famous saying "I need to do it myself, but I can't do it alone" is so true in all of our lives. We did not come to this life to live it alone. God's plan requires both giving and receiving. Faith alone is not enough. We need "works" to serve and to be served.[33] It is clear that we have imperfections of body, mind and intellect—that we are not perfect. For that reason, we are dependent on others. We must be self-reliant, but that does not mean becoming completely independent of the help of others.[34]

A just God has placed us here on planet earth where we experience suffering and imperfection all around us. Mortality is a necessary estate because in this life we experience something we cannot do any other place. The life we had before and the life we will have hereafter will leave our bodies, spirits, and minds in a more perfect state. We did not and will not have the opportunities to give of ourselves in the same way as we can in this life. What a simple truth of a gospel principle! As we suffer and serve in this life, we are fulfilling a very essential part of the gospel plan.[35] If there were not suffering in this world, there would be no need for service. Thus, the gospel plan would become completely irrelevant.

None of us are alone in this world. It is through compassion and charity that we can best understand this truth. Suffering can inspire in us the desire to ease the suffering of those around us. It can also teach humility, allowing us to gracefully accept the compassion and charity of others.

◅Chapter Three▻

SELF-WORTH

WE SUFFER TO UNDERSTAND THAT SELF-WORTH IS
FOUND IN THE SOUL

*"GOD ALLOWS US TO EXPERIENCE THE LOW POINTS OF
LIFE IN ORDER TO TEACH US LESSONS THAT WE COULD
LEARN IN NO OTHER WAY."*

~C.S. LEWIS

Perfection is not when there is nothing to add, but when there is nothing more to take away. The great artist, Michelangelo, created what is considered one of the most incredible sculptures the world has ever seen. When asked how he was able to create such a masterpiece, he replied, "I just chipped away all the rock that wasn't David."[36] God perfects us in the same way. Through trials, He chips away all of our selfishness and anger and sands down our pride and impatience until what emerges is us in our true form, of infinite worth, as God intended. Unlike the perfect outward image of the sculpture David, God is working to perfect our hearts and souls. To Him, that is where the beauty lies.

As mortal beings, we often see beauty on the outside. Body image and self-worth often go hand in hand. When

Melodee began to prepare for her mastectomy, and in the months of recovery afterward, she struggled greatly with her self-worth. Her body-altering surgery became a major test of self-worth, as it completely changed the body she had known for thirty-three years. Sure, she'd experienced sudden changes before her mastectomy, but they were mostly natural or reversible ones, like the drastic weight gain and loss involved with bearing children, or choosing to experiment with a vibrant hair color. With this major surgery, the sudden change was beyond her control. Cancer had forced her to choose between life and breasts.

Even before undergoing the painful changes from surgery, Melodee struggled. She worried that she would be losing a big part of herself, of her self-worth, of her womanhood. She had never really thought about it before, but the thought of losing her breasts became a great challenge. Breasts are a big deal, and to have them taken by disease was a hard thing.

"I'm still young," she thought, *"and I still want to feel beautiful. I've given up my hair, but that will grow back. Now, I'm forced to lose my breasts. They will be reconstructed, but they will always be different. My entire body will be different."*

Apparently the connection between body image and self-worth exists beyond the teenage years. Faced with this complete change in her body, Melodee was now having to cope with some of the same battles over body image and insecurities that she had felt in the years of her youth.

At one of those moments when she was struggling most with this concept, Melodee opened her email and found one from a fellow youth leader from church, asking for ideas to introduce their value focus for the coming month, Individual Worth.

Melodee would be in charge of encouraging the girls to complete experiences and value projects surrounding this concept, as well as helping the youth to understand its meaning. This could not have simply been a coincidence because this was also a concept that Melodee needed to grasp in order to better cope with the changes she would soon experience!

The scriptures gave her an amazing place to start. "Remember the worth of souls is great in the sight of God."[37] As she reviewed this passage, one she had read many times over in her life, she felt as if it had been written just for her at this time.

When she read it again, she added a few changes: "Remember, *Melodee*, that the worth of *your soul* is great." She turned, again, to another familiar verse:

"Know ye not that ye are the temple of God, and that the spirit of God dwelleth in you?"[38] Again, in her mind, she applied it to her own situation. "Have you forgotten, *Melodee*, that you are a spirit daughter of a King and that your spirit, *your soul,* is precious to Him? You are not this body. YOU are the spirit that dwells within that temple."

Even though changes beyond her control would be made to her body, she knew that her spirit could remain strong. She would struggle with the pain and ugly changes to her physical body, but she could still remain strong and beautiful on the inside. The simple reminder of her individual worth made the suffering easier to bear. She knew that she was watched over, protected, and known by a loving and merciful Father in Heaven. He numbered every hair on her head, though they were short and thin at that moment.[39]

Her stomach would soon be where her breasts once were, but she knew that her soul would remain of great worth. She had nothing to fear. "And fear not them which kill the body, but are not able to kill the soul."[40] After being reminded of this verse, she encouraged herself. "This surgery will change my body, but it will not destroy ME, for I am not my body. I am my soul and my soul is of infinite worth."

Her body would never be the same again, but her soul could continue to give thanks for her many blessings

I will praise thee; for I am fearfully and wonderfully made: marvelous are thy works; and that my soul knoweth right well.[41]

Not everyone will suffer through a body-altering surgery. However, many struggle to find their worth in this world. The challenges that make us question our worth are as unique as each individual. We all have physical flaws, scars, and genetic traits that are not perfect. There are also experiences that we suffer that cause our physical bodies to be less than perfect. All of that suffering is often trying to teach a simple truth: God does not look on the outside, for He sees our heart. The worth of our souls is great in God's eyes, and we must learn to see our own worth in that light. Some physical imperfections are greater than others and some can lead to emotional suffering and fear of men. Eventually, we must come to understand that our worth is not in the beauty of these physical bodies. It was less important that Melodee's body was scarred from her illness, for true beauty lies in the soul. It took true suffering to force her to finally see that beauty.

No one who has ever lived, is now alive, or will live in the future shares a fingerprint with anyone else. The Lord has infinite creations, but He has an individual plan for each of us. In speaking to Moses, God explained His greatness and also His love. "And, behold, thou art my son; wherefore look, and I will show thee the workmanship of mine hands; but not all, for my works are without end, and also my words, for they never cease. Wherefore, no man can behold all my works, except he beholds all my glory; and no man can behold all my glory, and afterwards remain in the flesh on the earth."[42]

William Grey expressed it well when he said, "When God molded Adam of the dust, He shaped him in the outward form of Himself; He gave this unique form to man alone. Besides this, God gave man dominion over his environment, and to do this job, He gave him abilities like His own. Man can think, reason, make decisions, and plan. He can originate and evaluate ideas and bring them to completion. He can communicate and express complex concepts that can be understood by other men. Mankind understands and marks the passage of time."[43]

As unique beings created in the image of God, we are of infinite worth. Through our trials we can come to recognize that worth and know that what we are facing is only the refiner's fire burning away our impurities and shaping us into who our Creator wants us to be.

ᑲᐤChapter Fourᕊᐣ

JOAN'S STORY

"BEFORE YOU CAN LIVE A PART OF YOU HAS TO DIE. YOU HAVE TO LET GO OF WHAT COULD HAVE BEEN, HOW YOU SHOULD HAVE ACTED AND WHAT YOU WISH YOU WOULD HAVE SAID DIFFERENTLY. YOU HAVE TO ACCEPT THAT YOU CAN'T CHANGE THE PAST EXPERIENCES, OPINIONS OF OTHERS AT THAT MOMENT IN TIME OR OUTCOMES FROM THEIR CHOICES OR YOURS. WHEN YOU FINALLY RECOGNIZE THAT TRUTH THEN YOU WILL UNDERSTAND THE TRUE MEANING OF FORGIVENESS OF YOURSELF AND OTHERS. FROM THIS POINT YOU WILL FINALLY BE FREE."

~SHANNON L. ALDER

Joan's story is an iconic story of suffering and survival. Her story has never been told to anyone, but was silently locked in her memory until she was persuaded to relate it in this book. Telling the story was traumatic for her, and she cried throughout the process. The time period in which much of Joan's story takes place was a dark time in the history of the South. Prejudice will be recounted. The abuse Joan faced is also graphic. Although she was abused as a child, raped at the age of fifteen, abandoned by her first husband at age thirty, had a brother killed in a car accident, and robbed at gunpoint in her own home, she remains very positive and has found a place of peace. Joan is sixty-five years old as we write her story. She looks much younger, is very energetic and lives life with a purpose. Telling her story has been cathartic for her and her greatest wish is that her story may help others overcome similar situations.

Because Joan's experience affected her psychologically, she required therapy. She recounts: "I went into therapy the first time when I was going through my first divorce at age thirty. My first memory was achieved through hypnosis. I was free, floating, flipping and stretching. It was amazingly wonderful. I have never felt that way again. Suddenly, there was this pounding and I was being slammed around. Then something hit my head really hard. I retreated. My next memory is of lying on a bed in my grandmother's spare room. I can completely describe the room, the bedspread, the smells, everything. My grandmother and mother were standing at the end of the bed while I lay on my tummy in the middle of the bed on a blanket. They were fighting, loud, angry words, pushing, slapping and I began to cry. My mother grabbed me by my arm and flipped me over, roughly removing my diaper. She screamed, 'You can make me change her shitty diapers but you can never make me love her.' As I write this, my hands begin to tremble. It was extremely impactful.

"My next memory was lying in bed between my grandparents. My grandfather was a smoker so he would wake in the middle of the night, raise the window by his bed and smoke before going back to sleep. I would wake up and scramble to sit beside him, swinging my legs and talking to him. He smiled at me, put out his cigarette, hugging me as he rolled us over. He whispered, 'Sleep now baby.' I smile as I write this. He was a gentle man."

Joan was the daughter of a single mom; born just ten days after her mother, Angela, turned sixteen. Joan's relationship with her mother mirrored Angela's relationship with Joan's grandmother, Sally. Theirs was a destructive cycle repeated from mother to daughter. The mothers were fiercely critical and manipulative with their daughters. They both manipulated their grandchildren into having harsh feelings toward their mothers. She describes the relationships as cognitively evil. The women would put on a positive face in public, hugging and kissing the children and saying that they were so lucky to have them. At home, however, things were very different; the children were abused, criticized, and made to feel worthless. Joan has a few good memories from her childhood, but the rest are mostly nightmares she has been required to confront and reconcile. She suffered in silence believing that her life was normal. Though Joan's life at times seemed unbearable, she survived; her story may now help others stay strong and heal their wounds.

When Joan was an infant and toddler, she and Angela lived with her grandparents, Sally and Sam, in Rayne, Louisiana. When Joan was three years old, her mother married a man named Ken and they moved to a small town outside of Albuquerque, New Mexico. Ken was one of eight husbands her mom would marry. This move took Joan outside the relative safety of her grandparents' home. Joan remembers her grandparents crying and screaming as she was driven away. In response, Angela called out to Sally, "You will never see your granddaughter again because Joan belongs to me. I can do whatever I want because she belongs to me."

This kind of emotional abuse was often coupled with physical abuse. Both were common in Joan's household. She would get slapped hard and thrown to the floor for just about anything. Angela would try to hide the abuse by not letting her go to school when she was bruised, but the teachers suspected it. She knew because they treated her differently from the other kids. By the time Joan was in first grade, her family lived in Shreveport, Louisiana. She was the only sibling old enough to go to school and was supposed to get up in the morning in complete silence, get ready, and leave without waking her mother. If Joan woke up Angela or any of the other children she would get whipped and have to stay home from school.

One day, Joan forgot her reader and was too afraid to go home and get it for fear of waking up Angela. She was crying hysterically before she even got into the classroom. Her teacher took her to the principal's office where the principal asked Joan what was wrong. The confession came flooding out of Joan. "I forgot my reader and my mom would be mad at me and I would get whipped if I went home to get it; but if I didn't go get it the teacher was going to punish me and I'd never be able to bring a book home again!" The principal just calmed her down, told her she wouldn't be in trouble, and sent her back to class.

A few days later a social worker came to Joan's house to check on the family. She mentioned what Joan had said at school and Angela immediately went into a rampage, claiming that Joan was a liar and had always been a storyteller. Of this incident, Joan relates, "I don't remember anything else the lady said but when she left, I was beaten. I could not attend school for what seemed like a long time because I had one bruise on my arm that took a long time to heal and a black eye that really hurt for a long time." That was all Joan could say about that day. Joan remembers her house in Shreveport, Louisiana. "We had some pretty horrible things happen there. My brother who is five years younger than me was a crying baby. When he would cry my mother would throw him into my arms and tell me to take him outside before she killed him. I took care of him, changed his diapers, fed him and played with him. He and I are still close today. When he was about three, my mother hit him so hard in the side of the head that he has no sight in his left eye. She told me it was my fault. I should have been watching him. I don't remember what he did, I just remember when they discovered his blindness she blamed me. After all, everything was always my fault. She told me every chance she got, 'You ruined my life' or 'Everything is your fault, or you are worthless.'" I was the scapegoat for everything.

The next year the small family moved to Gonzales, Louisiana, and lived with Ken's sister. While they were living there, everyone contracted the measles, and her mother became pregnant again. One night Joan woke up in a panic to screams and cries while her mother loaded them into the car and moved them, yet again. This time the family was living in their car in the woods. They would clean up at a gas station every morning and be taken to school. Joan felt embarrassed and was relieved when they moved back onto Sam and Sally's land a little while later. Her grandfather gave Angela an acre and helped pay for a house to be built. It was a small, unfinished house with no doors on any of the rooms and the only electricity and water came from Joan's grandparent's house. Two-by-fours were erected and covered with roofing paper. The sink was set in on top of boards positioned across two cabinet tops. Despite the condition, it was better than a car in the woods.

Soon the bill collectors began coming to the house. Joan was only in elementary school, but she was the one tasked with getting rid of them. Her mother would stand behind the door with a belt in her hand to enforce the lie that she was not home. The bill collectors would bombard Joan with questions about her mother until she got flustered. One time she began to cry so much that the man left. When he was gone, Angela slapped her so hard she hit the floor. She then began to kick Joan, telling her to get up because the man was coming back. Joan was hurt and angry and wouldn't get up, so her little sister was sent to answer the door. The man pushed passed her little sister and found their mother hiding behind the door. Her mother started screaming and swinging the belt, so he left again. The two girls were badly beaten after this incident.

(The following story does not pass today's test of political correctness, but instead reflects the memory of the way things were in the time frame in which this story occurred. Please see endnote 44.)

During this time, the children would occasionally spend the night with their grandparents. Typically, it was when they were bruised and couldn't go to school. On one occasion, Sam, Joan's grandfather came into their bedroom, got Joan and her brother and sister and loaded them up in the wagon. He took them across the railroad tracks to what he called "nigger quarters." The kids watched as a man was dragged from his house, beaten and a cross was set on fire in his front yard. Sam told the children that they needed to see what happened to people who didn't know their place. Joan was confused. "We played with that man's nieces and nephews," she thought. "Their grandmother comes over and helps my grandmother." Joan remembers that her grandmother would give the family food for helping, but never money because "niggers don't know how to handle money."[44]

When Joan was twelve, her grandfather died. Shortly before his passing, he had a fight with Angela, and he hit her with a shovel. It was clear that Joan's abuse was part of a cycle. Once Sam was gone, Joan's life truly became a living hell. She then realized that her grandfather had been protecting her and her siblings, that he was the reason her mother didn't harm them too badly. Joan was finally seeing Angela's true colors, and it wasn't a pretty sight. Angela was a bitterly negative person, always saying that no one did anything right and that the kids were never good enough. She hit them often with whatever she could find. Joan felt the need to protect her siblings but received many more whippings because she did so. On one occasion, Angela yanked her son's arm so hard that she pulled it out of its socket. Everyone, including her own children, was afraid of Angela and what she might do in a rage.

Joan tells a story that demonstrates the fear and anxiety that the children felt. "We were required to make our beds and clean our rooms before we went to school every day. If our cleaning job didn't suit her or she had a bad day or she was just feeling mean, she would trash the bedroom. There were about three or four of us to a room but it was always the oldest one in the room who was at fault. It was so devastating to come home from school and find the bedroom trashed. She would not say anything when we came in, she would just wait for us to find it. She would take everything off our bed, out of our closet, out of all the drawers in the dresser, off the wall, off the top of the dresser and pile it in the middle of the floor. She would take the mattress and box spring from the bed and stand it against the wall.

"I remember standing in the door, having tears rolling down my face and my mother would walk up behind me, grab my hair and pull my face back so I could see her. She would scream and start hitting me with her fist or with whatever she had in her hands. She would tell me how worthless I was, how I had ruined her life and how she should kill me to keep me from ruining anyone else's life. After she finished, I then had to take a cleaning mixture she made with hot water, Clorox, and anything else she had to put in it. I had to clean the bedframe, wipe the mattresses and put the bed back together. I would have to refold all the clothes and put them back in the dresser. I would have to hang up the clothes in the closet and put everything back on the wall or the top of the dresser.

"When I was finished, Mother would come to inspect. If the clothes in the dresser were not folded properly and placed in neat rows, she would throw them back on the floor. If all the clothes in the closet were not facing the correct way, all shirt fronts facing left, all pants with the waist pointing left, all dresses with the fronts facing left, she would throw them back on the floor. If anything got wrinkled during this process, I had to re-iron it before it could be put back in the closet. If we had to do this dance a second time, there was another screaming, slapping, hitting dance to go with it. We kids would have to keep everything spotless and do all our chores.

"We had a wringer washing machine and three rinse tubs in our backyard, just outside the kitchen window. When I got home from school, washing was my job: rain, cold, snow, it didn't matter, the wash had to be done. Wet clothes are very heavy and my hands would freeze in cold weather. I would have to take hot water in a bucket from inside the house to fill the machine and the rinse tubs. After all the clothes were washed, I had to hang them on the clothesline. I hated Tuesdays and Fridays, washdays. By this time there were six of us and George was a baby with lots of messy diapers. Angela would stand at the kitchen window and yell at me to hurry up because the baby needed changing or the dishes needed to be washed."

As Joan grew older, the hurt, stress, and loneliness began to seep into her soul and she longed for an escape. During this time of her life she would sneak out of the house at night, lie under a big oak tree just outside her bedroom window, and look up at the night sky. She would pray, "God, if you are really there, either take me out of this house or let me die." She repeated these same words so often, that her prayer soon became simply "You know what I want. Amen." Then one day a huge storm came, lightning struck that tree and killed it. It had to be removed. Joan thought that was her answer; the tree mattered and she did not. That was when she stopped praying altogether.

After her grandfather died, her grandmother, Sally, began an all-out war with Angela. That battle lasted the rest of Sally's life. Sally started telling Joan that her mother hated her, that Grandma was the only one who loved her, and that she was the only one who cared what happened to her. Joan's mother was always in a fit of violent anger and Joan would get the brunt of a great deal of the anger, being the oldest. Her stepfather was an alcoholic who worked off shore on an oilrig. He would be home seven days and gone seven days. When he was gone, the children's lives were a living hell; when he was home, she ignored them. They would go to Sally's house to play and Angela would tell Joan to be home by four o'clock to start dinner or do some other task. Sally would keep Joan until 4:15 or so, telling her how much Angela hated her. Then she would get home late and Angela would scream and beat her, reinforcing what Sally had just said.

Sally even talked Joan into running away one time. Joan says, "I put some clothes in a bag, put them outside my bedroom window, waited until everyone was asleep and eased out of the house. I went to my grandmother who was waiting for me on her porch. She put me to bed and the next day told my mother she didn't know where I was. One of my sisters saw me in the window and told my mother. My mother pushed my grandmother down and dragged me from the house. I couldn't walk for several days without pain because I was beaten so badly. I remember her screaming as she hit me, 'You always cause so much trouble! You deserve to die!' Those vile and hurtful remarks were always followed by the classic, 'You ruined my life!'"

One night Angela and her husband were arguing and Ken pulled a gun on Joan's little brother, who was three or four years old at the time. Ken told Angela to give him some money that she had hidden or he would kill the boy. Ken fired the gun over Joan's brother's head. There was chaos of yelling, pushing, and hair pulling while Joan snuck out with her brother and they hid together. Her brother was shaking uncontrollably. Their mother finally gave her husband the money, and he left. The next morning Joan asked her mother why she let that happen and Angela just told her that she was a liar, she was making it up, and everything bad that happened was just her imagination. "What is wrong with you?" she would say.

The Rayne Baptist Church was across the street from Sally's house so when they lived near her or with her, they had to attend church. Angela would make them get dressed and send them to Sunday school. After Sunday school, she would be waiting in the chapel in their pew. The children were to file in silently, hug her, and sit quietly next to her for the remainder of the service. She always sat on one end of the pew and Joan sat on the other end. If anyone talked, fell asleep, or caused any trouble during the service, she would look at them and they would freeze for they knew when they got home there would be trouble. If the little ones caused any problems, the oldest child sitting next to them would get the belt when they got home. Joan always tried to keep the little ones next to her so that she could help them, but it didn't always work, so church was hell and after church was deeper into hell.

When Joan was thirteen, the bank repossessed the house on her grandparent's property, and the family moved to a trailer in Monroe, Louisiana. It didn't take long before they were back to living in the car in the woods. Joan and two of her siblings were expected to steal food so that the family didn't starve. Their mother would drive them to the store and the kids would go in under the guise of buying some penny candy while they very discretely put food into their pockets. Wieners were Joan's favorite. Early in the morning, Joan's stepfather would drive the car to nice neighborhoods, follow the milk truck and Joan would steal milk from front doors so the babies would have milk. Luckily, it wasn't too long before Joan's stepfather got a new job, and they moved to New Orleans, Louisiana, for about six months.

Around this same time, Angela had begun allowing Ken to use Joan as his toy. Angela figured out that if she did this, he would be less violent with her and the other children. It started very innocently. Joan would sit on his lap, and he would be playful with her. This "playtime" soon escalated to more inappropriate behaviors. Joan was uncomfortable and scared but had to play along or she would be made to feel guilty. She had no choice, but to let these things happen to her. Eventually, the playing was not enough for Joan's stepfather. When she was fifteen, before she even hit puberty, he raped her. She was traumatized. The next day, they took Joan to the hospital. While Joan kicked and screamed, the nurses asked Angela if it was possible that Joan had been raped. Rather than protecting her daughter, Angela discounted the entire idea of the violation that had happened. She told the nurses and doctor that Joan was sneaking out with boys to have intercourse and that she had tried to talk to her daughter about her "behavior," but Joan wouldn't listen. Angela even said that Ken would have to sleep in Joan's room to prevent her from sneaking out. This is also what Angela told the other children, creating the opportunity for further trauma to her oldest daughter. Eventually, Joan was given so many drugs to calm her down that she couldn't move. The nurses all left the room, and Joan's stepfather asked his wife to go get him coffee. He then molested Joan in the hospital room. Joan felt abandoned, alone, and hopeless.

Joan relates some of her emotions and feelings from this time, most of which was hopelessness. "There was no hope for me. I truly didn't matter because I was nothing. So I decided to accept my new role to cause less trouble. They released me from the hospital after a couple of days to go back home and he stayed away from me for a few days until I healed. Then he started coming to me again. My sister started sleeping in another room. She was told he had to sleep with me to keep me from letting boys in the house in the middle of the night because that was dangerous. I have vague memories of having intercourse pretty often after that for what seemed like a long period of time. I had not even had my first menstrual cycle. As far as I know, he never used any protection. I remember one time feeling sick first thing in the morning and he told me I had to go to school or my mother would think I was pregnant.

"The thought of being pregnant horrified me. I didn't want my life ruined. So I went to school. Shortly after that, my mother took me to the doctor to get a shot to start my cycles. She monitored them closely. I remember him telling me one time that boys my age wanted new stuff and I was used goods so I would always belong to him. I didn't feel anything anymore. This was my new normal. As you might imagine, I have relived this night and the following years over and over again trying to find where my fault might be, trying to understand these actions, and trying to decide if I caused this in some way."

According to the Stanford rape story that appeared in USA Today on June 22, 2016, an actual rape may take several minutes for the attacks to end but for every rape victim, "…it takes just a moment —a millisecond—to cross the threshold from someone who was not raped to someone who has had the most private parts of their mind and body violated in an irreversible way." That is "a moment that can never be undone or justified. A moment that will live on within them forever." [45] This is precisely the way that Joan felt. Her stepfather's actions were irreversible and would have a lasting impact on her.

Throughout this time in her life, Joan could do nothing to ease her suffering. She lived in a world detached from reality. Before she was raped, Joan lived in reality. She was aware of herself and could make intelligent choices. After the trauma of being raped, she developed a condition known as dissociative disorder which clinical psychologists define as memory loss (amnesia) of certain time periods, events and people. Some people develop mental health problems, such as depression, anxiety, and thoughts of or attempts at suicide. Some develop a sense of being detached from themselves. Joan could sense what was going on around her but could not control it and she blocked it out of her consciousness. It became an out-of-body experience. For the next four years, Joan's stepfather used and abused her. Joan describes herself as feeling nothing during this time. She seldom went to school during her tenth grade year. He made her feel like she was his property and that she couldn't make choices for herself. It was a devastating time that haunted Joan for much of her life.

At some point after this incident, Joan and her family went on a trip to see her grandmother. Because of the power struggle between Sally and Angela, Joan was often pressured into telling her grandmother the awful things that happened to her. Under great pressure, Joan told Sally about the rape. Her grandmother was livid, and there was lots of screaming and slapping. Her grandmother seemed to believe that this was Joan's fault, that she was too loose with her body. Joan was confused. This woman was supposed to love her, yet she blamed her for things that were out of her control. Still, she was safer with Sally than with Angela and her husband, so Joan stayed with her grandmother for a period of time. Though there were no beatings, she was manipulated and degraded psychologically.

Sally told her that she needed to go to college or she would never amount to anything. This brought Joan back to reality. Maybe there was help for her; maybe she could control her surroundings. At school, Joan stayed away from boys. She had a goal and school became a means to reach that goal. After a few months, Angela came to get Joan, and she was forced to live with her attacker again. She felt that it was easier just to allow him to have access to her than deal with the beatings. As damaging as this situation was, Joan felt a renewed drive to better her life. Rather than missing school and feeling nothing, this time she began to work hard in school, and she was even able to earn a scholarship to Louisiana State College. What joy she felt! After everything she had to deal with, here was an opportunity to change it all. She would be able to escape her situation and control her own life.

After the first two weeks of school, Joan's assigned roommate went home sick and never came back. In early October, Joan became sick, as well. Her first worry was that she might be pregnant. She went to the infirmary to get a pregnancy test, and it came back negative. Joan didn't know what else might be causing this illness, but she felt very ill and so exhausted. When she got back to her room, she fell asleep. She woke up three days later, back in her bed with her housemother, or dorm supervisor, shaking her. She had hepatitis. Joan's aunt Laverne, drove up to get her because her mother wouldn't come to pick her up. Joan describes Aunt Laverne as "a piece of work." "She moved into my grandmother's house after my grandfather died. She took over all my grandmother's holdings and money, remodeled the home, and basically took control of my grandmother's life." It seems Laverne's natural inclination would be to go get Joan rather than allow Sally to.

On the way home they stopped to see a doctor, who immediately admitted Joan into the hospital. She stayed there for two months. While Joan was in the hospital, Sally contacted her biological father, pleading with him to visit Joan. He did visit and told Joan that he was her father. Joan had discovered a few months before that Ken was not her biological father, which was a great shock. When she graduated from high school, her guidance counselor at school informed her the diploma would have to be in her legal name. Despite her knowledge of her father, Joan was stilled surprised to see him in person.

Her father tried to have a relationship with her, but Joan felt some bitterness toward him. Why hadn't he come to save her from her living hell? Where was he all those years? She later found out that he had health issues and that her grandpa Sam threatened to kill him if he tried to see her. *"Great. More dysfunctional family!"* Joan thought.

There was a silver lining in this confusing turn of events. After Joan's scholarship was cancelled because of her illness, her biological father was able to get her another one. Joan went back to school and stayed away from all the boys. Joan was a pretty girl. Boys seemed interested in her, but she ignored them. She was determined to concentrate on her studies. That didn't stop the girls from disliking her. Many of them were promiscuous and jealous, but somehow Joan got the bad reputation. Rumors were exaggerated, and Joan was friendless.

Then one night, her stepfather Ken showed up at her dorm, yelling for her to get in his car and run away with him because she belonged to him. Joan felt fear and embarrassment. "This certainly isn't going to help the way the other girls see me," she thought. And she was right; Ken's visit seemed to somehow solidify her tarnished reputation. So she began dating the next boy that asked--a track and field star. Suddenly, the girls began liking her. She was no longer a threat. After a couple weeks of dating, Joan and her boyfriend began to go to motels. For Joan, the intimacy meant nothing. It was just a physical activity, like playing a board game. Intercourse was nothing to her and meant nothing. It was nothing new, nothing exciting. She had lived with it her whole life; she was almost detached from the act. But her boyfriend gave her the attention she sought. He talked to her and complimented her and wanted to hear what she had to say. He made her feel important.

Soon enough, the couple got the unpleasant surprise that Joan was pregnant. They got married, but Joan didn't enjoy motherhood or marriage. To her, it was just an extension of her childhood; changing diapers, calming the baby, and constant intercourse. Despite his words to her before their marriage, Joan's husband was similar to her stepfather. He was a drug addict and unfaithful. Joan thought that this would have to be her life now. She would deal with it and pretend that everything was all right, as she always had. After the baby was born, Joan began working at a bank, and her husband went back to school to finish his degree. He became a teacher and a coach. They had another child while they both continued to work. Eventually, they moved back to Rayne, so that he could coach at the high school there. It was no accident that they moved close to her family. His intentions had always been to leave her. After 9 years of marriage, it was over. Joan was devastated. After all that she had endured for him, all of

his promises, the brave face she had put on, and still he was
gone.

A few months later, Joan's brother, who as a young
boy had a gun fired at him, was killed in a car accident. He
had alcohol and cocaine in his system. Joan felt the burden of
guilt because she helped him buy the car and she loaned him
money. The sheriff asked Joan to accompany him to inform
Angela. When they got to her mother's house, Joan walked
into Angela's room, and her mother's husband (now stepfather
number four) woke up shouting a string of profanities at Joan.
Under the pain of losing the brother she spent her life
protecting and standing up for, Joan went to her mother and
told her the bad news. Angela punched her, sending her flying
across the room. She began to attack Joan, calling her a liar.
The sheriff pulled Angela off Joan, and she screamed that this
was Joan's fault, that she killed her son. Part of Joan couldn't
help but agree. Angela and Joan didn't speak for several
months.

Around this time a much older man started showing
interest in Joan. He was a contractor and seemed to be a good
man. He lived with his parents since he was just coming off a
divorce like her. Joan describes their relationship as such: "We
married shortly after we met because again, I was pregnant. I
lost the baby and our marriage fell apart when he started
getting drunk and coming home to raise hell. One night a
friend of his called me from a bar and told me he was too
drunk to drive. I needed to go get him. I knew there would be
hell to pay if I left his truck at the bar so I got my fourteen
year-old son, Ian, out of bed. I had him get behind the wheel
and drive us to the bar. This was the first time he had driven a
vehicle. The friend helped my husband into the truck. I drove
the truck and my son drove my car back to our house. Several
weeks later, this husband pulled a gun on Ian. Flashing back to
the memory of my now dead brother being shot at as a child, I

made a decision. That was the end! I had already lived this nightmare! My husband got up to go hunting with his friend one morning and that was the day my children and I moved out. This marriage lasted less than two years."

Joan expressed that she made some of the worst decisions a woman can make. She lived a very immoral, loose life. Joan shares, "I had several abortions because the person I was married to or the person I was seeing at the time did not want a baby. It would have been inconvenient to bring another child into the world. My immorality knew no limits, married men, younger men, it made no difference. Intercourse was a way to get attention, to create a sense of being needed, and to get what I wanted or needed from a man. I needed to be seen, I needed to be noticed, I needed to be wanted, I needed to be desired and intercourse was the vehicle I knew how to use. It had worked my whole life to get what I needed or wanted." Because of her childhood trauma, sex was not a symbol of a loving, faithful relationship.

Joan did not enjoy being a mother. It was a burden, a role she had to fulfill. As her mother so eloquently put it, "This is your bed so now you have to lay in it." And lay in it she did. Joan did all the things a mother is supposed to do, said all the right things, cuddled, kissed and cared for her boys, but her heart was never in it when they were little. She was a better mother than Angela, seldom hitting her boys. Her sons never knew of any of the men in her life except their father and her second husband. When the boys got older and could help with chores, help with problem solving, or help with finances, they became partners in her life. Joan enjoyed being a mother to older boys.

Around this time in her life, Joan had a realization. She tells, "So many times in my life I pleaded with God to take me, to save me, to offer me some type of comfort, or to just kill me and put me out of my misery. But shortly after my second divorce, I realized this adult misery was my doing, my creation, and my life. I couldn't blame anyone for the things that were happening to me now. I believed that God did not exist and even if He did, He never had and never would watch over me. This realization empowered me. I started to make different choices. I knew I could not trust anyone or anything. I could only rely on myself. I finished my accounting degree. I was determined I would never be poor again and I would not have to answer to a man. I would be self-sufficient. I stopped seeing men completely. I realized no one cared about me, my life or my children but me. I was responsible, and I could choose where I wanted my life and the life of my boys to go from here."

From that point on, Joan was determined to be self-sufficient. Once she had gained this freedom, she moved with her boys to Shreveport, Louisiana. Her oldest son got a scholarship to go to Northwest Louisiana University, but only lasted one semester because he didn't want to live so far from Rayne, Louisiana. It was around this time that Joan found out that Angela had been manipulating her son and telling him awful things about her ever since he was little, much like her grandmother had done to her. Her son didn't want to move back in with her, so Joan allowed him to live with Angela. She didn't want to continue the manipulative and damaging tradition her mother and grandmother had created.

Soon after that, Joan thought that her life was missing something. She decided to audition for a local theatre because she had always loved singing. Joan soon became friends with the pianist, Isabel, at the theatre. "Both Isabel and her children had a special light about them," she said. Joan began asking questions, and soon discovered that Isabel was a member of the Church of Jesus Christ of Latter-day Saints (LDS). Isabel sent the missionaries from her church to visit with Joan. While Joan was meeting with the missionaries, she was also forming a great friendship with Isabel. Isabel thought it might be a good idea to set Joan up with one of her friends, David, who also had been through a divorce. Joan began seeing David frequently and eventually fell in love with him. She was a bit precarious about the relationship; all of the men she was ever attracted to had a horrible fault or problem. She also felt confused. Before she had moved to Shreveport, she stopped seeing men and decided that she would be completely self-sufficient. Her decision to be taught by the missionaries was a decision she made for herself. She felt that she could either learn from the missionaries or be with David, but not do both. She was trying to change her life, but she was also falling in love with this man. The longer they were together, the more deeply they fell in love and Joan overcame her wariness and chose to marry David. Angela opposed the church, so she was very supportive of Joan marrying this man. She would say, "Joan, you don't need to worry about this religious stuff; marry him! You can change him later." Joan later found out that her mother had burned a Book of Mormon that Joan's brother brought home from college and she understood why Angela had supported her marriage.

At this time in her life, Joan felt like she had it all together. She had a good job, her boys were doing well, she had nice friends, and she was comfortable. However, the missionaries and her new husband were causing her to re-examine her feelings toward God. Maybe He did care about her? Maybe Christ did die for her? But, she was also confused. Where had God been all of her life? She decided to join the church, but her heart really wasn't in it. She participated in everything, but was never truly converted. It was all a façade.

David got a new job, and they moved to Salt Lake City, leaving her boys and their lives behind.

1996 was the year from hell. In March, she had a complete hysterectomy resulting from endometriosis that caused her intense pain. In June, she was fired from a good job that she loved. This was also partly caused by the endometriosis; her doctor couldn't find the right hormone combination and the resulting behavior got her fired. In September, her husband got a job in Houston, Texas, and they moved across the country again. In October, Joan's oldest son was killed in a car accident.

The death of her son caused so much pain, anguish, desperation, and horror for Joan. All of the proceedings were a fog. It felt like it was all happening to someone else. A few days later, his death finally hit her, and she shut down. Joan stayed that way for nearly a year. Her old friend dissociation had returned to help her. She went through the motions necessary in her life, but has no memory of them. The second year after his death, she began to feel again. What she felt was guilt, anger, frustration, doubt, pain, and above all, questions. Why him? Had she done something to cause all of this? Why did the horror of this life never seem to end? She believed it wouldn't until she wasn't on this earth anymore. She begged her husband to divorce her, so that she could end her life and not affect anyone. Joan felt that a part of her soul had died with her son. She was empty. She tried to comfort herself, but nothing eased the pain.

Even after many years, the grief never stops. She will always love him, but the mourning for her son and his lost potential will always be there as well. It made the events in her other son's life hard to bear knowing that her oldest son would never experience them. Even twenty years after his death, she still thinks of him daily. She can now remember the good things in his life and not be constantly crippled by the thought of him.

During her grief, Joan had a profound dream. She was walking through a part of Rayne that she knew very well, but it was different and dangerous. Everyone else was desperate around her, but she was not afraid. She looked to her left and saw a man beside her. In a beautiful voice he said, "Lo, I am with you always." She woke up crying and she knew the man she had seen in her dream was God, who had always been with her. He knew of the events in her life, He had been with her all through her tragedies, her grief, and her mistakes. He knew all of her thoughts and behaviors. She began to pray and ask God why He was only coming to her now. She had survived everything that came to her, so why was He coming now? Now she felt she didn't need His help; she could handle this.

The promptings started small, but they were clear. Joan felt that she should attend massage school. This didn't make any sense; she had an accounting degree, she was able to finish school and raise kids at the same time, and she's worked for years. She would be able to find another job; she just had to finish grieving. But the promptings didn't stop and she finally decided to trust that this was God's plan. Her decisions hadn't always been good, so she thought she would give His idea a try. She prayed for guidance. Her husband reminded her that she hadn't worked in a couple of years and it might be difficult to pay for school. After researching the cost, Joan agreed that they could not afford for her to attend massage school. She went back to God and asked what she should do now. A couple weeks later she received a flyer in the mail for a massage school that would accept college credits. She spoke with the school and they accepted her credits and said she could finish the school for $2000. She felt prompted to sign up right then, so she did. Her husband was still reluctant, but he had bought some stock in a company and then sold it so they had a little extra money, but he wasn't sure how much.

On the first day of classes, Joan prayed and went to class. She didn't have the money but she felt that this was the right thing to do. The school didn't ask for the money on the first day and then for several days after. One morning she prayed and asked how she was able to attend massage school for free. That same day the administrator told her that her fees needed to be paid. She said that she would pay the next day. She again asked God, "What now?" When Joan checked the mail that afternoon there was a check from the brokerage firm for $2067. She thanked God. The next day when she went to pay, the receptionist told her that she also needed to pay for the textbook, which was $67.20. She wrote the check and was able to attend school for only twenty cents out of her own pocket. She followed the promptings from God, and He provided.

That experience was the beginning of a fulfilling relationship with Heavenly Father. Throughout her current life, He has guided her to help others and to be helped by others. As she trusts in Him, He provides for her. She says that she is still a mess and she still has times when she thinks and feels inappropriately and times when she wants to die. But her Father is patient with her. He works with her and she feels His love. She believes that Satan is alive and dangerous and works to destroy her. She also has faith that her Father will help her walk through the fires that she faces. She is still a member of the LDS faith and community. Though she doesn't understand all of the rituals of the church, she has faith that God will help her to understand and be at peace. She feels that Heavenly Father knows what she has been through, understands the way she feels, and is patiently working with her. She trusts fully in Him now.

Joan's life has never been easy. It has been ugly and full of shame and guilt, but God strengthened her along the way so that she was able to endure it. Everyone has challenges through which they learn and grow. Although the choices of others and her own caused Joan much pain and suffering over the years, she was thankful for her relationship with God. For years she had turned her back on Him (as she thought that He had turned His back on her), but as she began to follow Him, she realized that He was there all along allowing her to grow into the person she needed to become. The love that she feels from this relationship brings Joan great joy and helps her continue to endure through the struggles that life brings. Joan has forgiven her mother and harbors no hard feeling toward her. She visits her often and remains the anchor in the family.

Chapter Five

Growth

We Suffer to Encourage Growth and Change

"It is always the simple things that change our lives. And these things never happen when you are looking for them to happen. Life will reveal answers at the pace life wishes to do so. You feel like running, but life is on a stroll. This is how God does things."

~Donald Miller

Patricia Pitterle, a public speaker and prolific writer, believes "that it is important to realize that hardships and difficulties come to us largely for three reasons. Sometimes, it is because of our own sin or something we did to bring those circumstances to pass. Sometimes, it is because of the sins of others. Someone else has done something that has had consequences for us in our daily experiences. Sometimes, the hardships and difficulties are just a part of everyday living. It is just something that happens. We need to make the effort to learn and grow from our afflictions."

Tribulations encourage growth and change. We often do not understand or even notice the growth until looking back many years later. At certain times, however, the pain of suffering can actually lead us to make changes. Joan's realization that her choices were giving her a life that she was unhappy living helped her to grow and live a life that she is now proud of.

Lobsters are a natural example demonstrating how suffering leads to growth. It may sound strange to talk about lobsters in a book on suffering, but like all of humanity, a lobster deals with discomfort its entire life. In fact, it is this suffering that will signal the lobster to begin a period of growth. Lobsters must shed their old shells, hide under a rock for a time, and allow a new shell to grow. During this molting process, a lobster must first withdraw from its old shell. The withdrawal begins when the large flexible membrane that joins the carapace and abdomen stretches and splits. At the beginning of the molt, the membrane holding the gastroliths (stomach stones) break, and the calcium is thrown into the stomach. From there it is re-absorbed so that it may help in the immediate re-hardening of the new shell. Escaping from its old shell may take the lobster anywhere from several minutes to half an hour, depending on environmental conditions and the size of the animal. Once free of the old shell, the growth may proceed.

Over the next few hours, the lobster, which resembles a black rubber toy, will absorb water and will swell to reach its new, larger size and begin to grow a shell to match its larger body. The new shell has everything the old shell had, including all the same appendages, gills, mouthparts, antennae, antennules, eyestalks, and pleopods, as well as every hair, spine and bristle! Amazingly, a lobster even has the ability to regenerate lost appendages. For example, a lobster may "throw" a claw to escape a dangerous situation, such as a fight with another lobster. After its next molt, the claw will begin to regenerate, and eventually a new claw will replace the lost one.

Although no creature enjoys pain, in the case of a lobster, discomfort is the indicator to begin making a change. A lobster would be unable to grow, to become stronger, or to renew broken parts without that initial pain. This cycle of pain, growth, more growth, additional pain, and so on, is a sign of a great life. By surviving a relatively short amount of discomfort, the lobster is able to become more than it was before. Similar to these creatures, humans experience suffering the minute they are born. They are shaped by the stresses of life throughout mortality. Joan's unhappiness caused her to step back, take a look at her life, and decide to make a change.

Growth and change for humans often involves adversity, but this suffering can make us stronger. John Bytheway has explained, "When the winds of adversity come, remember one thing - kites fly against the wind. Kites don't fly in spite of opposition. Kites fly high because of opposition. In fact, they couldn't fly without opposition." Bytheway has also taught, "Something wonderful happens when we really know, without a doubt, that God loves us—our questions completely change. Instead of asking, 'Why did this happen to me?' We should say 'Well, I know God loves me; I know that. So what can I learn from this experience?'"[46] Whenever we feel the stress and challenges of this life, we can turn that pain into a way to learn and grow, following in the ways of the lobster.

Joan's trials began at birth. Because of the physical and emotional difficulties she faced throughout her life, she grew into a strong, independent woman. Her childhood struggles shaped her into a protector and a light for her siblings, as she demonstrated courage to stand up to her mother. When she was a teenager, her trials taught her resilience and how to be self-motivated to overcome the horrible things in life. In adulthood, Joan learned the importance of being responsible for her decisions and doing her best. All of these lessons led her to the one that we must all ultimately learn if we want to find true peace and happiness – God lives, loves her, and is watching out for her. Though most of her life she doubted Him, Joan grew into a faithful woman who is close to God and it is precisely because of her struggles, not despite them, that she gained this relationship with Him.

As we read the scriptures, we understand that Christ requires much of us. However, the scriptures also promise that we can do all things through Christ, and we will be strengthened to overcome any challenge. [47] God's grace is given to those who make a willing commitment to do all that He asks. Grace is not the absence of God's high expectations. Grace is the presence of God's power. This power helps us leave behind our old selves and our struggles and begin to change.

Spencer W. Kimball explained that the trials we experience can be a source of personal growth. "Is there not wisdom in giving us trials that we might rise above them, responsibilities that we might achieve, work to harden our muscles, sorrows to try our souls? Are we not exposed to temptations to test our strength, sickness that we might learn patience, death that we might be immortalized and glorified?"

"If all the sick for whom we pray were healed, if all the righteous were protected and the wicked destroyed, the whole program of the Father would be annulled and the basic principle of the gospel, agency, would be ended. No man would have to live by faith. If joy and peace and rewards were instantaneously given by the doer of good, there could be no evil—all would do good but not because of the rightness of doing good. There would be no test of strength, no development of character, no growth of powers, no free agency, only satanic controls" [48]

The human skeleton is another one of God's natural metaphors. Our bones demonstrate a distinct relationship between stress and strength. Bones are living tissues. Even after the skeleton is fully developed and each bone has grown to its maximum length, the cells continue to be broken down and reformed throughout our entire lifetime. This process involves two specific cells: osteoclasts and osteoblasts. Osteoclasts are responsible for breaking down bone (reabsorption) while the osteoblasts follow and form new bone. The speed at which osteoclasts break down bone is inherently faster than the rate at which osteoblasts can form bone, which makes sense because new bone can't be formed unless it is broken down first. However, this discrepancy causes the need for other factors to intervene in order to ensure that the osteoblasts are working as fast as possible. The strength and density of a bone is entirely dependent upon this ratio between the rate of bone reabsorption and the rate of bone formation.

One major factor in the growth of bone is physical activity. Wolff's Law states "bone tissue places itself in the direction of functional demand," meaning that bone tissue will be broken down and reformed more quickly in places where the bone is used and stressed. This is precisely why astronauts lose bone mass in space. They are weightless, so there is no stress placed on their bones, no demand for the bones to grow. Because reabsorption occurs faster than formation, their bones lose strength. Many studies have shown that active populations have a higher bone density and strength than sedentary populations. This can even be shown in the skeleton of a single person. A professional tennis player will have a significant increase in bone mass on their playing arm vs. their non-playing arm. So quite literally, if you don't use it, you lose it.

The stress that we place upon our skeleton, the harder our bone tissue has to work, is what makes our bones strong and resilient. If there was no stress placed on them, they would be broken down and we would be left with brittle, fragile bones. But as we exercise them and place stresses upon them, they grow, becoming stronger. We experience this same phenomenon in our spirits. If we were to sit idly by, experiencing no pain or hardship, we would be delicate and frail, having no strength or substance. As stresses and trials are placed upon us, we can become strong and resilient and our experiences can shape us. As our bones follow Wolff's Law, our spirits also grow in the direction of functional demand. The trials that we face allow us to grow in the area that we need it most. If we struggle with patience, our trials can help us to become more patient. If we struggle with obedience, our trials can strengthen us in that area. If we allow Him to, God can take the stresses and trials that are placed upon us and use them to help us grow into the person that He ultimately wants us to become.[49]

Without the tests of faith, we cannot grow. Growth will only occur if we learn to recognize the signal that God is ready to teach us. Joan recognized these promptings from God. Because she chose to follow God's advice, she was blessed and taken care of. We truly can become better and be more prepared to take on any of life's challenges. Sheri Dew[50] explained, "If you're serious about sanctification, you can expect to experience heart-wrenching moments that try your faith, your endurance, and your patience." Don't get discouraged if a quest for more patience includes the testing of that patience. It will become easier over time. The trials we face, if we face them with resilience and the faith to endure, can work to make us stronger and bring us closer to God. Only through this suffering can we truly grow into the people God would have us become.

Chapter Six

LOVE OF GOD

WE SUFFER TO BETTER TO UNDERSTAND THE LOVE OF GOD

"MAN APPROACHES GOD MOST NEARLY WHEN HE IS IN ONE SENSE LEAST LIKE GOD. FOR WHAT CAN BE MORE UNLIKE THAN FULLNESS AND NEED, SOVEREIGNTY AND HUMILITY, RIGHTEOUSNESS AND PENITENCE, LIMITLESS POWER AND A CRY FOR HELP?"

~C.S. LEWIS, THE FOUR LOVES

Every person who has ever lived and ever will live will receive great blessings. It is up to the individual to learn to recognize God's blessings in their own lives. God loves His children. It is His work and His Glory to bring to pass their immortality and eternal life.[51] In order to qualify for exaltation, each person must be tested and perfected, but suffering does not have to be pure agony: "There hath no temptation taken you but such as is common to man: but God is faithful, who will not suffer you to be tempted above that ye are able; but will with the temptation also make a way to escape, that ye may be able to bear it."[52] Through her life-long suffering, Joan eventually learned that this law could apply to her trials and tribulations.

Not only did God love and bless her, He loves all of His children. It is for each of us to learn to understand the love God has for us.

Like all who suffer, Joan often wondered why things happened in her life. It became clear that sometimes you will not get a complete answer to that question. Instead, she learned to just keep pressing forward. Eventually all her questions could best be answered, "Because God loves you." He loves us, perhaps best because He allows us to endure suffering in order to make us better.

During the darkest storms, it can be difficult to feel the love of God. However, God is our refuge and strength, a very present help in trouble. "Therefore, will not we fear, though the earth be removed, and though the mountains be carried into the midst of the sea; Though the waters thereof roar and be troubled, though the mountains shake with the swelling thereof. Selah." [53] By looking for the love and light, even during the storms of life, we begin to understand that with God's help we are able to overcome whatever comes our way.

God's love is unchanging and ever present, just as He is. Scriptures remind us "…we have known and believed the love that God hath to us. God is love; and he that dwelleth in love dwelleth in God, and God in him." [54] Never was a more important declaration made to the world than "God is love." God doesn't just love; He is the very essence of love. Love is the essence of his existence, His very being, and infuses all His Godly attributes because God's very nature is love. [55]

God loves us, but that love does not keep us from all pain or suffering. In fact, God's plan of happiness for his children includes tests and trials. The convert Paul suffered great trials in his effort to spread the gospel of Jesus Christ among the Jews and the Gentiles. "…Five times I received from the Jews thirty-nine lashes. Three times I was beaten with rods, once I was stoned, three times I was shipwrecked, and a night and a day I have spent in the deep. I have been on frequent journeys, in dangers from rivers, dangers from robbers, dangers from my countrymen, dangers from the Gentiles, dangers in the city, dangers in the wilderness, dangers on the sea, dangers among false brethren...And he said unto me, My grace is sufficient for thee: for my strength is made perfect in weakness. Most gladly therefore will I rather glory in my infirmities, that the power of Christ may rest upon me. Therefore I take pleasure in infirmities, in reproaches, in necessities, in persecutions, in distresses for Christ's sake: for when I am weak, then am I strong."[56] Paul was unshakeable in his trials and he knew that the pains he suffered were all part of God's plan for him because He loved him.

Similarly, Joan's life was full of trials and great suffering. She could have easily given up, believing that there was nothing in this life worth living for and no one to love her, and at times she almost did. The realization that God does love her made all the difference. Life is an experience to teach that truth. It does not always turn out the way we want it to, even when we are doing what is right. Paul recognized that bad and good things happen to good and wicked people and that life is sometimes very unfair. Paul testified that Jesus Christ has the power to comfort us in our trials and will make all things right in the eternities. It is important to walk by faith in the Savior's love.

Our Father in Heaven knows that we must experience some pain and suffering in this life, but He will also never leave us comfortless. In addition, there is no pain, no trial that He has not experienced. This lesson was taught to another historical figure, Joseph Smith, while he pled with God at a time of great suffering.

On October 27, 1838, Lilburn W. Boggs, governor of Missouri, issued an order that read in part: "The Mormons must be treated as enemies and *must be exterminated* or driven from the state, if necessary for the public good."[57]

Four days later, Joseph Smith and several associates were betrayed into the hands of the Missourians at Far West, Missouri. For the next several weeks these men were abused and insulted, forced to march to Independence and then to Richmond, and incarcerated in Liberty Jail in Missouri. These men had not been convicted of any crime; nevertheless, they were held in the jail for several months.

Liberty Jail was much like a dungeon. The outer walls were stone masonry construction, two feet thick. The inner walls and ceilings were hewn oak logs, about a foot square. There was about a foot of space between the outside masonry walls and the inside oak walls. This space and the space above the upper ceiling were filled with loose rock to discourage escape. The only openings in the lower level were two iron barred windows, two feet wide and six inches high, and an opening in the ceiling to the upper room with a heavy wooden door. A hole in the floor of the top level was the only way to get to the lower level. The only way out of the jail was through a trap door in the ceiling. The ceilings on both levels were so low that two of the men who were confined there were never able to stand up straight. The upper room had two larger iron barred windows, two feet wide by one-foot tall, along with a heavy oak door. Outside the door was a small platform with a stairway down to ground level.

Joseph Smith, Jr., and his eight companions were imprisoned in Liberty Jail for four and a half months during the coldest part of the Missouri winter. There were narrow openings, which provided the only light in the prison. Unfortunately, these openings also let in the cold. Conditions were horrible. The prisoners were often sickened by rotten or poisoned food. Along with these deplorable conditions, Joseph and the others also worried for their families and the society of saints who were being driven from their Missouri homes in the midst of winter.[58]

Food was scanty, of poor quality and frequently poisoned. Some of the prisoners suspected that they were sometimes fed human flesh, but comments by the guards regarding 'Mormon beef' probably had reference to cattle stolen from the Mormons. Their friends on the outside were occasionally able to bring them wholesome food.[59]

No bedding was provided, so the prisoners were forced to sleep on the stone floor with only a bit of loose straw for comfort. The prisoners were allowed visitors from time to time. Alexander McRae recorded visits by Brigham Young, Heber C. Kimball, George A. Smith, Don Carlos Smith, Benjamin Covey, James Sloan, Alanson Ripley, and Porter Rockwell. In March, Frederick G. Williams came with President H. Buell, but the jailer, concerned that tools could be passed, denied them entrance.[60]

"The food given to the prisoners was coarse and sometimes contaminated, so filthy that one of them said they 'could not eat it until they were driven to it by hunger.' On as many as four occasions poison was administered to them in their food, making them so violently ill that for days they alternated between vomiting and a kind of delirium, not really caring whether they lived or died.

"In the Prophet Joseph's letters, he spoke of the jail being a 'hell, surrounded with demons ... where we are compelled to hear nothing but blasphemous oaths, and witness a scene of blasphemy, and drunkenness and hypocrisy, and debaucheries of every description. We have ... not blankets sufficient to keep us warm; and when we have a fire, we are obliged to have almost a constant smoke,' he said. 'Our souls have been bowed down' and 'my nerve trembles from long confinement,' Joseph wrote. 'Pen, or tongue, or angels' could not adequately describe 'the malice of hell' that he suffered there. All of this occurred during what, by some accounts, was considered the coldest winter on record in the state of Missouri."[61]

It is difficult to comprehend the conditions that were imposed upon the brethren who were enclosed within this dungeon-prison for 128 days. It was a dark, dismal, filthy, wet, foul-smelling, vermin infested hole. The only sanitary facilities were slop buckets. Journals speak of the physical trauma - toothaches, earaches, pneumonia, hunger, colds, unsanitary conditions, stinging eyes, etc.

Of the many trials of Joseph Smith, imprisonment for five months was certainly one of the most severe. As personally unpleasant as incarceration conditions were to endure, they were to him not nearly as weighty a matter as were the hardships of the people he served. The reports of cruelties - the whippings, the beatings, the rapes, and the plundering of homes and farms - were overwhelming. Then finally, the forced march out of the state in wintertime caused him to ask, "How long shall they suffer these wrongs and unlawful oppressions?"

While in the miserable jail, Joseph learned that his sufferings were still not comparable to those of the Savior, as the Spirit whispered to him: "The Son of Man hath descended below them all. Art thou greater than he?"

Elder Orson F. Whitney said, "The Prophet was lying in a dungeon for the gospel's sake. He called upon God, 'who controlleth and subjecteth the devil,' and God answered telling him that his sufferings should be but 'a small moment.' 'Thou art not yet as Job,' said the Lord, 'thy friends do not contend against thee.' Job's friends, it will be remembered, tried to convince him that he must have done something wrong or those trials would not have come upon him. Job had done no wrong; it was 'without cause' that Satan had sought to destroy him.

"God told Joseph 'If thou art called to pass through tribulation; if thou art in perils among false brethren; perils among robbers; perils by land and sea; if fierce winds become thine enemy; if the billowing surge conspire against thee, if the very jaws of hell shall gape open the mouth wide after thee, know thou, my son, that *all these things shall give thee experience and shall be for thy good.*' There is the reason. It is for our development, our purification, our growth, our education and advancement, that we buffet the fierce waves of sorrow and misfortune; and we shall be all the stronger and better when we have swum the flood and stand upon the farther shore."[62]

Jeffrey R. Holland spoke of this event, "The important lesson from Liberty Jail is that everyone, including the righteous, will be called upon to face challenging trials. When that happens we can sometimes feel that God has abandoned us. As individuals, as families, as communities, and as nations, probably everyone has had or will have an occasion to feel as Joseph Smith felt when he cried from the depth and discouragement of his confinement, 'O God, where art thou? … How long shall thy hand be stayed …? Yea, O Lord, how long shall [thy people] suffer … before … thy bowels be moved with compassion toward them?'

"Whenever these moments of our extremity come, we must not succumb to the fear that God has abandoned us or that He does not hear our prayers. He *does* hear us. He *does* see us. He *does* love us. When we are in dire circumstances and want to cry, 'Where art Thou?' it is imperative that we remember He is right there with us—where He has always been! We must continue to believe, continue to have faith, continue to pray and plead with heaven, even if we feel for a time our prayers are not heard and that God has somehow gone away. He *is* there. Our prayers *are* heard. And when we weep, He and the angels of heaven weep with us."[63]

God loves us. Joan eventually came to this knowledge. Each of us can do so, as well. Even through great suffering, God loves us and never leaves us alone. He wants nothing more than for us to return to live with Him, having learned and become what we came to earth to learn and become. He wants us to be perfect, to be made whole, and to continue our progression. We can only become who He wants us to be by passing through tests and trials, by pushing against the winds of change, and allowing God to pull us through.

> *GOOD TIMBER DOES NOT GROW WITH EASE:*
> *THE STRONGER WIND, THE STRONGER TREES;*
> *THE FURTHER SKY, THE GREATER LENGTH;*
> *THE MORE THE STORM, THE MORE THE STRENGTH.*
>
> *~DOUGLAS MALLOCH, "GOOD TIMBER"*

Chapter Seven

BETH'S STORY

*"IT IS IMPORTANT TO REMEMBER THAT SETBACKS,
FAILURES, AND TRAGEDY ARE A PART OF LIFE. WHETHER
WE MANAGE TO FIND JOY AND SUCCESS IN THE DAILY
STRUGGLE OF LIFE IS LARGELY DEPENDENT ON OUR
ABILITY TO PERSEVERE THROUGH EVEN THE TOUGHEST
ADVERSITY WITHOUT EVER GIVING UP."*

~KEEP INSPIRING ME

Beth is a stalwart individual who is admired by many. She is a person who never complains yet on the inside hides scars that never healed. She was no exception to the refining fire of trials. Beth has been an example of faith and hope throughout her entire life. One author's family is good friends with her and has seen firsthand the trials in her life and how she has responded to them. Her story is one that has strengthened and helped many people. Throughout her life she was the perfect model of peace and hope. She had unshakeable faith in her God and was an inspiration to a great number of people. Her father relates that the greatest lesson she taught was that when you are at the end of your rope, tie a knot and hang on. Beth hung on!

Beth's trials began early in life. As a child, Beth hated needles. Like most children, she was delighted when she missed vaccination day at school and didn't have to get a shot. However, that joy was short-lived when, at ten years old, the excruciating pain of polio attacked her.

According to the World Health Organization (WHO), Poliomyelitis (polio) is a highly infectious viral disease, which mainly affects young children. [64] The virus is transmitted person-to-person and spread mainly through the fecal-oral route or, less frequently, by a common vehicle (e.g. contaminated water or food) and multiplies in the intestine, from where it can invade the nervous system and can cause paralysis. Initial symptoms of polio include fever, fatigue, headache, vomiting, stiffness in the neck, and pain in the limbs. In a small proportion of cases, the disease causes paralysis, which is often permanent. There is no cure for polio; it can only be prevented by immunization.

Beth's muscles were stricken immobile as the disease destroyed her nerve centers. For four long months, Beth underwent special medical care. Her muscles began to awaken, signaling the start of an even longer stretch of time spent in physical therapy. Eventually, she could be fitted with braces stretching from her hip to her shoe. Her torso was bound tightly by a corset in order to hold her spine straight. She felt like the tin man! She missed one day of school and this was her punishment – a life confined to supports and braces. It felt like just yesterday that she could run and jump all on her own. Now she couldn't stand or move. Her heartache was heavy, but her resolve was stronger. She knew that these were the cards she was dealt and she had no choice but to do her best with what she was given. She chose to face this task with faith and hope, and that decision made all the difference.

Trials continued to come fast and furious for Beth. She was told that her corset would not be sufficient to continue to support her back. She would require a spinal fusion. Her feelings were mixed. On one hand, this was devastating! This meant that the treatment wasn't working and her braces weren't supporting her. Surgery and recovery would be a nightmare! On the other hand, maybe this would work! Maybe she wouldn't have to feel like the tin man anymore. There was a glimmer of hope. For a month prior to the surgery, Beth was placed in a plaster cast from her shoulders to her legs. This prison was so much worse than the simple corset that she was accustomed to wearing. This cast was highly uncomfortable, pressing into her legs and limiting circulation while restricting the motion of her shoulders. When the time of surgery approached, the doctors cut a small hole in the back of her cast while the surgery was performed.

According to the Mayo Clinic, spinal fusion is typically an effective treatment for fractures, deformities or instability in the spine. But study results are more mixed when the cause of the back or neck pain is unclear. In many cases, spinal fusion is no more effective than nonsurgical treatments for nonspecific back pain. It can be difficult to be certain about what exactly is causing back pain, even if scans reveal a herniated disk or bone spurs. In addition, many people have X-ray evidence of back problems that have never caused them any pain.

Even when spinal fusion provides symptom relief, it can eventually result in more back pain in the future. Immobilizing a section of the spine places additional stress and strain on the areas around the fused portion. This may increase the rate at which those areas of the spine degenerate.

Such was the case with Beth. Three days later, the same surgery was done on the lower half of her back. For the next two years, Beth calmly wore the plaster prison in which she was encased. Not only was it restrictive and uncomfortable, it wore down her skin from bruised to bleeding and added an extra burden onto her already braced legs. Over and over, Beth and her family were required to return to doctors for checkups. The doctors would x-ray her spine and adjust the cast accordingly when the spine was not straight. She endured this cast while showering, sleeping, and every other second of her life for two years.

When the day to remove the cast came, it was a special day for Beth. She would finally be free! After two years of confinement, she would finally be able to move! Her faith and hope had paid off; she could see the end of the tunnel. Then suddenly, the tunnel caved in around her. Less than a month after her cast was removed, Beth's spine began to collapse. The darkness of the tunnel returned. Could she handle another operation? Another 2 years of the plaster prison? She decided that she could and she would. The tunnel may have caved, but she never would. So she kept persevering down the path and two years later, after four years of incarceration, at fourteen years old, she was freed a second time. The joy was, again, overwhelming.

As was common in Beth's life, the tunnels never seemed to end, and not long after the second cast was removed, Beth's back began to collapse again. She thought her heart might collapse along with it. But the stalwart girl, who had been through so much, taught her father a lesson during this trial. The night before her third operation, Beth's dad found her sitting in her wheelchair. As she saw his worried expression, Beth said, "Daddy, everything is going to be just fine. I am really a very lucky girl. There are some who have much bigger problems than I do." Beth's faith was greater than her struggles.

For another two long years, Beth endured her third cast. As the end of yet another tunnel approached, her family was planning a vacation to Europe. She begged the doctor to take the cast off a month early so she could visit Europe, and he eventually agreed. This time, her surgery stuck. What a triumph! At the age of sixteen, Beth had already endured more than most do in a lifetime.

The family's trip to Europe was a respite after all that they had faced in the previous six years. Beth loved every minute of it. Once they returned to the states, Beth's doctors planned more surgery for her legs in order to help her muscles re-learn how to function. They manipulated her muscles and nerves in an effort to bring back her strength. These surgeries left Beth bed-ridden for six months. To make things worse, they ultimately didn't work. Beth and her family were crushed. Though she still stayed resolute and faithful, after this disappointment, Beth was determined not to undergo any further surgeries. The grief and pain were too much to handle.

Beth spent the next few years completing her high school and college degrees. She continued to use her braces and undergo physical therapy to strengthen her muscles. After finishing school, Beth began to wonder about her prospect for a family. She had the opportunity to do service and missionary work in her congregation of the LDS church. Because of her physical limitations, she needed someone to accompany her. A man named Zachary offered to help Beth. As the two spent time together, Zachary began to see past Beth's physical trials and into the beautiful and resilient heart that she had. He saw that her trials had refined her into a very special woman. They made the decision to be married. It was an answer to Beth's prayer and a blessing in response to her father's pleading. Beth soon found out that she was pregnant. Though her past of polio, surgeries, and weak bones and muscles left many in her family worried, Beth was confident their baby would be safe, and she was right. Beth bore a beautiful child and devoted herself to motherhood. The family was genuinely happy. As Beth and her husband were expecting another baby, they felt that despite their struggles, their life was wonderful. After many years of turmoil, the happiness they experienced was a great blessing.

However, this family did not have the luxury of a "happily ever after" just yet. Their second child died at birth and the heartache was more real than anything Beth had ever felt. The only thing that kept her going was her faith in God and His grace. She knew she would see her angel again. Through this tragedy, the family stayed strong. It was another hand dealt that Beth had to do her best with, another tunnel to push through. The family recovered from their heartache and Beth gave birth to another daughter.

In the two years following the loss of their baby, misfortune struck the family again. Zachary was diagnosed with Hodgkin's disease. According to the Mayo Clinic, Hodgkin's lymphoma is a cancer of the lymphatic system. The lymphatic system drains excess fluid from the blood and protects against infection. Hodgkin's lymphoma is different from other forms of lymphoma.[65]

The cause of Hodgkin's lymphoma is unknown. It is likely related to complex genetic and environmental factors that lead to alteration of the immune system. There are some compelling pieces of data to suggest that a virus causes it, and the Epstein-Barr virus (EBV) has been considered.

While Zachary was undergoing treatments, testing, chemotherapy, and surgeries, Beth remained as faithful as ever. Though the family struggled, Beth was able to lift the weight on their shoulders and make the burden bearable. Zachary pulled through after many months and began to work again while Beth gave birth to another baby boy. It wasn't long until Zachary had another attack of Hodgkin's disease. "When will it end?" Beth thought. "Have we not been through enough?" She didn't want to see her sweetheart in such pain. This was the man that saw through her braces and weak body to the beautiful soul inside. He saved her from loneliness; he gave her a family. She didn't know what she would do if she lost Zachary. But he continued to get worse until there was nothing more to be done. The family was in the wake of yet another tragedy. Beth had lost her legs, lost her back, lost her muscles, and lost children, but nothing compared to the pain that this loss caused. Zachary's death was hard on Beth, but she again made the choice to push through and hope for better things to come. Her faith in God and her faith that she would see her children and husband again helped her to be resilient despite what she was facing. Though at the time of Zachary's funeral she was a pregnant widow with four children, Beth was still an example of tranquility to all who attended.

Soon after facing the death of her husband, Beth faced the death of yet another child quickly after birth. The suffering seemed endless, but the faith that she built over the years enabled her to be an example of endurance and peaceful strength.

Beth married again and was able to have more children. The trials and suffering that Beth endured were many and include multiple sclerosis, breast cancer, and the lingering pain from polio. Beth passed away on August 23, 2016, as this book was being written. She was preceded in death by her first husband, four children, and her stepson. She is survived by her second husband, four children, four stepchildren, five siblings, and nineteen grandchildren. She was a blessing to all she met. Her compassion and humble service allowed many to feel the love of God through her. In the course of writing this book, the authors have been touched by her ability to survive the numerous trials in her life with a happy heart and helpful hands. Her legacy and example will strengthen others for generations and give us all the hope to press forward with faith." Throughout her entire life Beth was a valiant example of faith, endurance, courage, and the ability to tie a knot at the end of her rope and hang on.

Everyone's suffering is individualized, and though it may be painful at the moment it will all be eased. "There is no physical pain, no spiritual wound, no anguish of soul or heartache, no infirmity or weakness you or I ever confront in mortality that the Savior did not experience first. In a moment of weakness, we may cry out, 'No one knows what it is like. No one understands.' But the Son of God perfectly knows and understands, for He has felt and borne our individual burdens."[66]

Chapter Eight

HOPE & FAITH

WE SUFFER AS A TRUE TEST OF FAITHFULNESS

"THE LORD COMPENSATES THE FAITHFUL FOR EVERY LOSS. THAT WHICH IS TAKEN AWAY FROM THOSE WHO LOVE THE LORD WILL BE ADDED UNTO THEM IN HIS OWN WAY. WHILE IT MAY NOT COME AT THE TIME WE DESIRE, THE FAITHFUL WILL KNOW THAT EVERY TEAR TODAY WILL EVENTUALLY BE RETURNED A HUNDREDFOLD WITH TEARS OF REJOICING AND GRATITUDE."

~JOSEPH B. WIRTHLIN

I f this mortal life were always easy, there could be no accurate gauge of faithfulness. God does not want his children to suffer, but understands in His wisdom that there is often no other way to test and to try us. Joseph Smith taught, "For a man to lay down his all, his character and reputation, his honor, and applause, his good name among men, his houses, his lands, his brothers and sisters, his wife and children, and even his own life also— counting all things but filth and dross for the excellency of the knowledge of Jesus Christ—requires more than mere belief or supposition that he is doing the will of God; but actual knowledge, realizing that, when these sufferings are ended, he will enter into eternal rest, and be a partaker of the glory of God. ...

"A religion that does not require the sacrifice of all things never has power sufficient to produce the faith necessary unto life and salvation; for, from the first existence of man, the faith necessary unto the enjoyment of life and salvation never could be obtained without the sacrifice of all earthly things. It was through this sacrifice, and this only, that God has ordained that men should enjoy eternal life; and it is through the medium of the sacrifice of all earthly things that men do actually know that they are doing the things that are well pleasing in the sight of God. When a man has offered in sacrifice all that he has for the truth's sake, not even withholding his life, and believing before God that he has been called to make this sacrifice because he seeks to do his will, he does know, most assuredly, that God does and will accept his sacrifice and offering, and that he has not, nor will not seek his face in vain. Under these circumstances, then, he can obtain the faith necessary for him to lay hold on eternal life.

"It is in vain for persons to fancy to themselves that they are heirs with those, or can be heirs with them, who have offered their all in sacrifice, and by this means obtained faith in God and favor with him so as to obtain eternal life, unless they, in like manner, offer unto him the same sacrifice, and through that offering obtain the knowledge that they are accepted of him. ...

"From the days of righteous Abel to the present time, the knowledge that men have that they are accepted in the sight of God is obtained by offering sacrifice. ...

"Those, then, who make the sacrifice, will have the testimony that their course is pleasing in the sight of God; and those who have this testimony will have faith to lay hold on eternal life, and will be enabled, through faith, to endure unto the end, and receive the crown that is laid up for them that love the appearing of our Lord Jesus Christ. But those who do not make the sacrifice cannot enjoy this faith, because men are dependent upon this sacrifice in order to obtain this faith: therefore, they cannot lay hold upon eternal life, because the revelations of God do not guarantee unto them the authority so to do, and without this guarantee faith could not exist."[67]

Having truly sacrificed and yet endured well proves sincere faithfulness to Christ. Scripturally, Christ is often referred to as the Bridegroom and those in His gospel are the brides.[68] Being born again in Christ is as if entering into a covenant, a companionship similar to marriage. This becomes an easy comparison for faithfulness, as a strong marriage is one where spouses are faithful to one another. The proof of this faithfulness is most accurately displayed through the most trying tests. Let's say that a husband remains faithful to his wife on a business trip. He has kept his covenants. How much more of a test would it be for that same husband to have remained faithful to his wife while on a business trip to Las Vegas, where his boss wants to hold meetings in a strip club and wants to pay women to go back to hotels with his employees? To have remained faithful in the more difficult circumstances better proves the level of commitment. The harder the test, the greater the score. When we suffer greatly and still remain faithful, our Father in Heaven can truly see where our heart lies. For, as Henry B. Eyring taught, "The great test of life is to see whether we will hearken to and obey God's commands in the midst of the storms of life. It is not to endure storms, but to choose the right while they rage."[69] Beth is an example of this stalwart faithfulness. Despite all of her struggles and the many times she could have cursed God and lost trust in Him, she continued to believe and be true to those beliefs.

Another example of the effectiveness of earthly tests is the tree of life.[70] For if a person was able to reach the tree, or eternal life, by simply walking down an easy path, one free of mists of darkness, temptations, ways to fall off and become lost, or the mocking from one's fellowman, it would not be as great of an accomplishment to have remained on the path. Having endured the most difficult suffering along the way makes the arrival at the destination that much sweeter.

Although each person will have their own path in mortality, their own level of suffering, and their own individual tests, it can be difficult to accept these differences without comparing one to another.

Though difficult to resist the urge to compare the severity of trials between different individuals and question God's fairness, one must learn to see his or her own trials independent of the trials of others. All have difficult tests throughout their lifetime. Only God is omniscient; only God sees the full picture. What we see of the trials of others, and even of our own suffering is often just a glimpse of the entire story. We are required to learn to press forward, enduring, even when the trial seems more than we can bear.

Dieter F. Uchtdorf has often taught of the need for patience in suffering. "Patience means accepting that which cannot be changed and facing it with courage, grace, and faith. It means being 'willing to submit to all things which the Lord seeth fit to inflict upon us, even as a child doth submit to his father.' [71] Ultimately, patience means being 'firm and steadfast, and immovable in keeping the commandments of the Lord'[72] every hour of every day, even when it is hard to do so." The way may be difficult, painful, or beyond our ability to withstand, but in the times of greatest darkness, we are learning to have hope for the dawn. The strongest storms often produce the most magnificent rainbows. Beth became this magnificent rainbow for others. Because of her hope during hardship, she was able to give hope and light to others, including one of the authors. Beth's father said that she was a great example to others. He calls her "the greatest teacher." Many people have heard her story and drawn strength from it. When she was at the end of her rope, her faith and hope gave her the ability to tie a knot at the end and hang on.

The storms of life are raging, often metaphorically, yet sometimes in reality. Man has always strived to understand and explain, scientifically as well as scripturally, the severity of storms and the destruction seen on earth. Often, scientists see "gloom and doom" for humanity. Best-selling economist Robert Heilbroner said in 1974, "The outlook for man, I believe, is painful, difficult, perhaps desperate, and the hope that can be held out for his future prospects seems to be very slim indeed."

What are we to learn from the storms of life in the trials we face? Why do tragedies and challenges, often from natural causes, seem to destroy and damage all that man attempts to build? Why attempt to construct anything, if, as the experts predict, it will all be brought to an end in the near future? Perhaps much of the devastation and difficulty on earth is simply testing faithfulness and individual commitment to "...[pressing] forward with a steadfastness in Christ, having a perfect brightness of hope, and a love of God and of all men."[73]

Interestingly, different individuals can often reach completely opposing conclusions about the same event. For example, one person might view a natural disaster as evidence that God does not exist. According to Shankar Vedantam, an American journalist, and science correspondent for NPR, "Invariably, however, believers usually experience a strengthening in their faith after a disaster. There may be a time of questioning, and some believers may see their faith shaken deeply, but for most, tragedy brings greater commitment to religious faith, not less."[74]

In Personality and Social Psychology Review, Kurt Gray and Daniel Wegner suggest that suffering may cause religious believers to accept even more strongly the reality of God than they did before because the human mind is designed to seek explanations for the phenomena we see around us.[75] Such was the case with Beth. The more she suffered the more she yearned for spiritual understanding. Trials may actually train our minds to become stronger, to better understand the purpose of life. Thus, the most difficult challenges are testing our resolve, pushing us to endure, even when life is at its most demanding. The true test of suffering is faithfulness, and the rewards are enormous.

Beth's life and choices have shown that there is always faith and hope, even when there is nothing else. Her storms allowed her the opportunity to come closer to God and as she did so, she was able to feel peace and strength despite the whirlwinds in her life.

Chapter Nine

CRAIG'S STORY

"TELL YOUR HEART THAT THE FEAR OF SUFFERING IS
WORSE THAN THE SUFFERING ITSELF. AND THAT NO
HEART HAS EVER SUFFERED WHEN IT GOES IN SEARCH OF
ITS DREAMS, BECAUSE EVERY SECOND OF THE SEARCH IS A
SECOND'S ENCOUNTER WITH GOD AND WITH ETERNITY."

~PAULO COELHO, THE ALCHEMIST

Craig is a person who suffered deeply because of the suffering and choices of those that he loves. Craig was thirty-eight years of age and his wife was thirty-five when they adopted two beautiful girls. Their dream of having children came true. They did their best to raise them to be happy, kind, and self-reliant. Unfortunately, things don't always turn out the way they are planned. As all parents know, a child's suffering, whether because of their choices or random circumstances, will cause their loving parents great sorrow. Because he was unable to change his adoptive daughters' decisions or relieve their suffering, added burdens were placed upon his shoulders. He felt the weight of questions, wondering if his daughters' choices and struggles were because of his parenting or their birth parents' decisions. He didn't know what he could do to help them and could only stand by and watch them struggle through life. In Craig's words:

"Our deepest moments of suffering can only be appreciated by those fellow sufferers who relate to our experiences. Suffering is a common lot with everyone. Our sufferings are all different, yet they are similar in the feelings and heartache experienced. Many suffer in ways that they can only communicate with people at an emotional level. My experience and research may be helpful to those who have struggled in raising adopted children as our family has."

As with all adoptive parents, families enter in the adoptive process with the illusion of successfully raising productive, God-loving members of society. Craig began at an early age to teach his kids about Jesus Christ, the church they belong to, and obedience to all the Commandments. They were very consistent, and as with most parents, were fairly successful in the beginning.

The first shock came when their oldest daughter became pregnant and was kicked out of college because she failed to meet the school honor code. As well-meaning parents, Craig and his wife were crushed when they got the news. They felt like their 18 years of teaching had been betrayed and their financial investment had been wasted. The couple totally questioned their ability to teach moral values by example and word. They had done their best, but still felt that they had failed their children, their church, their God, and themselves. What a crushing blow. Fortunately, their daughter's baby was successfully adopted into another family in which the couple couldn't conceive. This helped Craig feel as if the trial had become a blessing to someone else. He says, "The light began to come on for me after the successful adoption of our daughter's baby and her marriage to a great guy and the gift of another child."

"The heart crushing experience turned to a blessing after one of our darkest moments. The gamut of feelings from anger and hopelessness to abandonment was gone after many hours of therapy and prayer. My love for her never changed, but many questions for myself arose like, 'Was I a bad father? What were my mistakes? If I cannot do this basic thing, what can I do? I am a failure.' This inner self-questioning, doubting, and anger was difficult."

Craig is able to take solace now in knowing that his granddaughter was a great gift to another couple. "I feel like my daughter repaid the debt by blessing another childless father and mother."

Craig and his wife's second adopted daughter caused them even more heartache. The same emotions and questions weighed on them yet again, but this round lasted much longer than 9 months. Their youngest daughter was raped at thirteen years of age and then became very sexually active by the time she was fifteen. At seventeen, she was out of control, and her parents had her picked up in the middle of the night and transported 1000 miles away to a school designed to bring order to total chaos. They imprisoned her out of concern for her safety, future, and happiness. Craig shares, "You can't imagine those emotions, those inwardly probing questions of personal failure." When she was released at eighteen, things took a turn for the worse. She soon became involved with a dangerous boy who was a thief, drug addict, and sexual pervert. On one occasion, she was the driver in a robbery using Craig's vehicle. If she was out of control before, she was completely unbridled now.

Craig's fears and emotions were heartbreaking. "There was a time when we didn't know whether we would ever see her in the morning. We didn't know if she would overdose, commit suicide, or be killed in some bizarre sexual perversion. Imagine the feelings of failure after spending every day of her life teaching her of Jesus Christ and His loving commandments and watching her reject it.

"These heartaches caused us to make a great effort to overcome them. My wife has been praying 24/7 for the last eight years. I pray and endure every day. I have seen a psychologist every two weeks for the past eight years. I've searched and searched many hard hours to find books in an attempt to understand the deep issues here. I also donate ten hours per week for the past eight years to my church to feel close to God. We pay $10,000 each month for my daughter's care at the recovery school. Each of these activities has been an effort to relieve the suffering. There was no greater motivation than to find relief from feeling those burdens."

Finally, it seems they are seeing a little hope at the end of a long tunnel of darkness. Their daughter has a good job that requires specialized training. She personally put the effort in to achieve this schooling and her parents are very proud of her accomplishments. She has come so far from her post recovery school associations and decisions. Craig and his wife are so proud that she is beginning to make the choice to become a contributing member of society. She has become grateful for all of her parents' support and has begun to pray, which makes them beam with happiness. She has come a long way from the choices and circumstances of her youth.

Craig tells, "There was a time when I felt so much anger towards that young man who caused our family so much suffering that I wanted him to suffer as we did. Now, instead of intense anger toward him, I feel sorry for him, for those he continues to rape, and his eternal judgment.

"Despite all of the suffering that we went through, I was able to find a silver lining. The burden I carried was my motivation to find answers and keep moving forward, and that had its reward. This great mercy came from the Lord when I learned of a psychological discovery that even our daughter's trained psychologists were unaware of."

Starting in 1970, and evolving over decades, several German psychologists and others studying newborn behavior discovered that emotional imprinting began in every unborn child roughly at three months from conception. This means that the emotional core values of each and every human being is transferred from mother to child just as DNA would transfer genetic traits. To make it brief, children receive most of their own feelings of personal worth while still unborn.

Craig later found their youngest daughter's birth mother and she confirmed to them what psychologists took years to determine. She told them of the great anxiety, depression, fear, and hopelessness created by the divorce from her husband at the time of her pregnancy. These feelings were transferred to Craig's daughter in the womb. Their youngest daughter's level of comfort before birth was a disaster of filth, rejection, and addictions. For their daughter to fully reprogram all of the core values established during her womb experience will be a lifetime challenge.

Through this research, Craig found answers to his hopeless questions. The suffering he felt wasn't entirely his fault. It wasn't entirely his daughter's fault either. On that happy day, they learned that emotions can be cured. Both Craig and his daughter can be made whole again. Craig shares,

"There are answers to life's deepest suffering. God is real. He knows our struggles and he gives us answers. I can't find blame with my children's birth mothers because where does it stop? At which generation did these toxic emotions begin to be passed from one mother to the next to the next to the next? Where is the curse broken? It begins with me as I share my research with others and choose to forgive. This is my gift to you. There are answers, there is hope, God loves you, and overcoming trials can make us better."

Craig wrote a poem for his daughter during his deepest sorrow. Accompanying the poem is an essay his daughter shared on Father's Day many years ago. It exhibits his suffering alongside the joy he felt from the talk his daughter gave.

"Dear Daughter:

Oh God hear the tears of my heart

Oh God see the dampness of my pillow

Oh God feel the emptiness of my soul

Oh God the minions have stolen her

Stole her far away to a dark place

They've cleverly wrapped chains, one by one around her pure soul. They covered her in filth; they turned her loving tongue into a stinging nettle.

The minions have her, they encircled her, covered her so I can't recognize my sweetheart even close before me.

She is an empty cistern before me.

Oh God, turn her heart to thee, cover her in the blood of thy agonies that she might be cleansed

Rescue her from the claws of the minions; fill her emptiness with Thy joy of life

Oh God let her heart see their awful grasp

Oh God let her pillow be dampened for Thy agonies in her behalf

Oh God hear the tears of my heart

Oh God see the dampness of my pillow

Oh God rescue the emptiness of my soul

Love, Dad"

"My dad loves plants and animals. He sells trees, shrubs and flowers for a living and I know that if he didn't love animals that I wouldn't have my horses, cats and dogs. He takes me to the golf course sometimes, and I get to drive the little golf cart, and I really love it when he rides down a creek near our house with me on our horses. He supports me in everything I do, and it helps me do better.

"He helps me with my schoolwork, and is very patient with me. He makes sure that all my choices are good and he makes sure that I follow the gospel. He prepares fun and educational family home evening lessons that everyone has a part in. Sometimes he reads stories, and we all get to listen. He even will ask questions about the story's message, and how we can apply it to our lives."

His poem and her essay contrast starkly opposing feelings. Sometimes our sorrow is caused by our choices and the consequences of those choices. Other times, our sorrow is caused by the choices of others. No matter what the cause of our suffering, we can always choose to have faith, lean on Christ, and become better.

Chapter Ten

KIMBERLY'S STORY

"SUFFERING HAS BEEN STRONGER THAN ALL OTHER TEACHING, AND HAS TAUGHT ME TO UNDERSTAND WHAT YOUR HEART USED TO BE. I HAVE BEEN BENT AND BROKEN, BUT - I HOPE - INTO A BETTER SHAPE."

~CHARLES DICKENS

People often forget about the family members who suffer through the sufferings of their loved ones. Even one degree of separation from the person who is suffering can lead to great pain and challenges that are difficult to bear. In addition to the actual hardships that are faced when someone you love is in the midst of tribulation, feeling helpless to solve the problem or guilt over one's own suffering can add to the burdens.

Kimberly is a woman who has been tried because of her husband's choices and his consequent suffering. She is a close friend of the author. She grew up her whole life as many do, trying to do her best and always trying to become better. Today she strives to live by the advice to just love others, no matter what.

Kimberly's husband, Rob, was exposed to pornography when he was a very small child. He was only eight when he was riding the bus and he was shown an image that forever changed his life. At the time, he didn't know what it was or how harmful it was; all he knew was that he had never seen it before and, as most children do, became curious. For the following years Rob was repeatedly exposed to it until his curiosity got the better of him and he began seeking it out for himself. All this time he kept it hidden, burying it as deeply as he could until it became engrained in his life. His family and friends had no idea what was plaguing him. It was something that was shoved into the darkest corner of his life, until it could no longer be contained there and began to consume him. It was a stress relief, a boredom relief, a way to release anger, and turned into a very severe addiction. This lasted for years.

Rob's entire youth years and part of his childhood were stolen from him because of pornography. He was not close to God, he was unhappy, and he had a twisted view of relationships and intimacy. Though he never did anything to violate a woman, he had been robbed of the beauty that God intended intimacy between a husband and wife to be. This is something that Rob will have to live with and fight for, for the remainder of his life.

When Rob was nineteen, he decided that he was not the person that he wanted to be. After years of keeping his addiction buried, he swallowed his pride and moved forward. He turned to God and his church leaders for help. Through repentance and constant support from those who loved him, Rob was able to clean up and go on a mission for the LDS church.

How wonderful that experience was for him! He was able to gain a true testimony of Jesus Christ after years of being distant from Him. He was able to serve and love those around him and find renewed purpose in life. Rob still struggled with the images that had been literally burned into his mind, but he was overcoming them and feeling the love of God. The two years that he served God was a blessing and a stark contrast to what the previous 11 years had been.

However, addictions can never just be willed away. When Rob returned from his mission, those images began to plague him again. Slowly, he slipped back into old habits and the addiction had control. After over two years of sobriety, the struggle still hadn't ended. He made efforts to stop. He had a real desire to put his past behind him and move forward with school and a career, but pornography plagued him. It had been engrained into everything he did for years. Similar to the effects of an alcohol addiction, his brain had rerouted his instincts to turn to pornography when he was stressed, anxious, angry, or simply bored. How could he overcome it? His brain was literally rewired. Rob shares, "I felt like I was drowning and there was no escape. I constantly fought hard to clear my mind and keep those thoughts at bay, but at times it was too much and I succumbed. The shame of giving in was so much worse than the drowning, but because my mind was addicted, I couldn't turn away. I would feel ashamed and make a renewed effort to overcome, but then I would sink back into the negativity and drowning again. The feelings of guilt that followed each concession just fed into the cycle by causing stress and low self-esteem. I desperately wanted out, but I wasn't sure it would ever end." Luckily, Rob is a man of great faith and continued to make great efforts to overcome his addiction.

In his efforts to move forward with his life, Rob moved out of the circumstances he was in and went to school. There, he was lucky enough to meet his wife, Kimberly. She loved him from the very beginning. The more time they spent together, the more she felt like there was something that he wanted to tell her but he wasn't. She trusted him, though, and knew by his actions that he was someone she would be blessed to spend her life with.

Eventually, Rob told her of his addiction. By this time, he hadn't succumbed to his addiction in months and was doing well again. But her heart still sank, both for herself and for Rob. Kimberly relates, "This was a new hurdle I had never faced before. I loved him and wanted to be with him for eternity! Yet this made me nervous. I didn't know how to handle it or what to expect. What I did know was that I loved him and would support him and be there for him, no matter what. That knowledge was enough for me to decide to stand beside him." The more Rob told her, the more compassion she felt towards him. Her heart filled with even more love for this man when she saw how much the addiction hurt him and how hard he was working to overcome it. Within the first year of their marriage, Rob decided that he again needed the help of church leaders to overcome his addiction.

He did his best to keep Kimberly out of it, but she insisted on being involved. Every time Rob told her that he was struggling, it took a lot of effort on her part to not be personally hurt. She felt like he was pushing her out of his struggles and it made her feel like she wasn't important enough to help, but on the other hand, when he told her his honest feelings, she felt betrayed and hurt. It was difficult for Kimberly, but she had great faith in the Savior and knew that her husband could find relief if he kept pushing and kept working. She prayed for strength to have compassion and see her husband as Christ would. As she worked on this, she was able to see the value in the advice, "just love him." Kimberly has been able to see her husband's success and progress. She has let go of the feelings of betrayal and hurt that so often burden relationships in these circumstances. She knows how hard he is working and sees the pain in his eyes when he struggles. She is able to see that he is the victim and that he needs her.

While her husband was undergoing therapy and the repentance process, Kimberly made the choice to undergo her own therapy and repentance process at the hands of the Great Physician. He has filled her heart with love and compassion for Rob rather than bitterness and resentment. Kimberly has realized that his addiction and the chemical changes that occurred in his brain because of it have nothing to do with her. Rob loves her and would give anything to have those images and memories removed and he is giving everything to work through it. The pain and heartache that she first felt when she learned of his addiction was largely selfish. Now it is for her husband. The selfishness that caused her to feel betrayed has now been turned into selflessness that leads her to comfort and console Rob. Because his strivings are sincere and diligent, Kimberly knows that Rob is the victim and it would only make him feel guiltier if she were to victimize herself as well. Kimberly was lucky to fall in love with a man who truly tries to do his best every day and sees his wife as motivation to stay strong.

Of this experience, Kimberly says, "I learned compassion that I could not have learned in any other way. The man I love was fighting so hard to keep his head above the water. He was desperate. How could I ever turn my back on him? At times I did feel betrayed and his actions felt like a personal blow, but when I saw the sincerity of his struggle in his eyes, I knew that I was not the victim. Once I realized that, a whole new spectrum of light opened up for me. I was able to serve Rob in a way that my previous selfishness hindered. I was able to help him get his footing when he was slipping. I was able to be a light for him and help him clean out the dark corners that had once consumed him. When I began seeing him with compassion and true charity, I was changed and he gained a new resolve to change."

In his efforts to overcome the plague of pornography, Rob regularly meets with his ecclesiastical leader, attends meetings, and meets with a therapist to help disentangle his youth and childhood from his addiction and move forward with his life now. Though it isn't always easy, Kimberly is able to forgive her husband and support him through his struggles. She has great faith that if she is able to forgive him and love him so selflessly in this painful situation, how much easier is it for the Savior, who understands to an exact degree what Rob is facing, to forgive him, love him, and lift him up above these struggles.

It took many prayers, tears, and selfless choices, but Kimberly no longer suffers directly because of Rob's actions. The weight she now carries is to see her husband suffer and not be able to take it away. She shares, "I know that my husband tries so hard to find relief, but sometimes it just doesn't come and he must endure through the heaviness. I know that he feels terrible guilt for his thoughts and actions. I know that he wants nothing more than to erase those memories from his mind. Because of the compassion I have been able to learn by letting go of my pain and realizing his efforts, I feel Rob's pain even more deeply. I share the weight that he carries now. The consequences of his actions still cause me pain, but in an entirely different way. My efforts to help him have caused me to suffer with him even more deeply when he feels the weight more heavily. I believe that this must be a tiny glimpse of what the Savior feels for Rob. I know I am far from perfect in my efforts to be charitable, but at times I am able to feel for Rob a part of the love that the Savior feels for him. This understanding did not come easily or quickly, but it was worth it to be able to support Rob and show him the love that he needs in order to overcome this burden."

Some of our deepest moments of suffering come from the sufferings of those we love. It can be difficult, painful even, to watch those we love most as they struggle and suffer. The tests and trials of loved ones can lead to our own suffering. This type of pain can be difficult, as you often have little control over a solution or relief from suffering, but you can learn to live day by day, or moment by moment. As we continue to have faith in our loved ones and in our Savior, we will be able to find relief. Their choices may not change and their struggles may not cease, but we can find peace and understanding. This is a lesson for which Kimberly is eternally grateful.

Despite the suffering that they both endure, Rob has made great strides in overcoming this addiction. The desires and memories are less frequent and vivid. His progress is a testament to the power of our agency and the power of the Atonement. The words are true that Christ himself spoke, "If thou canst believe, all things are possible to him that believeth."[76]

Chapter Eleven

AGENCY AND CONSEQUENCES

WE SUFFER BECAUSE GOD ALLOWS US TO MAKE REAL CHOICES

"WHEN YOU CHOOSE AN ACTION, YOU CHOOSE THE CONSEQUENCES OF THAT ACTION. WHEN YOU DESIRE A CONSEQUENCE YOU HAD DAMNED WELL BETTER TAKE THE ACTION THAT WOULD CREATE IT."

~LOIS MCMASTER BUJOLD, MEMORY

In this life, God puts the burden of choice squarely on our shoulders. Delbert L Stapley[77] said, "One of God's most precious gifts to man is the principle of free agency—the privilege of choice which was introduced by God the Eternal Father to all of his spirit children in the premortal state. This occurred in the great council in heaven before the peopling of this earth. The children of God were endowed with freedom of choice while yet but spirit beings. The divine plan provided that they are freeborn in the flesh and become heirs to the inalienable birthright of liberty to choose and act for themselves in mortality. It was essential for our eternal progression that we be subjected to the influences of both good and evil.

"As sons and daughters of our Heavenly Father, we have this gift of free agency to use in our mortal lives. We must be tried, tested, and proved to see if we will choose the right and do all things whatsoever the Lord our God shall command us. As spirit children of God, we have built-in powers of conscience sufficient to develop our free agency in right choices and to acquire qualities of goodness, humility, and integrity of purpose."[78]

No principle in time or eternity is so cherished as the right of agency, the right to consider alternatives and make choices without compulsion. A war was waged in heaven over our agency—a war that was transferred to earth. Satan is determined to blind, bind, and lead captive through ignorance and sin everyone he can. Understanding our agency is imperative for our spiritual survival and fulfillment in Christ.

The gift of agency gives each person the freedom of choice, but not the ability to control the consequences of those choices. Former Senator Patrick Moynihan, a rare intellectual in the United States Senate, chided his college students by reminding them that everyone is entitled to their opinions (choices), but no one is entitled to their facts (consequences). Some of our suffering in this world is a direct consequence of poor choices. However, many would argue that the suffering from illnesses is not a consequence of poor choices. Some suffering is a result of our personal choices, yet other trials are just a result of natural forces.

Though some trials are within our control, the gift of agency does not come with the ability to handpick those trials that are not. It does, however, provide the opportunity to show gratitude, regardless of the trials we face. How could Craig and Kimberly be grateful or positive during their trials when the natural instinct is to be resentful? Bitterness is a choice we are given, one that can often lead to more troubles. Instead of remaining bitter, there is also a choice available to develop an attitude of gratitude during times of great stress. This is possible, but not always easy. Even if it is difficult to be grateful for the trials we face, there is still the opportunity to be grateful for the lessons we learn, the support we receive, and the other blessings that God sends us.

Through suffering, we are changed as we learn to train our minds to choose gratitude. We begin to understand that even in the most difficult trials, there is always a silver lining, always hope. Craig saw this silver lining on multiple occasions. When his first daughter was pregnant, he was able to see the blessing that the baby would be to another family. When he was so heavily weighed down by the choices of his second daughter, he was able to find motivation to move forward and relieve the burden, rather than falter underneath it and allow it to consume him. Kimberly also began to see the silver lining when she chose to have faith in the Savior's ability to cure all illnesses and allowed herself to forgive and love her husband. In some of the most difficult trials in life it may seem as if there is no escaping the darkness. When there seems to be no choice but to give in to pain and fear, there is always something better. That choice is to find the strength within to turn to the light, to reach for the hands that are yearning to help, or to pull yourself up by the bootstraps and keep on going. Craig's and Kimberly's stories are the perfect examples of how choosing to have faith is always the better path to take.

Thomas S. Monson stated, "We can lift ourselves, and others as well, when we refuse to remain in the realm of negative thought and cultivate within our hearts an attitude of gratitude. If ingratitude be numbered among the serious sins, then gratitude takes its place among the noblest of virtues."[79]

Steven Hopesharer[80] gave good advice on how to

approach suffering. "When prisoners of war return home, many of them have indicated that the main thing that helped them to survive with the least amount of mental anguish was their attitude which, in most cases, involved a belief in a God who was in control of their lives in spite of their circumstances. We notice that same attitude being manifested by those who were persecuted in the Bible like Paul, Steven, and most vividly by Christ Himself. He conferred with His Father about everything, particularly His suffering. Even while on the Cross, in a last comment and act of faith, He said, 'into Thy hands I commend my spirit.'" This positive attitude made all the difference for Craig and Kimberly.

When we face trials that come as a direct consequence of our choices, it is important to remember that we can always choose to repent and do better. When we face trials that do not come as a direct consequence of our choices, we can choose to endure, being grateful every day for the blessings we receive.

On many occasions, our suffering comes as a result of the choices of others. These choices can directly affect us in a negative way, causing us to have a trial to overcome. Both Craig and Kimberly suffered because of the actions of their family members. The choices of others can also cause us sorrow as we feel compassion for those we love and suffer with them. We must watch as loved ones suffer, thus adding to our own pain. Craig and Kimberly faced this trial as well. Through the negative consequences from the actions of others, there is often much suffering from no fault of our own. All of this "second hand" suffering can be frustrating, as we feel powerless to control the storms.

One of the most challenging choices that can cause suffering to those closest to us is that of the consequences of addictions. Addictions are largely defined by their fruitless struggle to overcome diminishing returns. A diminishing return is when a large quantity of something is not proportionately satisfying as a small quantity. For example, eating a single piece of cake is satisfying; eating ten slices of cake is not ten times as satisfying. Each subsequent slice will be less satisfying than the last.[81]

When a person is addicted, they often recognize that their addiction is unsatisfying, but continue consuming in hopes that they can obtain the pleasure or satisfaction that they associate with the activity. The addictive substance may be accompanied by withdrawal symptoms that create demand for the activity even when it's inherently unpleasant; this chains addicts to their behavior and makes it difficult to stop even when they no longer enjoy it.

Addiction can be a difficult topic to understand and most of what the scientific community has uncovered about addiction seems to go against the Christian belief regarding "free agency." Addictive things such as alcohol, drugs, and pornography are choices at first but can become addictions when a person becomes dependent on them. Addictive behavior robs an addict of the ability to choose for his or herself. After repeated use of these substances, an actual physical change occurs in the brain causing dependence on the substance. This physical change remains with the individual for the remainder of his or her life. However, this does not excuse the individual from the choices they made in the past that led to this suffering. If they allow it, the individual can become a slave to the addiction, letting it dictate every choice they make. Fortunately, the change in the brain that is caused by addiction can be controlled and overcome and the burden can be lifted. The process is long and difficult and will continue to cause suffering, but we know that Christ "descended below all things"[82] and therefore "is perfectly positioned to lift us."[83]

The struggle of addiction does not just affect the individual with the addiction. As Kimberly's story illustrates, addiction can cause great suffering for the loved ones of the individual as well. The suffering is a mixed bag of emotions and questions. "Why did she choose to take this path? Is there anything I can do to help him? Is she treating me this way because of the addiction or are these choices her own? Why does he have to suffer so much to overcome this? Will there ever be any relief?"

Experts agree that families where addiction is present are oftentimes painful to live in, which is why those who live with addiction may become traumatized to varying degrees by the experience. Broad swings, from one end of the emotional, psychological and behavioral spectrum to the other, all too often characterize the addicted family system. Living with addiction can put family members under unusual stress. Normal routines are constantly being interrupted by unexpected or even frightening kinds of experiences that are part of living with drug use. [84]

Drug addiction and alcoholism are addictions that most people are familiar with, but there are many addictions families suffer from. The fact is that any addiction, from drugs and cigarettes to shopping and gambling, can have disastrous social and financial consequences. When the addict has a family, the cost of the addiction can wreck the home and have long-lasting effects on every person he or she touches.

Marni's biological father was an alcoholic, during her pre-teen/teenage years. She relates "He could drink beer and generally be fine – most times, he was usually happy and only occasionally sad. However, when he drank Jim Beam, he became very mean. I would avoid him when he drank that, because he could become verbally and sometimes physically abusive. Looking back at that situation through adult eyes, I'm assuming my father drank the heavier stuff to help him cope with his and my mom's marital issues. He was very unhappy. However, because my mom tends to default to an overly sensitive and angry personality when she's drunk – no matter what it is that she drinks – the fights between them could get very bad. I remember that they were so bad; I spent almost a whole summer living at my best friend Sarah's house to get away from it all. I hated coming home and hearing/seeing the both of them go at it, so I tried to avoid coming home altogether."[85]

During early childhood years, living in this intense emotional environment can set up a fear of feeling or patterns of attachment that are filled with anxiety and ambivalence. In their youth, children of alcoholics or drug dependent parents (COAs) may feel overwhelmed with powerful emotions that they lack the developmental sophistication and family support to process and understand. As a result, they may resort to intense defenses, such as shutting down their own feelings, denying there is a problem, rationalizing, intellectualizing, over-controlling, withdrawing, acting out or self-medicating, as a way to control their inner experience of chaos. The COA may be difficult to identify. They are just as likely to be the president of the class, the captain of the cheerleading squad, or the A student, as they are to act out in negative ways.[86]

Unless one makes a diligent and dedicated effort to combat their addiction, as Rob did, the consequences that they and their family members face will continue to spiral until the addict is filled with regret and their loved ones are filled with resentment.

Effective counseling programs have adopted the AA model in treating addiction that starts with admitting that you, of yourself, are powerless to overcome your addictions and that your life has become unmanageable. Pornography promises thrills and sexual satisfaction. But it fails to deliver on these promises. It can't give *anyone* deep and lasting fulfillment. It is a figment of the imagination but is often acted upon.

Pornography is anything you see, read or hear that's designed to cause sexual arousal. It includes many types of media — magazines, books, movies, music, the Internet and more. Sometimes, pornography can even lead you to do things you never imagined. Consider Gene McConnell.[87] He was an ordinary businessman with a wife and daughter, but fascination with pornography became the fuel that caused his normal life to explode. "It began to ruin my marriage, my business, everything," explains Gene. "It started with strip-tease or topless bars, then to massage parlors and prostitutes. Finally, I started fantasizing about what it would be like to actually rape a woman. I tried it one night when I saw a woman who 'fit' the scenario in porn. Fortunately, I didn't go through with it. After being reported and arrested by the police, I spent some time in jail."

Images burned into your mind? A bed filled with strange faces? Going off the deep end? These consequences happen all the time in varying degrees. The fantasy world of pornography is like a big carnival pulling people in every day with promises of great thrills only to place them on a lonely roller coaster of excitement and emptiness, arousal and anxiety.

When God created us, He gave us a desire for love and intimacy that we could satisfy only in a relationship with Him and, to some degree, through a special relationship with one partner. It breaks God's heart to see His children bypass these relationships in pursuit of mere images—lifeless reproductions that can arouse but never give or receive love.

King Solomon said, "Can a man scoop fire into his lap without his clothes being burned?"[88] Along those lines, can you repeatedly bring sexually arousing images into your head without consequences? You may not be physically burned by sexual images, but psychologists argue that those images can actually be burned into your *mind*. Emotional arousal causes the release of a hormone called epinephrine in your brain that chemically burns the pictures into your permanent memory.[89]

Despite the mighty physical changes that addiction causes, the power of God can restore a person to complete spiritual health, but one must decide to turn their will and life over to the care of God the Eternal Father and His Son, Jesus Christ. Both Kimberly and Rob chose to do this on both sides of the addiction. They stand as a testament that it is only through the healing power of the Atonement that some diseases can be healed.

The question that is often asked by support groups is how do I help someone with a pornography addition? This is a question asked by parents, spouses, and kids. Even though loving the addict is the simplest answer it doesn't mean it's easy. Kimberly learned that being able to truly take this advice comes after much prayer and effort.

The choices of others often have unforeseen consequences that affect those around them. How often have we heard, or even said ourselves, "This won't hurt anyone. I'm the one making the choice so I will be the one that faces the consequences." This idea is false. When it comes to addictive substances or habits, the effects can spiral out of control. Even those choices that don't spring from or lead to addiction can affect those around us in harmful ways. Both Craig's and Kimberly's stories teach that the choices of others can cause us to suffer, as direct results of those choices, but also as we watch our loved ones struggle.

Life has plenty of suffering caused by our actions or the actions of others. Because of the wonderful gift of agency, we sometimes have to deal with the not-so-wonderful effects of poor choices. We often face tests that, like the Savior's, were not direct consequences of our own choices. Many of the reasons behind these trials cannot be explained and might affect us through no fault of our own. It might even truly seem that the harder one tries to stay strong and overcome suffering, the more difficult life can become. Take great comfort from the words of Jeffrey R. Holland. "If for a while the harder you try, the harder it gets, take heart. So it has been with the best people who ever lived."[90]

CℐℴChapter Twelveℭℜℴ

Comforter

We Suffer to Allow the Holy Ghost to Truly Comfort

"Why would we need to experience the Comforter if our lives are already comfortable?"

~Francis Chan

When the storms of life are raging, and there seems no light in sight, the only thing one can do is learn to feel the comfort that can come from God. The scriptures teach of the role of the Holy Ghost. Christ promised that the Father would send the Comforter in Jesus' name, a gift of peace. When the Holy Ghost is allowed to do his job, he will bring to our minds the remembrance of the peace of the Savior. Pondering on this peace will heal our hearts, and we will not be troubled, or afraid.[91]

The Holy Ghost is a powerful gift that provides unlimited use of inspiration and guidance. The Holy Ghost can bless every life in countless ways. Among the many roles of the Holy Ghost, we have been promised that he will "teach [us] all things,"[92] "guide [us] into all truth,"[93] and testify of Christ.[94] Especially when we have no other source of hope, or are suffering because someone we love is not making the best choice, we can rely on the Comforter.

Robert D. Hales expanded upon the need to ponder when he taught, "Pain brings you to a humility that allows you to ponder. It is an experience I am grateful to have endured. ... I learned that the physical pain and the healing of the body after major surgery are remarkably similar to the spiritual pain and the healing of the soul in the process of repentance."[95] Much of our suffering is not necessarily our fault. Unexpected events, contradicting or disappointing circumstances, interrupting illness, and even death surround us and penetrate our mortal experience.

Opposition is part of Heavenly Father's plan of happiness. We all encounter enough to bring us to awareness of our Father's love and of our need for the Savior's help. Often, we can be brought to this awareness in no other way than through suffering. Some adversities are individual. Others are common to large numbers of our Heavenly Father's children, but all trials are necessary to teach us to learn to heed the still, small voice and receive the peace the Holy Spirit offers. If Craig's and Kimberly's struggles taught them anything, it was this.

So many on this earth are in need of peace. "Peace comes from knowing that the Savior knows who we are and knows that we have faith in Him, love Him, and keep His commandments, even and especially amid life's devastating trials and tragedies."[96] When we take the time to feel the peace from the Comforter, it is easier to do those things that will help us endure great trials, even the most painful.

"Often, but not always, comfort comes from the removal of pain. If the painful trials are not completely taken away, the Comforter can still bring healing peace. As Dallin H. Oaks taught, "Healing blessings come in many ways, each suited to our individual needs, as known to Him who loves us best. Sometimes a 'healing' cures our illness or lifts our burden. But sometimes we are 'healed' by being given strength or understanding or patience to bear the burdens placed upon us. All that will come may be 'clasped in the arms of Jesus.' All souls can be healed by His power. All pain can be soothed. In Him, we can 'find rest unto [our] souls.' Our mortal circumstances may not immediately change, but our pain, worry, suffering, and fear can be swallowed up in His peace and healing balm."[97]

Kimberly experienced this very thing during her efforts to be strong. She felt of the Holy Ghost's soothing relief. He enabled her to overcome her feelings of selfishness and prompted her with feelings of comfort and peace to be able to more fully understand her husband's struggles and reach out to him in compassion. Craig also felt the influence of the Holy Ghost in his life and often expressed, "How wonderful it is to have had the blessing of the Holy Ghost in my life throughout my trials."

Often the greatest trials are those that cause pain and sorrow in this life, but we can also feel the warm, peaceful comfort from the Holy Spirit. Kent F Richards was a witness to a great deal of pain in his profession, and he shared some of his experiences. "...As a surgeon I found that a significant portion of my professional time was taken up with the subject of pain. Of necessity I surgically inflicted it almost daily—and much of my effort was then spent trying to control and alleviate pain."[98]

Richards actually caused pain in order to heal it. As a result, he often pondered the purpose of pain and stated, "None of us is immune from experiencing pain. I have seen people cope with it very differently. Some turn away from God in anger, and others allow their suffering to bring them closer to God. Like you, I have experienced pain myself. Pain is a gauge of the healing process. It often teaches us patience. Perhaps that is why we use the term *patient* in referring to the sick."[99]

Dr. Richards pondered one night while lying in a hospital bed, this time as a patient and not as a physician. As he pondered, the Holy Ghost was able to teach him truths about pain. Richards came to understand that during His mortal life, Christ *chose* to experience pains and afflictions in order to understand us. Perhaps we also need to experience the depths of mortality in order to understand Him and our eternal purposes.

Henry B. Eyring echoed these truths. "It will comfort us when we must wait in distress for the Savior's promised relief that He knows, from experience, how to heal and help us. ... And faith in that power will give us patience as we pray and work and wait for help. He could have known how to succor us simply by revelation, but He *chose to learn by His own personal experience.*"[100]

When we learn to understand this truth about Christ, the Holy Ghost can bring a comforting peace that we will never be alone, for there is One who truly understands all suffering. Dr. Richards felt the power of this truth. "I felt the encircling arms of His love that night," he relates. "Tears watered my pillow in gratitude. Later, as I was reading in Matthew about Christ's mortal ministry, I made another discovery: 'When the even was come, they brought unto him many ... and he ... healed *all* that were sick.' He healed *all* that came to Him. None were turned away."[101] All can feel the great blessings of comfort; all can be healed in their very souls through the peace of the Christ.

Craig and Kimberly both found healing through the Savior and the comfort of the Holy Spirit. It took time for both of them, but the pain that was inflicted upon them by their loved ones turned into a lesson. They were able to draw nearer to God and the pain was relieved through selfless love for their family members. If it weren't for the pain that their trials brought, the Holy Ghost would not have had the opportunity to teach them.

Richards goes on to say, "Children are often more naturally accepting of pain and suffering. They quietly endure with humility and meekness. I have felt a beautiful, sweet spirit surrounding these little ones. Perhaps, this is one reason why the Savior teaches the importance of becoming like little children, developing meekness and learning to be submissive. When we are able to develop these qualities, we are more likely to be closer to the Holy Ghost and more able to feel the peace and love the Holy Ghost is able to provide in times of trouble.

"To all of us the Savior said, 'Behold, ye are little children and ye cannot bear all things now; ye must grow in grace and in the knowledge of the truth.' 'Fear not, little children, for you are mine.' 'Wherefore, I am in your midst, and I am the good shepherd.' Our great personal challenge in mortality is to become 'a saint through the atonement of Christ.' The pain you and I experience may be where this process is most measured. In extremity, we can become as children in our hearts, humble ourselves, and 'pray and work and wait' patiently for the healing of our bodies and our souls. As Job, after being refined through our trials, we 'shall come forth as gold.'"[102]

⟪Chapter Thirteen⟫

Melodee's Story Part 2—The Return

"I encourage patients and families to continually look for the miracle but don't try to define it. In other words, if the only miracle we are looking for is the big one—the one where there is a miraculous cure—then we will most likely miss the other miracles that are unfolding before our very eyes, each and every day."

~Deacon Wayne Charlton, Cancer Center Chaplain

After Melodee was officially cancer-free, life did not suddenly get easier. Stephen took a new job, a little over an hour from their current home. They decided to move to be closer to family. That summer was filled with unpacking boxes, swimming at the neighborhood pool, exploring their new surroundings, and enjoying a lake vacation. It wasn't until the end of the summer that Melodee even had to think about her next blood work and cancer screening appointment.

Even though her home was now further away, Melodee did continue to travel to Dr. Nabhi's office for her follow-up visits.

The three-month checkpoint was all clear. Still cancer free!

The six-month checkpoint was good news, as well.

At the nine-month checkpoint, some of the results were inconclusive, and Melodee complained of pains in her lower abdomen, which could suggest a hernia, as well as pain in her left breast, almost like it was underneath, or in the bones. Dr. Nabhi ordered a STAT CT scan, just to be precautious. Thankfully, the scan revealed no evidence of disease and no hernia, but did highlight some existing gallstones. Melodee passed her nine-month checkpoint, but was advised to meet with Dr. Plack to assess the gallstones before they became a problem.

"Why am I feeling so much pain in those areas, though? Shouldn't there be a reason?" Melodee was cautiously optimistic, but also curious.

"The pain under your breast could be from underwire bras. Switch to bras with no wire or sports bras and monitor your pain level. The other pains could be adhesions, scar-like tissue that can form after a major surgery, especially after the one you had. You could speak to your plastic surgeon if you continue to be in great pain."

It sounded to Melodee like this was an example of a doctor who didn't have all the answers and was truly "practicing medicine," and she brushed the advice to the side. Melodee was free of cancer, which was all that really mattered. She was now on the official countdown to the big one-year checkpoint, when she would transfer to a doctor closer to home. She had been told that one-year cancer-free was a big deal and meant the chances of recurrence were greatly reduced.

In the next few months, her extended family celebrated with a reunion at Disneyland. Stephen and Mel took an early anniversary trip, as well as a weekend trip to attend a concert. On the flight home, Mel began to complain about an upset stomach and increasing pain, but she figured it was a result of the poor food she had been eating on her recent trips.

The following Monday, Stephen was scheduled for elective surgery, one that would require a hospital stay. Melodee put her own pain on the backburner to focus on Stephen's recovery. Stephen returned home, and Melodee's condition continued to worsen. Finally, after being up all night, suffering from intense pain in both her belly and in her upper back, accompanied with nausea, Stephen convinced Mel to go to the emergency room. Tests confirmed that she had some gallstones that were blocking her ducts and needed to be surgically removed. Melodee was kicking herself for treating Dr. Nabhi's advice so lightly. She now required two emergency surgeries, one to remove her gall bladder and another to remove three stones from her ducts.

The lab work for Melodee's one-year checkpoint was due the following week. She would have the follow-up with Dr. Nabhi the week after that. When the nurses saw the results of Melodee's labs, they jokingly asked if she had been out drinking immediately before having her blood work done. Some of her numbers were much higher than they should be, and alcohol could cause such elevation. Her doctor was not pleased with the elevated levels in her lab report, either. When Dr. Nabhi asked what had been going on in the previous months, Melodee explained her gall bladder issues.

"Didn't I tell you to get that taken care of before it became a problem?" Dr. Nabhi scolded. "Some of your numbers are alarming for cancer markers, but those are the same numbers that can be elevated because of gall bladder problems. The gallstones explain these higher results, but I'm not happy about this at all. Take care of yourself!"

Mel expected this reprimand. Life had been so busy, and the stress of more unplanned medical emergencies added to her frustrations. She just really needed some good news today. She needed the relief of passing another screening. Thankfully, that's exactly what she got! Melodee had finally reached the big milestone; she was now one-year cancer free!

Dr. Nabhi explained that Melodee would only need blood work once every six-months and could possibly move to being evaluated once a year. That was the answer Mel had been waiting for.

It was time to make a huge change. Near the end of this appointment, Melodee expressed her gratitude to Dr. Nabhi for the past two years of care, explaining that she planned to transfer to a new oncologist. This had more to do with location than anything else, but since it was more difficult to travel the distance to Dr. Nabhi's office than to a cancer center only minutes from her home, Mel had decided to transfer. She said a tearful goodbye to the wonderful staff who had helped make her battle a success. She was especially going to miss Lila and Jan, who had become more like loving family than nurses, but it was time to close that chapter of life.

The summer of 2015 was supposed to be a celebration of being cancer free. For the first time in a long time, Melodee and her family started making plans that did not revolve around cancer treatment or surgeries! Between swim lessons, summer camps, and other various activities, Mel nearly forgot to schedule an initial appointment at the cancer center that came highly recommended by several of Stephen's new coworkers. Thankfully, she was able to snag an appointment in the middle of July.

However, June did not go as planned. The week after the last appointment with Dr. Nabhi, Melodee threw her back out. She could not seem to recall how it happened, just that she woke up one morning and it hurt to sit up in bed. She could not bend well, and walking tweaked her back with every step. Stretching, a heating pad, and rest seemed to help, so Mel figured she had just pulled a muscle. Then, everyone started to get sick. All three boys went to the doctor with strep throat and ear infections. Toward the end of the week, Melodee's throat started to hurt, so she took antibiotics as well. Instead of seeing improvements, she got significantly worse—crazy night sweats, fever, chills, no energy, and a return of the same back pain. She went back to the ER. She was quite dehydrated, had low potassium, and both a kidney and UTI infection. The doctor said this also "probably" explained her back problems. With a new prescription, Mel seemed much better near the end of the week.

Her new oncologist, Dr. Flanner, was a breath of fresh air! Not only was her office much closer to home, her demeanor was different, more sensitive and caring. Mel liked Dr. Flanner from the start, and felt confident in her decision to transfer. Mel most likely needed "The Cancer Nazi," (Dr. Nabhi's moniker) while in the trenches of fighting cancer. Now, Dr. Flanner's more tender, loving demeanor felt better suited for the caregiver who would keep track of her future. Dr. Flanner reviewed Melodee's chart and even suggested measures Melodee might take to help her body stay cancer-free, beyond just medication. Mel felt blessed in her choice to switch doctors. She had again been matched with one who believed in faith-based practices and seemed to be put in her path for the right reasons at the right time. They scheduled an appointment for five months into the future and said their pleasant good-byes. Mel was pleased with her choice and looked forward to enjoying her new, officially cancer-free, life.

However, Mel's body had other plans. Her back continued to be a source of pain, but she did not have time to let it get her down. July was a busy month, as her oldest son had chosen to be baptized as a member of their church. Family and friends were coming into town, and she was in charge of putting together a big party to celebrate. That weekend was a beautiful and happy time.

After the celebration ended, her pain continued to increase. Melodee had a constant inner battle, wondering if she should see another doctor or return to the ER for more tests. With no new symptoms, only worsening pain in more extensive areas, she figured these doctors would just send her home, thinking she was only coming in to fill a pain pill addiction. Mel managed to talk herself out of going.

"Surely, I'll get better. I've been pushing too hard. I just need to stretch and take things easy. Perhaps, if I switch between a heating pad and ice packs the pain will eventually subside."

A few days later, Mel was spending the day swimming with her boys at their grandparents' home. She remembered that her cell phone was inside, and Stephen was going to be off work soon. Not wanting to miss his call, she hurried in through the back door to grab her phone, not taking much time to dry off. As she stepped onto the new wood floors inside the house, her wet foot slid forward, causing her to lose balance and crash down, half of her body hanging outside of the doorframe. She immediately felt a shock of pain that flowed up through her back and seemed to radiate down to her bones. Between the tears, she shook her head, thinking, "Well, at least *now* I have a reason to go to the ER!"

Not able to move, she called out for help.

"Steve?" She called to her father-in-law with no answer. "STEVE!" She yelled at the top of her lungs, even though just that effort was painful. He couldn't hear her. After several attempts of calling out "KYLE!" her son heard and came quickly.

"What's wrong, Mom?" Kyle seemed confused and a bit panicked.

"Get Grandpa," Mel instructed. "I slipped, and I need help to get up."

They both came back quickly, dripping wet. With help from both her father-in-law and her oldest son, Mel was able to stand. The pain was almost unbearable, and she knew she needed medical attention. Steve made a call to Stephen, got the other boys out of the pool and dressed, and planned to drive Mel to the ER. Meanwhile, Mel knew she couldn't show up at the ER in her drenched swimsuit, but she also did not have the ability to bend or the range of motion required to stretch and peel off a wet swimsuit or to pull dry clothes on. Asking her father-in-law was only a last resort, so she begged Kyle to help. Although he was reluctant, Mel was so grateful her young son agreed to assist his mother in that moment.

Steve led Mel to the car and drove straight to the ER, where Stephen was able to meet them, having gotten off work early. Mel was given something to manage her pain and had x-rays to check for fractures. Trying to lie flat on the table and hold completely still worsened the pain! Thankfully, the x-rays revealed no broken bones. From the description of symptoms, the story of the fall, and her locations of pain, the doctor made a diagnosis of an SI (sacroiliac) strain. She was instructed to "take it easy" and was referred to a pain specialist if the symptoms did not improve in five days.

Thankfully, Stephen worked with such a specialist, Dr. Olan, who was able to squeeze Mel in for an appointment later that week. During the exam, Dr. Olan assessed all the areas that were causing pain. Mel felt a combination of aches and sharp stings in her sternum, around through her ribcage, in her shoulders, in both her upper and lower back, in her hips, and down through her upper thighs. This amount of pain most likely did not all seem to be a consequence of her recent fall, and Dr. Olan was concerned about possible fractures that might have been missed by the x-ray. He ordered an MRI, which was scheduled for July 27th, exactly two months after her one-year cancer-free date. The test in her new hometown had been much easier to schedule and access, as it was minutes from her home, not hours.

Three days after the test, Dr. Olan called to request a meeting. Mel thought this was odd, especially because she knew he was working with Stephen at the time. Why didn't he just tell Stephen the results and set up another appointment?

She was taken directly back to Dr. Olan's office when she arrived. He met her shortly after, a much shorter wait time than before.

"How are you feeling?" he began.

"Not bad. The pain is a little more controlled." Mel answered.

"Well, the MRI did show what I predicted. You have a fracture in two of your thoracic vertebrae. But, the reports explain something more concerning. The MRI also found metastatic lesions."

Mel's heart rate skyrocketed, and she was nearly speechless. She had no idea what "metastatic lesions" meant, but it sounded a lot like "metastasized," which had an awful word-association to cancer.

She managed to ask, "What exactly does that mean?"

"Unfortunately, it looks like your cancer is back, now in your bones. The scan found evidence of metastases in your entire spine, your sacrum, and your right ilium. They recommend further evaluation to assess your entire skeletal system. I spoke directly with the pathologist who told me, off the record, that what he saw extended beyond the areas I had specifically ordered in my referral."

Mel felt like she couldn't move. She couldn't breathe. She texted Stephen, "Call Me ASAP!" and the phone rang a minute later.

"I'm here at Dr. Olan's office."

"That's weird. I just saw him. Why didn't he just tell me your report?"

Mel could barely breathe, barely speak, but she managed to spit out "My cancer is back, and it's in my bones." Between sobs. She couldn't say it, but kept thinking, *How could this be happening? I did everything I was supposed to do! I am supposed to stay cancer-free!*

Thankfully, Dr. Olan was a great friend with Dr. Flanner, the oncologist Melodee had met a few weeks earlier. Because of that appointment, Mel was an existing patient, and Dr. Olan was able to secure the last appointment of the day. It was good to have connections!

The drive from one hospital to another was lonely and terrifying. It took every ounce of courage not to turn the car around and run away from it all. Just when she thought cancer was behind her, it had returned with a vengeance. The wave of fear and uncertainty that had plagued her after her original diagnosis, now over two years before, seemed small in comparison to the tsunami that threatened to crush her today. The fear and anger were almost paralyzing, and to make matters worse, history seemed to be repeating itself:

She was meeting with an oncologist before they had the complete reports of cancer, again.

The doctor was leaving on vacation the next day, again.

Instead of a simple answer to her symptoms, she had received a devastating diagnosis, AGAIN!

Mel had nearly cried all her tears when she met Dr. Flanner (and Stephen) at the Cancer Center.

"First of all," Dr. Flanner began, "how have you been able to walk around? You must be amazingly tough or have a crazy-high pain tolerance to have been dealing with this for so long!" Here was that calm and caring persona, for which Melodee had already felt much gratitude.

Stephen answered before Melodee could, "She does!"

Mel began with the only question she could muster. "How could this have happened? Why didn't this show up with my labs, which I JUST had TWO months ago? Or on the CT scan I JUST had in March?"

"I don't think this is something that has been going on for six months," Dr. Flanner explained. "You have an aggressive cancer, so it quite possibly has only been growing back for those few months. At the time of your last scan, cancer cells might have not yet formed lesions large enough to generate suspicion. Let's pray that it is only in your bones and hasn't yet made it to your brain."

Her doctor was hopeful they had caught it early.

"How lucky I am to have broken my back!" she joked. Mel never thought she would be grateful for a broken spine, but it was that injury that helped lead to her correct diagnosis, as painful and frightening as it was to discover.

In the week that followed, Mel scheduled a brain CT, a PET scan, and a meeting with a radiation oncologist to gather more information. While Dr. Flanner was on vacation, Mel even sought a second opinion through Dr. Nabhi, which led to another MRI, CT, and a biopsy of her spine. The diagnosis was perfectly, undeniably clear: It was definitely cancer.

A NEW PLAN

There was no escaping the diagnosis. The biopsy from the lesion in her spine was positive for breast cancer markers. Melodee had Stage 4 breast cancer. Stage 4 cancer has no cure.

At the first appointment with Dr. Flanner, after she returned from vacation, they put together a game plan.

"The best course of treatment would be to start with radiation, most likely focused on the area of your spine with the largest metastases, focused mostly where you have the compression fractures. This will strengthen your bones and protect your spinal cord at the most fragile point. After ten days of radiation, we will move forward with a different type of chemo than you had before, Taxotere, which is in the same family as the chemo you had in 2013. You will also be given Herceptin and its sister drug, Perjeta. Taxotere is given in six rounds, once every three weeks. Halfway through and after its completion, we will conduct scans to monitor your body's reaction to the drug. If that chemo doesn't work, there are a few more options to try. In addition, research is always coming up with new breakthroughs. Even if we exhaust all of the current available drugs, we could look for clinical trials. However, let's pray that the first treatment melts your cancer away."

Mel was not looking forward to experiencing the side effects of chemo all over again. The nausea, the loss of hair, and the weakness: it was not a fun experience.

Dr. Flanner continued, "If this chemo is successful, you will continue only the infusions of Herceptin and Perjeta for…" there was a long pause, as if Dr. Flanner was calculating. "Well, for the rest of your life."

"How long will that be?"

"Remember whenever cancer metastasizes, that it breaks from the area of its origin and begins growing in another area, it is always Stage 4," Dr. Flanner explained. "Unfortunately, there is no cure with Stage 4 cancer. We can fight it back, like a virus. We can treat some of the side effects. But you will never truly be cancer free."

"What are my chances of living five years, ten years, or fifteen-plus years?"

"Do you *REALLY* want to know? Patients and spouses come in all the time asking that very question; they insist on knowing. When I answer, they wish they had not known."

Mel didn't hesitate. She wanted to know what she was up against. "I'd rather know what I'm dealing with, so I can come to terms with the reality of time I can expect."

"The average life span is three to five years."

Seeing the tears welling up in Mel's eyes, Dr. Flanner clarified. "I'm not saying that's how long *you* have to live. I'm just saying that's the 'average.' All I can tell you is the average, but we don't know now where you will be. We do not have a great deal of data of people in your age range, but young people tend to do better. So much depends on finding the right chemo, one that will melt your cancer away. We need to see how well you do with treatment and go from there."

Only three to five years?

That was much shorter than Mel had expected to be told, but she would rather have the truth. Cancer suddenly became much scarier the second time around. In 2013, she never feared death. From the beginning, her doctors had been confident that she would reach remission.

Knowing now that she would spend the rest of her life battling Stage 4 cancer was heartbreaking, especially since there was no way to predict how much longer she would live. She could understand Dr. Flanner's question about learning this news and why this information would not be pleasing to patients. This time around, discovering that she now had an incurable disease, Mel felt much more raw and emotional with this diagnosis of cancer than she had with the first. Any thought of cancer easily brought tears.

For the next few weeks, Melodee moved through several steps of the grieving process. In essence, she had just received a death sentence and was forced to grieve for the life she knew she'd lose. She'd already experienced shock and denial upon receiving the initial reports. She continued to ponder the same questions: "How can this be? How could this have happened? Is this a cruel joke, a dream?"

Anger was next. She was angry with doctors. How had everyone from Dr. Nabhi to Dr. Plack to Dr. Flanner and all the doctors in her various ER visits have missed this? She was angry with herself for not pursuing her pain, the one brushed aside by Dr. Nabhi, the one she had felt in her sternum and up under her breast, as if in her ribs. No, it was not pain from the underwire of her bra; it was cancer.

She was angry with God. "I did EVERYTHING I was supposed to do!" she cried. "I took further preventative measures than I HAD to do! I endured the pain and suffering of a bilateral mastectomy and a painful process of reconstruction, which was supposed to give me a 98% chance that my breast cancer would not return. I took Tamoxifen, even when I hated the side effects! I stuck to a low-calorie diet. I gave up sodas. I started working out almost every day! I've already been through this! I don't deserve this! My kids don't deserve this! Stephen doesn't deserve this!" Mel was frustrated that she had fought rigorously to become a survivor, only to begin the fight again after only one good year. It did not seem fair.

Sadness stayed around for quite some time. Melodee's sadness was mostly in relation to her family. She had waited so long to become a mother, and she felt that the blessings of that role were now going to be denied. There was still so much to teach and many more memories still to make. Her children were so young to be left without a mom, and she was afraid they would grow up with no real recollections of her, only those fuzzy memories that are just from pictures and stories they had been told. This broke her heart like never before, as she understood the importance of a loving and caring, and LIVING mother. "A child needs a mother more than all the things money can buy!"[103] Her boys needed their mother!

Melodee was also sad for Stephen. She had seen how difficult the first battle had been for him, and now he had to suffer further. His true love had a terminal disease, and there was no escaping it. Mel knew that Stephen wanted to be supportive and helpful. He also had needs and emotions. He was scared and angry and sad, as well. They had made so many goals and dreams for the future. How would they fit a lifetime of experiences into a few short years? How would Stephen find the time and energy to take over being both dad and mom in her absence? How would he be able to stay strong for the boys when he was alone and grieving? Questions like this were a nearly constant fear.

She met again with the radiation oncologist, Dr. Global, who worked closely with Dr. Flanner. Using the scans of her spine, he planned out the best location to target the radiation. That day, Melodee was tattooed with five small, blue dots: three evenly spaced down her chest and onto her abdomen, and one on either side of her waist. These would be the markers to stand as the guides used to perfectly line up her body for each session of radiation.

Because of the description of radiation Melodee had received in her first cancer battle—the image of burned and damaged skin, unfit for future surgeries, she had expected radiation to be a long and painful process. However, it literally took longer to lie down on the table and line up perfectly than it did to receive the actual radiation treatment. When the technicians left the room, the machine would rotate to the correct target points. It would then begin whirring. Mel counted to about seventeen seconds, give or take, each session. Then, the whirring stopped, the machine rotated back around to return to its original position. That was it. She repeated that process for nine more days, and that was that! Perhaps the radiation route would have been the easier the first time around after all! And, she had to wonder, would it have prevented her current predicament?

During the weekend after completing radiation, Melodee's anxiety over starting chemo again grew. She dreaded the pain and suffering that accompanied the treatments. She again sat alone on the floor of her room, in tears. In this rare, quiet moment, the spirit whispered a beautiful, comforting thought.

"Melodee, it is a gift to know that your life will be short. Use that knowledge to discover your mission, and live each day as if it were your last. The Savior knew His mission from the beginning, but He had to wait thirty years to fulfill it. He used the time between to bless the lives of others. When you know your purpose and live each day to reach it, *that is living*, even a day at a time."

Not everyone was blessed to have knowledge about his or her own timing and cause of death. In this light, Mel began to see how her ability to access and use this knowledge in her life was another small way she could strive to be more like the Savior.

At that moment, Melodee began to feel less sorry for herself. Although her earthly life might be cut short, she was grateful for the motivation to live each day as if it were the last, setting and reaching small goals, and to spend time each day trying to be more like the Savior and following His example. She was learning to accept the briefness of her mortal life, and to choose to make the most of whatever time she had left.

Melodee's cancer was a burden that most likely would never be removed, but the most important healing that would occur was increased faith and peace from above that replaces all fear.

Radiation and More Chemo

Although Melodee had come to terms with her terminal illness, often feeling added strength from the Lord, it was difficult to have complete hope for the coming years. No one could promise a cure, or even predict how much time for which she could hope.

Radiation had not presented any immediate negative consequences, but starting chemotherapy a few days after completing radiation seemed to escalate the side effects of both treatments. The area in her spine that was the target for radiation lay directly behind the lower range of her esophagus. Acid reflux and nausea from chemo irritated this radiated area, which felt like a combination of a sore throat and constant heartburn. Every breath, every swallow produced a stabbing pain down her entire throat. She forced herself to eat food only to stay alive, as she had no appetite, often felt nauseous, and the pain of swallowing made eating unbearable. She was prescribed a "magic mouthwash," a lidocaine-antacid-antihistamine solution. The "magic" was not as great as she had expected, for it did not erase the pain she felt from the pit in her stomach all the way up into her eardrums! Although she remained hydrated by forcing herself to drink plenty of water, it became a chore to eat enough calories to have any level of energy.

Doctors assured Melodee that the symptoms she was feeling were temporary; her esophagus would heal in a matter of days. However, nearly three weeks had passed since her final radiation, and she saw no improvement. In fact, Mel began to develop worsening symptoms and finally called to make an appointment with Dr. Flanner. The doctor had no available appointment times, but the nurses referred Mel to a primary care physician. They were concerned Melodee might have a possible infection which could delay her scheduled chemotherapy.

Since Melodee had no assigned primary care physician in her new city, she called around to find a doctor who was accepting new patients and had availability that day. Dr. Scott, another female doctor, very pregnant at the time, was a match.

She ordered a strep test, which came back negative. Doctor Scott wondered about a possible case of thrush. She placed a STAT order for a scope, which was the only way to diagnose the cause of the extreme pain. Later that day, Mel made an appointment with a gastroenterologist, Dr. Donald.

Dr. Donald's overall impression was that Melodee's symptoms were not completely matching up with her experience. In other words, it was taking too long for the expected side effects of radiation to wear off, and he was concerned about a different cause of Mel's pain. Unfortunately, Dr. Donald was leaving the next day for his vacation. (Really? What are the odds that yet *another* doctor was leaving so soon after Melodee's appointment?) Dr. Donald highly recommended a scope later that day, and in the interest of time, he suggested a scope without sedation. The doctor explained the procedure. During an EGD, or esophagogastroduodenoscopy, a scope with a light and camera at the end is lowered through the mouth and esophagus to look at the upper digestive tract. Having a husband in the field of anesthesia made Melodee feel as if she was going against the family business to agree to a non-sedated procedure, but it was too late to change her mind!

Moving downstairs to another part of the hospital, Melodee was led to the pre-op area and was instructed to put on a hospital gown over her clothes, as it would be a non-sedated procedure, only taking about five to ten minutes. A few minutes later, they rolled back to an operating room. A nurse gave Melodee three sprays of a "cherry" flavored numbing medicine and asked her to roll over on one side. She began explaining, "I will put a bite block in your mouth after you start to get sleepy...Oh, wait! This is a non-sedated procedure! You're not going to sleep." This was yet another clue that Mel should've waited for the drugs!

"Okay, Melodee, breathe deeply through your nose. The worst of it will be over soon."

Dr. Donald's idea of a "thin" scope was completely different than Melodee's. She had expected a barely noticeable tube, but forgot that the tube needed to be large enough to accommodate the small camera that fit inside. As the doctor pushed this tube down her throat, she tried to take deep breaths, as she was instructed. These breaths became more about trying to inhale deeply through her nose, while also trying not to vomit from the gag reflex, which was triggered in the minute it took to shove the tube completely down her throat.

Mel made it through the worst part and just closed her eyes and tried to picture herself on a beach somewhere in the Caribbean. Her tongue kept trying to swallow the scope that was already swallowed, and her body kept trying to warn her that she was choking. As drool and tears rolled down her face, Dr. Donald was able to take his necessary pictures and gather the biopsies. They had already told her "the worst part" was over, but the tube had to come back out. By that time, the numbing spray had worn off. She coughed and choked, as her throat was set free, finally feeling the signal that her suffering from the procedure had come to an end.

With no anesthesia recovery time, Mel was able to speak to the doctor right away and examine the pictures of her esophagus. Dr. Donald pointed out an area of an ulcer, which correlated with the area in her lower chest that Mel had been referencing each time she explained her pain. It would take a few days to receive the reports from the biopsies. Unfortunately, Mel was scheduled to start chemo the following week, which could irritate the ulcer further. Dr. Donald expressed his concerns about adding chemotherapy to her already irritated esophagus, but Melodee was determined to try to stick to her timetable. Dr. Donald was able to prescribe a new medicine for her to try. He promised to pass on any results he received as soon as he could, and instructed Mel to not be concerned if she didn't hear from him until the following week; while on vacation, he would have limited access to that information.

Dr. Donald walked Melodee all the way out of his office, something a physician had rarely done, and continued asking questions about her journey. His parting words lingered:

"I'm so sorry for this trial. I will be thinking about you in the days to come." He got a little choked up and added, "I will be praying for you, too."

This touched Mel's heart, and her eyes also filled up with tears. In the past two days, with two new doctors, she immediately felt cared for and loved by these humans whom she had never before met. It was, yet again, another example of how God was using other people to meet her needs and let her know that she was never alone.

She needed to hold on to that knowledge when Dr. Donald called Melodee the following Monday morning, asking her to come to his office that afternoon. She was anxious to hear results and suggestions to reverse the pain. The appointment began as many often do.

"How have you been feeling?"

"I still have a great deal of pain, and it's difficult to eat."

"I figured that would be the case. I received the pathology reports from your biopsies. Unfortunately, they found cancer in your throat. I'm so sorry."

Time froze again. She felt as if her life was completely out of her control. Was this a bad dream? It could not truly be happening. How could this be? How aggressive was her cancer if it continued to grow after radiation and in the midst of chemotherapy?

Mel felt hopeless. Maybe it was her time to die.

Melodee was scheduled for chemo the following morning, and Dr. Flanner personally walked back to the infusion area to pull her up to the front for an official appointment.

"I've consulted with Dr. Global over these pathology reports."

Mel could feel the waterworks starting already.

"I want you to calm your mind over this being a new tumor. Dr. Global and I both think a more likely explanation for these "irregular cells" would be cells in your throat that were still healing from radiation. It is more reasonable to believe that the biopsy could have snagged cells from your existing metastases than for a new throat cancer to have developed, especially while you are receiving chemotherapy. Your scans from only weeks ago showed no signs of disease in that area."

The fear had not completely subsided, but Mel was feeling a little less trepidation.

"Let's continue to monitor your pain and visit this again. You'll be having your half-way point PET scan in a few weeks, and we will know more then."

The PET scan was clear of activity in Mel's esophagus, and there was even better news, so incredible that Dr. Flanner called Melodee at home.

"This is good news. It is very, very good, as in the best results we could have hoped for! All of the areas of your metastatic lesions have shrunk, even further than fifty percent. Your body is responding so well to this chemo!"

What a relief! Now, Melodee just needed to keep pressing forward with the treatments, which were much easier after the ulcer in her throat finally began to heal, allowing her appetite to return.

Aside from that small scare of having developed a new cancer, which turned out to be a fluke, the next few months of treatments were much easier than Melodee had expected. She remembered how sick she had been by the end of her chemotherapy the first time around, due to her weakened immune system. This time around, she set low expectations and did not plan for an exact schedule of treatments. She predicted her blood work might come back too low for chemo, as it had before. This time she was set up to not be disappointed by hiccups in the process. Amazingly, none of these setbacks occurred. This time around, chemo was actually easy. Her only side effect of any great concern, other than hair loss, was an allergic reaction, a bumpy rash that popped up all over her body reminding her of acne, but that was more irritating and embarrassing than painful and debilitating. This was easy compared to 2013.

The first time around, her treatment seemed insurmountable, although surviving seemed attainable. Now, the tables had turned. The side effects of this chemotherapy were negligible, doable even, but the overall diagnosis felt impossible. If Melodee gave herself time to dwell on her fears, she often slipped into that dark place, the one with no hope. She felt as if this dark cloud was constantly following, waiting for the right time to strike. No one, not even the doctors, could give an exact time frame, and again, the unknown proved to be the most challenging part of cancer. Melodee completed the entire scope of chemotherapy treatment on time, with no delays.

She did, however, experience some dark days of doubt. With all odds against her, the only way Mel could come out of the dark place was to search for the light. No matter how bleak her future seemed, God was still blessing her immensely. If she looked closely, there was ALWAYS something to be thankful for, always a reason to smile, always hope. She learned to look on the bright side of life, to worry less about the little things and most of this life is "the little things" and to have faith for the future.

As she looked more closely for God's blessings, she was humbled at the small miracles so far:

She had not lost all of her hair, even her eyelashes and eyebrows, which were essential for the makeup she loved best.

She had caring doctors and nurses, who were faithful and God-fearing people.

She had not had to be completely homebound, as she was before.

There were countless acts of service that made her life easier.

Her boys had incredible teachers to fill the gaps in what Melodee couldn't do.

The list went on and on.

The more Melodee expressed her gratitude to God, the more she found for which to be grateful, as is often the case.

It seemed that the greatest work God had been performing was transforming Melodee through the cancer experience. Although her treatment was similar this time to last, she was stronger now. Although the outlook was less than favorable, she was able to still press forward in faith. She was learning to be more humble, more patient, more forgiving, less frustrated. This change of heart had taught Melodee to look for the small miracles that were happening all around her. She had no power to change her cancer. It was aggressive, it would most likely come back, and she would have both the emotional and financial burdens of cancer for her entire life. She could, however, change her outlook. God was working miracles on her heart. She knew God loved her and would not leave her comfortless. She began to stand as a witness of this testimony, and that began to touch the hearts of others.

Melodee had another PET scan at the end of December. Being so close to the New Year, Dr. Flanner promised to call when the results came in. Days and days passed, and Melodee was beginning to think the worst.

"They must be bad, if she can't tell me over the phone."

"If this chemo didn't work, will I start right back up again with another?"

"Will my hair ever have a chance to grow back?"

There was an uneasiness about the first appointment of 2016. Melodee was prepared for the worst. And, then it happened, those words Melodee never expected to hear:

"You're in remission."

"Wait....What? You said there was no cure!"

"I am so pleased with the way your body responded to chemo. The reports show no evidence of disease. You had a complete response to therapy!"

There were tears of joy and relief. Truly, nothing was impossible!

"You aren't done, though. You'll be in maintenance, receiving Herceptin and Perjeta indefinitely, every three weeks. You'll continue to have scans every three to four months and an echo around the same time. In addition to this maintenance, targeted treatment plan, Dr. Flanner did not want Melodee to completely get her hopes up. She explained, "I expect that your cancer will come back. I just don't know when and where, but it will come back. You have not exhausted all of your treatment options. As long as you are healthy enough and strong enough to fight, we will."

Melodee was realistic about her future, but for now, the unthinkable had happened. The miracle of remission was one Mel had never expected to receive. This miracle truly touched the hearts of those who had started to lose hope. It was in the truly miraculous that some were finally convinced of the power of God.

The response Melodee received at her announcement of remission was truly incredible. People were just as astounded as she had been to learn of this modern day miracle. "Truly, God is real, and He is still a God of miracles!" one of Melodee's dear friends exclaimed.

Mel had become faithful enough to know that the God of miracles is in the daily efforts of her life, but not everyone has "ears to hear and eyes to see."[104] When the truly miraculous occurred, even those with dulled senses paid attention. In her tremendous suffering, God's miracle had greater far-reaching power.

There were always the doubters. "But, what if cancer comes back?"

"It's not truly a miracle if it doesn't last, right?"

Mel didn't know all of the answers. She still assumed that someday cancer would take her life. For now, she was humbled by the miracle she had been given and looked forward to standing as a witness of God's mercy, for the rest of her days.

January 2, 2016 was Melodee's first date of remission, however, her fight is far from over. Melodee must stay faithful and continue receiving maintenance drugs to remain in remission as long as possible. She has learned that, even in her suffering, God loves her.

☞Chapter Fourteen☜

GRATITUDE

WE SUFFER TO LEARN GRATITUDE FOR OUR PERSONAL TRIALS

"IT HAS BEEN SAID, 'TIME HEALS ALL WOUNDS.' I DO NOT AGREE. THE WOUNDS REMAIN. IN TIME, THE MIND, PROTECTING ITS SANITY, COVERS THEM WITH SCAR TISSUE AND THE PAIN LESSENS. BUT IT IS NEVER GONE."

~ROSE KENNEDY

Perhaps one reason we suffer is to gain the ability to be grateful, even when life is most difficult. Melodee had heard inspirational speakers explain, "God knows you and will only give you the trials you can handle," or, "if all the trials in the world were put in a pile, you would probably still choose the ones you have because you know them." With a diagnosis of Stage 4 cancer, she wasn't so sure she wouldn't be swapping trials with someone else, if given the chance. In any group setting when the question is asked if anyone has scars, invariably everyone will raise their hand. Why? Because scars are a reminder of an individual's suffering, and everyone suffers. Everyone faces challenges, in one way or another.

Mel had also remembered being told about "the patience of Job." Why couldn't she have the patience of Job, a man who was bound to experience much greater suffering than she? What did she have to complain about?

Since she was stuck in a chemo chair for hours, Melodee decided to open up the Book of Job and read it entirely, perhaps giving her some advice on how to have patience in trials, or on how to not question God during difficult times. Perhaps she could find the answers she needed.

Chapter one started off in a discouraging way. Job is described as "perfect and upright." [105] There went all her hopes! Interestingly enough, with a bit more study, "perfect," in this case, does not mean completely without sin. It simply means that Job was faithful and tried his best, with the hope that he could someday be made perfect. "Okay, Mel," she cheered. "All hope is not lost!" Job was also blessed with a wonderful family and great possessions. If the story ended here, we could conclude that God always rewards us for our good behavior. Job was perfect; Job got blessings. The end.

But, as Melodee knew, that was not the point of this story.

As she continued reading, Melodee came upon the descriptions of some of the ways Job experienced suffering, including the loss of property, wealth, and children. And yet, "in all this, Job did not sin with his lips."[106] There it was. Job was better, more patient, and more perfect than she. She was complaining about an illness, and he had lost much more. She still continued.

"After this opened Job his mouth, and cursed his day." It went on to say that Job wished he had never been born because of his great suffering. She had never before noticed that Job complained. Job was a good person, he was enduring suffering, he did not want to curse God, but he still complained. He still asked, "Why?" He still experienced misery and bitterness in his soul, even fear. Job was starting to sound more and more like a normal human and not someone who never questioned the tribulations of life! He was troubled, but fell back on his faith that God knew him and loved him, and he should be grateful for a time to be tested by God.

As the book continued, Mel could see a pattern of growth and suffering. Job questioned, he had concerns. He figured that affliction is a part of this life, even if he wasn't happy about it. There was grief, pleading with God to release him from the pain, so he would not "harden himself in sorrow," pain, and anguish of soul.[107] He questioned when enough was enough. Job asked what he had done to deserve his trials. He became weary with "bitterness of soul." [108]

Somewhere along the way, Job must have come to understand his trials, still with the faith that God was mindful of him. To some, it would have seemed that there was no God, as Job continued to suffer, but he did not lose faith. He explained that he would be pouring out tears to God.[109] He was still not happy with his lot in life, but refused to blame God for his problems. He knew that all people would experience trials. God allowed Job to be tested to the brink, even though Job was a righteous and faithful man.

About halfway through the book, the tone seems to change. Instead of complaining, pleading for his life to end, or having bitterness of soul, Job stops to ask himself, "Where is now my hope?"[110] This rhetorical question could be heard from the mouths of any number of people in the midst of great suffering. "Do I still have hope in God, even when life is rough? Everyone else has it so much easier!" Job understood: God was making more of him than he could alone. He was being purified, made into gold.[111] If this was the way God needed to refine and purify his life, so be it." God understands what He is doing. If this is what I need to be made whole, then this is what I'll go through!

The patience that is important here is the patience Job *learned* through his suffering. It was not that he never questioned, never pleaded, never complained, and never expected more from life because of his good works. He went through those stages through the pages of the book.

Job embraced all the good and bad that occurred in his life as a gift from God. His experiences made him a better person. He was tested in the fires of afflictions. The story of Job should teach us that we don't have to be perfect now to be good, and that it is okay to question and not find happiness in trials at first, as long as you are willing to endure, to not shrink away, and to eventually learn the lessons the suffering is teaching.

Having finally understood that arriving at the point of patience in trials can be a process, even for someone with 'the patience of Job.' Mel also learned to start to be thankful for her own trials, for it could be much, much worse!

Hugh B. Brown relates a powerful story about being grateful for the trials we are called to face. "I was living up in Canada. I had purchased a farm. It was run-down. I went out one morning and saw a currant bush. It had grown up over six feet (two meters) high. It was going all to wood. There were no blossoms and no currants. I was raised on a fruit farm in Salt Lake before we went to Canada, and I knew what ought to happen to that currant bush. So I got some pruning shears and clipped it back until there was nothing left but stumps. It was just coming daylight, and I thought I saw on top of each of these little stumps what appeared to be a tear, and I thought the currant bush was crying. I was kind of simpleminded (and

I haven't entirely gotten over it), and I looked at it and smiled and said, 'What are you crying about?' You know, I thought I heard that currant bush say this:

"'How could you do this to me? I was making such wonderful growth. I was almost as big as the shade tree and the fruit tree that are inside the fence, and now you have cut me down. Every plant in the garden will look down on me because I didn't make what I should have made. How could you do this to me? I thought you were the gardener here.'

"That's what I thought I heard the currant bush say, and I thought it so much that I answered. I said, 'Look, little currant bush, I am the gardener here, and I know what I want you to be. I didn't intend you to be a fruit tree or a shade tree. I want you to be a currant bush, and someday, little currant bush, when you are laden with fruit, you are going to say, 'Thank you, Mr. Gardener, for loving me enough to cut me down. Thank you, Mr. Gardener.'

"Years passed, and I found myself in England. I was in command of a cavalry unit in the Canadian army. I held the rank of field officer in the British Canadian army. I was proud of my position. And there was an opportunity for me to become a general. I had taken all the examinations. I had the seniority. The one man between me and the office of general in the British army became a casualty, and I received a telegram from London. It said: 'Be in my office tomorrow morning at 10:00,' signed by General Turner.

"I went up to London. I walked smartly into the office of the general, and I saluted him smartly, and he gave me the same kind of a salute a senior officer usually gives—a sort of 'Get out of the way, worm!' He said, 'Sit down, Brown.' Then he said, 'I'm sorry I cannot make the appointment. You are entitled to it. You have passed all the examinations. You have the seniority. You've been a good officer, but I can't make the appointment. You are to return to Canada and become a training officer and a transport officer.' That for which I had been hoping and praying for ten years suddenly slipped out of my fingers.

"Then he went into the other room to answer the telephone, and on his desk, I saw my personal history sheet. Right across the bottom of it was written, 'THIS MAN IS A MORMON.' We were not very well liked in those days. When I saw that, I knew why I had not been appointed. He came back and said, 'That's all, Brown.' I saluted him again, but not quite as smartly, and went out.

"I got on the train and started back to my town, 120 miles (190 kilometers) away, with a broken heart, with bitterness in my soul. And every click of the wheels on the rails seemed to say, 'You are a failure.' When I got to my tent, I was so bitter that I threw my cap on the cot. I clenched my fists, and I shook them at heaven. I said, 'How could you do this to me, God? I have done everything I could do to measure up. There is nothing that I could have done—that I should have done—that I haven't done. How could you do this to me?' I was as bitter as gall.

"And then I heard a voice, and I recognized the tone of this voice. It was my own voice, and the voice said, 'I am the gardener here. I know what I want you to do.' The bitterness went out of my soul, and I fell on my knees by the cot to ask forgiveness for my ungratefulness and my bitterness. While kneeling there I heard a song being sung in an adjoining tent. A number of Mormon boys met regularly every Tuesday night. I usually met with them. We would sit on the floor and have Mutual. As I was kneeling there, praying for forgiveness, I heard their singing:

But if, by a still, small voice he calls

To paths that I do not know,

I'll answer, dear Lord, with my hand in thine:

I'll go where you want me to go.

(*Hymns,* number 270)

"I arose from my knees a humble man. And now, almost fifty years later, I look up to Him and say, 'Thank you, Mr. Gardener, for cutting me down, for loving me enough to hurt me.' I see now that it was wise that I should not become a general at that time, because if I had I would have been senior officer of all western Canada, with a lifelong, handsome salary, a place to live, and a pension, but I would have raised my six daughters and two sons in army barracks. They would no doubt have married out of the Church, and I think I would not have amounted to anything. I haven't amounted to very much as it is, but I have done better than I would have done if the Lord had let me go the way I wanted to go."

As we face the tasks ahead of us with the humility to recognize that "all things shall work together for [our] good"[112] we will become increasingly more grateful for the Almighty Gardener's trimming shears in our gardens.

If we can truly learn to see the silver linings, the bright side of suffering, even the greatest storms of life will become bearable.

Chapter Fifteen

TRUST

WE SUFFER TO LEARN TO RELY ON GOD

"I PLACE NO HOPE IN MY STRENGTH, NOR IN MY WORKS:
BUT ALL MY CONFIDENCE IS IN GOD MY PROTECTOR, WHO
NEVER ABANDONS THOSE WHO HAVE PUT ALL THEIR HOPE
AND THOUGHT IN HIM'

~FRANCOIS RABELAIS[113]

Perhaps if we turn to God and understand our relationship with Him, it will help us better understand why we suffer. God's fingerprint can be found everywhere. A scriptural reminder to all who might ask for signs that God exists: "…Thou hast had signs enough; will ye tempt your God? Will ye say, 'show unto me a sign,' when ye have the testimony of all these thy brethren, and also all the holy prophets? The scriptures are laid before thee, yea, and *all things denote there is a God*; yea, even the earth, and all things that are upon the face of it, witness that there is a Supreme Creator."[114]

Throughout the pages of the Bible, the character of God is explained. From the creation to John's prophetic vision concerning the end of times and the ultimate defeat of Satan, God reveals Himself. Everything testifies that God lives and is the creator of all things. Even the physical elements obey his word.[115]

It is impossible for us to define perfection based on our limited sphere of knowledge, so man has described God as omnipotent, omnipresent, and omniscient. As God's spiritual children, we can be assured that we have divine, eternal potential. Although mankind cannot completely reach perfection in mortality, we can learn about God and understand that He will help us in our sincere efforts to reach our true potential.

The term omnipotence refers to the all-powerful nature of God. Omnipotence is "almighty power; unlimited or infinite power; a word in strictness applicable only to God."[116] God is the all-powerful Lord who created all things and continues to sustain them. In the beginning, God created the heavens and the earth in one day.[117] God created everything that exists in the universe and on the earth, and did it in an amazing display of His power. He has the power to create all things, to control all processes in the universe, from the interactions of celestial bodies, down to the minute interactions of microorganisms.

Omnipresence is a theological term that refers to the unlimited presence of God or His ability to be everywhere at all times. Omnipresence is, "presence in every place at the same time; unbounded or universal presence; ubiquity." God is not limited to one altar, one temple or one geographic area. God reveals Himself in His word as being everywhere. God was present as Lord in all creation. Even the elements and the energy of the eternities obey Him.

Skeptics of our divine nature often ask questions, such as, "If God is in control of everything, why is there so much suffering and evil in the world?" or "If God is omniscient, omnipresent, and omnipotent, why does He allow anything that is negative in the world He created?" God's perfection and knowledge actually require Him to allow suffering to occur, not because He wants His children to feel pain, loneliness, or sorrow, but because He loves us and knows that many times we can be tested in no other way. Suffering is often necessary to stimulate growth. As God's spiritual children, we can be assured that we have divine, eternal potential. Although mankind cannot completely reach perfection in mortality, we can learn about God and understand that He will help us in our sincere efforts to reach our true potential.

Due to the nature of mankind, our true understanding of God is quite limited. In his understanding of human nature, Joseph Smith concluded,

"There are but a very few beings in the world who understand rightly the character of God. The great majority of mankind does not comprehend anything, either that which is past, nor that which is to come, as it respects their relationship to God. They do not know, neither do they understand, the nature of that relationship, nor consequently they know but little above the brute beast, or more than to eat, drink and sleep. This is all man knows about God or his existence, unless it is given by the inspiration of the Almighty. If a man learns nothing more than to eat, drink and sleep, and does not comprehend any of the designs of God, the beast comprehends the same things. It eats, drinks, sleeps, and knows nothing more about God; yet it knows as much as we, unless we are able to comprehend by the inspiration of Almighty God. If men do not comprehend the character of God, they do not comprehend themselves."[118]

Mankind's limited knowledge of the universe and of the nature of God set up a need for understanding and growth. In order to comprehend our own divine potential as children of God, we must learn about Him. Once we discover the qualities that God possesses, we can work toward our own perfection. Often, the path is an uphill climb, full of stumbling blocks, but this is the only way to better know our Father in Heaven, and thus our own eternal potential.

Isaiah asks the right questions. "Do you not know? Have you not heard? Has it not been told you from the beginning? Have you not understood since the earth was founded? He sits enthroned above the circle of the earth, and its people are like grasshoppers. He stretches out the heavens like a canopy, and spreads them out like a tent to live in. He brings princes to naught and reduces the rulers of this world to nothing. No sooner are they planted, no sooner are they sown, no sooner do they take root in the ground, than he blows on them and they wither, and a whirlwind sweeps them away like chaff. 'To whom will you compare me? Or who is my equal?' says the Holy One. Lift your eyes and look to the heavens: Who created all these? He who brings out the starry host one by one, and calls them each by name. Because of his great power and mighty strength, not one of them is missing."[119]

It is difficult to answer the question as to whether good and bad things happen to good and bad people. Michael Coren answers the question by stating "This question is sometimes asked in innocence by people with a genuine desire to understand what seems impossible to understand. Other times it's asked by people who have suffered or whose loved ones have known grief and loss. They honestly want to know: *How could God let this happen to me and to mine? Why wouldn't God stop this pain and help me?* After all, sometimes we experience devastating suffering. Just consider the Holocaust, the abduction and murder of a child, or the long and painful death of a kind and gentle person."[120] This question says nothing about God, but everything about human beings. It is up to each of us to learn to believe and put full trust in God.

We may not understand why, but we can trust in God's love and mercy and goodness. Jesus Christ has demonstrated God's love and mercy to us. If you put your faith and trust in Him, "you will not fear the terror of night, nor the arrow that flies by day."[121]

We have been given the promise that Christ will strengthen us when we rely on Him. Without being faced with challenges greater than what we could endure purely through our own strength, we would have no use for a Savior. The most difficult tests in life lead us to humility, which teaches us to rely on divine assistance.

Jeffrey R. Holland reflects that. "...It ought to be a matter of great doctrinal consolation to us that Jesus, in the course of the Atonement, experienced all of the heartache and sorrow, all of the disappointments and injustices that the entire family of man had experienced and would experience from Adam and Eve to the end of the world in order that we would not have to face them so severely or so deeply. However heavy our load might be, it would be a lot heavier if the Savior had not gone that way before us and carried that burden with us and for us.

"Yet in the cold, lonely hours in Liberty Jail Joseph said, 'Let us do all we can *and do it cheerfully.*' And then we can justifiably turn to the Lord, wait upon His mercy, and see His arm revealed in our behalf. What a magnificent attitude to maintain in good times or in bad, in sorrow or in joy!"[122]

Many of Christ's followers including His apostles and other historical figures who have suffered in the name of God have experienced great trials, horrendous persecution, and even death. They each needed to gain the testimony that the grace of Christ is sufficient to cover their pain and suffering, sufficient to transform them, and sufficient to help everyone as long as that transformation process takes place. Each of us must do the same in our own lives. When we come to this understanding, all we might experience can be put in the proper perspective.

Brad Wilcox explained that the scriptures teach us to rely solely on "the merits, and mercy, and grace of the Holy Messiah."[123] "Wherefore, how great the importance to make these things known unto the inhabitants of the earth, that they may know that there is no flesh that can dwell in the presence of God, save it be through the merits, and mercy, and grace of the Holy Messiah, who layeth down his life according to the flesh, and taketh it again by the power of the Spirit, that he may bring to pass the resurrection of the dead, being the first that should rise."[124] When we can learn to rely on God and His promises, no amount of earthly suffering can separate us from God's blessings.

Thus it was with Melodee. Whenever Mel became frustrated in her suffering or ever questioned whether God loved her or simply left her alone to suffer, she simply had to look for all the evidence in her life and in the world around that God is real and does not leave us comfortless. When we understand that we are never alone, that there is one who truly understands, our perspective on suffering can shift into using the strength of the Lord to overcome.

Chapter Sixteen

MIRACLES

WE SUFFER TO ALLOW GOD TO PERFORM MIRACLES

"BAD DAYS COME TO AN END...FAITH ALWAYS TRIUMPHS AND...HEAVENLY PROMISES ARE ALWAYS KEPT."

~JEFFREY R. HOLLAND

Miracles testify of God, as their occurrence is often striking and unexplainable by science. Miracles come when we least expect, and in response to great faith or for the convincing of unbelievers in the validity of God. This has often been the case in scriptural accounts:

Moses parting the red sea.

Manna from heaven.

Jesus causing the deaf to hear and the blind to receive their sight.

Jesus raising the dead.

There are countless miraculous stories in the scriptures, and often the greatest suffering precedes the most astonishing miracles. It would seem that God has the power to prevent all suffering in this world, but without true burdens to ease, his greatest blessings would not stand out in stark contrast. If there were no one in need of saving, there would be no one to save. Many suffer so that God's miracles can stand out in the chaos of this world.

In celebrating her own battle to overcome cancer and the miracle of remission, Melodee was often faced with doubters and resentment. Some asked questions like:

"Why didn't God heal me?"

"What about the times when God makes us wait for the miracles?"

"What if the miracles we pray for are not the ones answered?"

"How can God truly be all-powerful if He allows some to suffer and die, without stepping in to save?"

"Does God love some more than others?"

When describing the healing power of remission as a miracle in "winning against cancer," one woman responded, "What does it mean to 'win' against cancer. When you use that language, it implies those who die from cancer have lost, that they have not won the battle. It's insensitive to others to call remission a miracle."

The response to this line of questioning becomes its own form of miracle. This thinking is finite, assuming that God is not omniscient, omnipotent, and omnipresent. Through suffering, we are being led to the miracle of understanding the purpose of this life. If some die from suffering, while others are healed, hope is not lost. Those who pass from mortality with the understanding of God have still won the battle. The battle is not cancer; it is of overcoming trials and proving faithful. All can overcome by understanding that we "win" through becoming whole.

Becoming whole involves more than mortal existence; it extends into eternity, if we will but let our hearts be broken and repaired. Dying does not mean losing, for death frees the mortal body from pain; living does not equate winning, unless those who are blessed to continue in mortality use that miraculous opportunity and mission to witness to others that God is not dead.

While Melodee suffered through her battle with cancer, hoping for the miracle of healing, her husband Stephen also suffered. He stayed by her side through the lowest valleys and the highest peaks. He continues to experience the journey of trying to find the miracles in their lives. Some thoughts from Stephen:

"The worst time of my life was watching Melodee suffer through cancer. I thought a cancer diagnosis was bad and scary the first time, but now it's beyond devastating. The number one question you want answered is 'why?' 'Why is this happening to us? Why now? Why at all?' But, 'why' is the one question you know you may never get an answer to.

"Cancer and other challenges that seem to never end are hard. It feels as if you'll never get through. It becomes such a tough burden, one she'll carry for the rest of her life and one I'll have to carry after she's gone. When she suffers I suffer. When we suffer the whole family suffers. When the family suffers everyone around us suffers. Suffering is shared.

"It gets tough when you see someone you love have a disease. The illness takes them and changes them into someone you've never seen. At times, they become someone you have never known. You feel badly for them. Physically, they don't look the same. They can't do the things they normally could do. I used to be able to say, 'My wife is going to stay home with the children and do X or Y, and I'll work.' Now, she no longer can. A lot of the responsibilities that used

to be hers fall on me, in addition to the ones I already had. The illness can also change a person emotionally, alter their personality at times, and it's hard to witness because you know that person would not be acting that way if it weren't for their disease or the effects of it.

"Looking back, many of the days start to run together. After dealing with something for so long, it gets harder and harder to pinpoint exact examples of my suffering. I can't remember exact days, but I remember the feelings I had at certain times. I remember working the hardest 12-hour shift and coming home exhausted. I wouldn't come home to what I expected. Looking around, I could see that nothing had been done because Mel had been in bed all day. After working all day, I'd then have to make dinner and take care of the boys. This is all stuff I wasn't used to doing on a day-to-day basis, but then I HAD to do it. This stuff got tiring. I feel like I know a little bit about what being a single parent is like. It's hard. There's a reason there should be a mom and a dad in a household because it's nearly impossible for one person to do it all.

"It's also hard for me to express my feelings about all of this. I don't want to come across as someone who's crying and down all the time, when I am not the one who is actually going through the disease. At times, I don't want to say how I really feel or what I am really thinking because I don't want people to judge. I feel like others would assume that I am a jerk for complaining and that instead of feeling sorry for myself, I should be glad I'm not the one suffering. They don't always see that I am suffering, too. So, I just keep my mouth shut. I can keep stuff inside. I can, but I can also see how people snap or break because they can't keep it all inside. People just snap because they have to in order to get a break from the stress. So many times during Mel's battle, we would see how the patients' loved ones would leave; many women were divorced or newly single because the effects of living with cancer were too much to take.

"I get it, and I can see where some of these guys are coming from. There were days (and continue to be some) when I needed to get out-not out of the relationship, but out of the house and away from it all for a while. I needed time for me, when I didn't have to think about cancer or do anything other than relax and clear my head because I have all of this extra work and responsibilities thanks to my wife's limitations. Most of the time, she gets all the attention, but there were days when I just needed to take time for me. Granted, there's not much of it because most of the time I'm always concerned about my sick wife and my three boys who can't live without me. There would be times when I would reach my limit and say, 'I've got to get out for a little while. I need to go to a movie or have my brother come down and go play video games, play golf, go watch sports, or just hang out.' 'Me Time' gets me through. I learned that I have got to take time for myself in order to be strong enough to not snap, to be able to stay supportive when it's hard.

"Some of the frustration for me is in our relationship, as well. There are so many days when she has been sick or healing or weak or tired, for all the right reasons. At the same time, I feel so bad for Mel that she has lost a lot of what makes her feel beautiful, as well as most of the feeling and sensation in areas of her body involved in that relationship, too. This affects her both physically and emotionally, which adds to the burden and alters the level of intimacy we had before cancer. Even though this disease has affected me personally, it is so difficult to witness those physical changes and know that there is nothing that I can do to bring things back to where they used to be. I feel like she can never feel any pleasure out of our relationship because she has no sensation, and that is a great burden to me, as her partner. I feel selfish and don't *want intimacy to be so one-sided. And, I don't want her to feel burdened or like any of this is her fault or changes at all the way I feel about her.*

"Yes, her body looks different, but the reconstruction looks pretty close to what she had before and feels very similar. The biggest change is getting used to seeing her scars. That's what is different. Her abdominal scar is very noticeable; it's so big, and she can't hide it.

"It's hard to explain my exact feelings about her 'new' body because none of this changes her; the person I love. Also, I am used to seeing surgical scars from my profession. So, when I see Mel's scar, I don't look at it and say, 'That's hideous! I never want to see it'! It's just not what I'm used to seeing on Mel. It's an awful scar, a scarring reminder of a terrible time. But, I love her. I have never thought about leaving her, not even a little bit. A part of me does understand why people do leave, and I would never ask, 'How could you leave?' or 'How could they do that to her at such a difficult time?' I don't judge because I've lived it. I could see how someone could leave if they haven't completely covenanted to stay together and don't love someone one hundred percent. I love Mel beyond that, and cancer only made that more clear.

"I've learned that when you have a family, it's important to have two people who want to work at it together. I've lived through the stress of basically only having one person capable of fulfilling both roles, and I see why a partnership is so vital to success. It's too difficult with just one person to do everything. I don't know how people do it for years, after years, after years. I know I could be a single parent, and most likely will have to at a time in the future, but I know I would need help. I'd need the support of my family or I'd have to pay someone to clean my house or help raise my

children. I've learned that you can't do everything by yourself; you have to have someone help you.

"I've learned about the importance of having the service of others. My testimony of service has increased, both of giving service and being able to receive it. I absolutely know how important the help of others has been and how much it has meant to me and my family. Especially at difficult times, service is essential.

"I think my testimony on service increased, but I think my testimony on church and God has been basically what it was before cancer. I know having faith in God and following Him is right, but going through something like cancer changes your perspective. It's the right thing to attend church meetings and be active, but being active doesn't equal having a testimony. Especially during cancer, we had to adjust our lives to do what was best for our family. There was basically a full year when it was impossible for us to attend church, as Melodee and our family had to cut down on exposure to germs that would be hard on her weakened immune system. Maybe other people thought we didn't believe and that cancer made us not want to go to church. It didn't change our faith in God, but it added some limitations on what worshipping looked like. Even now, if there is a day when Mel is just so exhausted and she needs time to rest, we will stay home.

"I feel like people annoy me more than ever before. I get frustrated with people who complain about stupid stuff to me. I feel like responding, 'Oh my gosh! If {that} was my only problem, life would be great!' If people are complaining about little stuff now, they don't understand that life can get MUCH harder in a snap. I try not to argue with people over the small stuff. I don't have time for that. Life is too short. There is too much stuff going on for me to get upset at people over little things.

"I worry about our boys. They are innocent, yet they are going to have to suffer through all of this. They will still have to suffer in the future. I feel like the Lord has blessed us now that Mel's alive, but she's not cured. She will never be cured. However, God blesses our kids. I'll be able to look back in many years to come and see more of the many ways that they have been blessed. The Lord will step in and bless the boys wherever I can't. He will do it through other people or in ways I can't understand because I can't be there all the time. Now, our boys might not have their mom in the future, but I know the Lord will make up the difference. That is something I have prayed for. Our children have no earthly idea what it will be like in the future and what they will have to go through. I worry about them, but I also know that they are resilient.

"The hardest thing for me by far was finding out when cancer came back the second time. We did everything we were supposed to do! She was supposed to live longer, but instead we got no break, no relief. The first time we were told, 'You're going to make it if you do what we tell you. It will be a year and a half of hell, and then you'll be fine.' Sure, we had one-year of remission before cancer came back. A year sounds like a long time, but in reality, we had NO RELIEF. In that year, we moved to a new place, and I took a new job. Nothing about that was restful. We were told Mel would be fine, but she wasn't fine. She'll never be fine. I've watched her go through this already, and the second time is worse. We now know her time is limited. Before, we had hope that she could beat it. Now, there is very little hope. The only hope is for a few more years with us. Maybe it will be five years, instead of two. And, if we make it to five years, maybe it will be a few more. But, her life is now on short term. This disease will kill her. But, she's a fighter. She seems to have done really well through this struggle, a lot better than many other people would.

"Cancer came back a lot quicker or faster than it ever should have, so I don't feel that Mel has experienced this great miracle. However, I am not saying that little miracles didn't happen and don't continue to happen along the way. We found cancer a lot sooner than we probably would have because of her fall. Our family has been blessed to have come through this cancer twice and still be together. Her body has not made a miraculous turnaround, and it has definitely been more suffering than surviving. There have been little things that have helped us all make it through. She's the miracle.

"When you go through hard things, you have to ask yourself, 'Are you going to follow God or not?' That's the question of life. When you ask, 'What is the test?" that's the answer. God will do it to all of us. That's the test. He says, 'I'm going to put you through this. It's going to be hard. You're going to suffer. And, you're going to do one of two things; you're either going to follow me or you're not.' When life is hard and we are tested, that seems to be when everyone questions themselves. Questioning is normal. That's God's plan. That's the test. That's the fork in the road. God will purposely put you in a situation [or several] when you have to decide which way you will go and what you are going to do when the path is not easy. I have gone through some bad times, and there are still times I question God, but I know that I am blessed. Maybe someday I'll get to that fork in the road and see that it becomes easier, and I don't have to question all the time. I don't believe that God is punishing us through anything we've done or haven't done. It's part of the test, not punishment. I feel like this trial has been the complete opposite of punishment, for we have been so blessed. Even though we already beat cancer once, it's back, but this is just still part of the test. We thought we were done, but Stage 4 is perhaps that extra bonus question on the last page of the exam.

"The hardest thing overall is seeing what cancer has done to Melodee. It has changed her. It has changed her whole appearance. From her head to her toes, there are a hundred little things cancer has done to her, to her mind, and to her body. I have not enjoyed watching the pain; I hate it. There is no relief. She feels good only for a week or two each month, but we have been strengthened to get through this.

"I don't know whether Melodee being cancer free is a 'miracle.' It could just be the medicine working the way it should. I have a hard time seeing the small things as 'miracles,' but I'm learning to be grateful for every day we have together. I guess you get to a point where you understand that every moment is truly a blessing. I am most grateful that Mel's still here. She's still making it day by day, and we are still fighting this. She is still able to do some of the things that she truly enjoys and she can still be a normal mother and wife. Those things are miracles today, compared with what we were facing during chemo. Part of the miracle in my life is God helping me learn to recognize all the blessings as miracles."

"I have learned most of all that you have to enjoy every single day you are given. You need to enjoy life, even as difficult as it can be at times. Life is way too short to put things off until the future, to procrastinate. Yes, you need to plan and prepare and save for the future, but not at the expense of making memories and enjoying life in the present. If you go through life putting off goals or telling yourself, 'I don't have time or money or means to do X or Y now. I'll wait until I'm older,' you might miss out. If you procrastinate your joy and your experiences until a future day, that day may never come. What are you going to do then? See all the sights and live all the dreams by yourself? You want to see and do these things with someone you love, so don't put it off. Live your dreams one day at a time.

"I have had a lot of questions, but I have never questioned God's love. And, I have never questioned my love for Mel."

We often expect miracles to be grand, amazing, undeniable proof that God exists and is in control. The miracles we don't always see are those small changes that happen each day, the tender mercies that keep us safe in our day-to-day lives. We want to complain and curse God when bad things happen, but if nothing bad ever happened, there would be no need for miraculous change.

"Faith precedes the miracle,"[125] and miracles most often occur "after the trial of faith." If hardships and trials were not a part of mortality, the miraculous healing of such suffering would lose its effectiveness. There would be no need for the power to save, no prayers for blessings of healing, no humility of man's nothingness, no success in being rescued from destruction. There must be an opposition in all things.[126] Without the storm, we could not have adequate gratitude for the calm. Man needs suffering to truly appreciate the serene.

◌𝒫Chapter Seventeen𝒞◌

PEACE

WE SUFFER TO ACCEPT MORTALITY AND FIND PEACE IN WHAT IS TO COME

"I USED TO THINK OF DIVINE PUNISHMENT AS DANTE'S HELL. NOW I THINK OF IT MORE LIKE THE SEPARATION FROM GOD."

~BILLY GRAHAM

There is no escaping death. All who have ever lived and will ever be born will one day die. In the meantime, life is full of challenges. "Many are the afflictions of the righteous: but the Lord delivereth him out of them all."[127] The only promise to help us through the suffering, especially the kind that can lead to the end of mortality, is peace, aid, and strength from above.

For years before, one of Mel's biggest fears had been enduring the death of her husband or children. Now, she was faced with leaving them behind, and it nearly broke her heart to think of being the cause of her greatest fear playing out in their lives. There seemed to be no way to accept this fear, no way to overcome the crushing dread. One day she received an email from an acquaintance at church. It was the start of the peace she needed, one that would drive out fear.

Melodee,

I have been hesitating to write or talk to you about this, but I wanted to let you know that I have a different perspective than many on the cancer battle you are fighting. My mom died from breast cancer when I was seven (almost eight). I was the youngest of three boys. My dad stayed single for almost eight years after her death and raised us (and did a great job given the circumstances). So, I know a little about what happens from a kid's perspective. I am hoping and praying you have ten to fifteen years instead of the three to five average. While my mom was not on this side of the veil for my baptism, graduations, marriage etc., she was/is on the other side of the veil, and I believe she was able to see these events. I also believe she was still mothering and protecting me from the other side. I don't think we fully understand all that our relatives on the other side do to protect us. I encourage you to fight the good fight against this cancer. That in itself will be a legacy to leave your boys.

This message was an answer to a prayer. Whenever Melodee pondered the thought of leaving her children without a mother, she could not hold back the tears. Now, she began to cry tears of relief, of happiness, and of understanding that she could continue to be a mother from the other side, an angel watching over and protecting her boys throughout their lives. Although Mel still felt sad for her family, she did not need to fear death. Death was just another part of life. Sure, there would be grief and sorrow for those she would leave behind. However, when Melodee reached the point in her journey when she was close to death, experiencing the greatest suffering from cancer, her loved ones would plead with God to "ease her pain," or "release her from this suffering." So often she had heard phrases like, "at least he is no longer suffering" or "she is in a better place" when referring to someone who had recently passed from this life. Why would those phrases exist about the next life if it were not truly better? Mel understood, like never before, that suffering was an earthly principle; she was meant for a better place.

After this tender mercy, when sadness or the fear of death and of what she would miss, this hymn came to her mind:

FEAR NOT, I AM WITH THEE; OH, BE NOT DISMAYED,

FOR I AM THY GOD AND WILL STILL GIVE THEE AID.

I'LL STRENGTHEN THEE, HELP THEE, AND CAUSE THEE TO STAND, ...

UPHELD BY MY RIGHTEOUS, OMNIPOTENT HAND.[128]

This hymn and the corresponding scripture reminded Mel that she need not fear--not death, not hardships nor loss, not anything of this world. Neither should she linger in despair or discouragement. She reminded herself to keep holding onto faith in Christ, for he will never leave anyone alone and will provide the strength needed to withstand any trial. "Be strong and of a good courage, fear not, nor be afraid ... for the Lord thy God ... will not fail thee, nor forsake thee."[129] We need not fear, for we are never alone. We need simply call upon the Lord--in times of need and in times of thanksgiving--and He will hear and answer. As the scriptures say, "I sought the Lord, and he heard me, and delivered me from all my fears."[130]

Mel could feel peace. The Lord would hear her prayers, as well as the prayers of others on her behalf. She was coming to understand that, "Healing blessings come in many ways, each suited to our individual needs, as known to Him who loves us best. Sometimes a 'healing' cures our illness or lifts our burden. But sometimes we are 'healed' by being given strength or understanding or patience to bear the burdens placed upon us. The healing power of the Lord Jesus Christ—whether it removes our burdens or strengthens us to endure and live with them like the Apostle Paul—is available for every affliction in mortality." [131]

True healing, being made whole, can only be felt through the process of suffering. It is through pain and anguish that we see the flaws of this world and begin to understand that we were all meant for a better place.

Everyone on this earth must discover his or her mission in life. Every single person that has ever lived and ever will live on this earth will suffer. In fact, all have been diagnosed with a terminal illness: "MORTALITY." Death is inevitable, but often the path toward mortality teaches us to long for the "better place," so often promised.

When we look around this world, it is easy to question, "Why do bad things happen to people who seem undeserving of them?" or "Why does God allow good things to happen to bad people?" Romans 5:8 declares, "But God demonstrates his own love for us in this: While we were still sinners, Christ died for us." Despite the evil, wicked, sinful nature of the people of this world, God still loves us. He loved us enough to die for us. Because He has walked the path before, the best way to learn to accept and rejoice in the trials of this world is to "trust in the LORD with all your heart and lean not on your own understanding; in all your ways acknowledge Him…" In doing this, we can all experience how He can make each of our "paths straight." [132] Although none of us is perfect, through this straight path God has laid out for us, we will be forgiven and promised an eternal home in heaven. What we really deserve is hell. What we are given is eternal life in heaven if we come to Christ in faith. [133]

In order to understand the path laid out on our behalf and the suffering that Jesus endured, we must imagine gathering all the pain, sufferings, hurts, disappointments and sins of every person who has lived, is currently living and will ever live, and heaping them upon Him. One can appreciate the sufferings that individuals go through in their individual capacities, but it is impossible to imagine one individual taking upon himself the sufferings of all mankind. That was Jesus' calling. He understood mortality and suffered that we all might grasp the finite nature of this earth and become willing to trade it in for eternity.

As Jesus prayed in the Garden of Gethsemane, He began to tremble because of the pain. An angel came to strengthen Him. He suffered so much that he sweat drops of blood. He was suffering for all of our sins so that we can be forgiven if we repent. A doctor's version of the physical changes that occurred in Jesus' body during the atonement can be found in *A Physician's View of the Crucifixion of Jesus Christ* by Dr. C. Truman Davis. The graphic imagery might give greater appreciation for this level of suffering and bring to light the gratitude each of us might gain in understanding that no trial we experience will equal His level of anguish. The scriptures were kind to shield us from the explicit details of the suffering that truly occurred.

The physical trauma of Christ's suffering unfolds as Luke the physician relates, "And being in agony he prayed more earnestly: and his sweat was as it were great drops of blood falling down to the ground."[134] Hematohidrosis is a rare condition in which a human being sweats blood. Though rare, this condition is well documented. Under great emotional stress, tiny capillaries in the sweat glands can break, thus mixing blood with sweat. Jesus Christ experienced hematohidrosis while praying in the garden. This process alone could have produced marked weakness, and possibly shock. The emotional trauma for Christ must have been infinite in application and infinite in stress.

It has been emphasized that Jesus' most challenging experience came in Gethsemane. In 1982, Marion G. Romney observed that Jesus suffered "the pains of all men, which he did, principally, in Gethsemane, the scene of his great agony was equivalent to the cumulative burden of all men, in Gethsemane that He descended below all things so that all could repent and come to Him"[135]

Christ not only suffered physical pain, he endured emotional stress, as well. He was betrayed by those who loved Him most. The kiss from Judas sealed His fate. Not only was Jesus betrayed by Judas, he was denied by his disciples. "Then took they him, and led *him,* and brought him into the high priest's house. And Peter followed afar off. And when they had kindled a fire in the midst of the <u>hall</u>, and were set down together, Peter sat down among them. But a certain maid beheld him as he sat by the fire, and earnestly looked upon him, and said, This man was also with him. And he denied him, saying, Woman, I know him not. And after a little while another saw him, and said, Thou art also of them. And Peter said, Man, I am not. And about the space of one hour after another confidently affirmed, saying, of a truth this *fellow* also was with him: for he is a Galilaean. And Peter said, Man, I know not what thou sayest. And immediately, while he yet spake, the cock crew. And the Lord turned, and looked upon Peter. And Peter remembered the word of the Lord, how he had said unto him, Before the cock crow, thou shalt deny me thrice. And Peter went out, and wept bitterly." It was too late for Peter. Despite the many hours that he spent with Jesus, despite the many miracles that he witnessed and despite the love, which Jesus showed to Peter, he could not support him in the end.[136]

The horrible mob beating occurred a second time - by a band of Roman soldiers. According to Dan Corner,[137] "To state that Jesus was *flogged* is to say that he was beat bloody with a whip with nine lashes that had sharp objects at the end of the lashes to bruise and tear the flesh. Also, it was not the Jews who flogged Jesus. If it had been, they would have been restricted to only 39 lashes. Instead, it was the Roman soldiers who were not under any Scriptural regulation for this kind of punishment. They could have far exceeded the number of blows the Jews would have given. Sometimes *flogging* alone would kill the victims. Jesus was beaten and disfigured beyond recognition. Of all the clear Scriptures already cited which show the terrible way the Lord Jesus was treated, none are more descriptive in an overall way than the following prophecy: "As many were astonished at thee; his visage was so marred more than any man, and his form more than the sons of men."[138] Many die from scourging alone, but Jesus rose from the sufferings of the scourge that he might die upon the cruel cross of Calvary.

Along with the physical beatings Jesus went through, there was also the mockery and insults from various evil people at different times. "All they that see me laugh me to scorn: they shoot out the lip, they shake the head, saying, He trusted on the Lord that he would deliver him: let him deliver him, seeing he delighted in him."[139]

"And they spit upon him, and took the reed, and smote him on the head. And after that they had mocked him, they took the robe off from him, and put his own raiment on him, and led him away to crucify *him.*"[140] Jesus carried his own cross until he collapsed from the weight and pain and mounting agony of it all. "And as they came out, they found a man of Cyrene, Simon by name: him they compelled to bear his cross."[141] When it actually became time for Jesus to carry his own cross to Calvary, he had already been up all night and endured multiple brutal beatings and a flogging. With the pain, loss of blood and lack of sleep, the Lord was in a severely weakened physical state. He started carrying the cross but was unable to carry the heavy weight under those circumstances. In addition, Jesus fell while trying to carry the cross, which means that dirt must have also covered his bloody and bruised body. This only added to the horrible sight he was to look upon at this point and as he hung from the cross dying.

Finally, on a hill called Calvary—outside Jerusalem's walls—while helpless disciples looked on and felt the agonies of near death in their own bodies, the Roman soldiers laid Christ upon the cross. "And when they were come unto a place called Golgotha, that is to say, a place of a skull, They gave him vinegar to drink mingled with gall: and when he had tasted *thereof,* he would not drink."[142] With great mallets they drove spikes of iron through his feet and hands and wrists. Truly he was wounded for our transgressions and bruised for our iniquities.

Then the cross was raised that all might see and gape and curse and deride. They cast lots.[143]

Jesus was alone. Judas betrayed him, the Eleven denied him, and the Father forsook him. "My God, my God, why hast thou forsaken me? *Why art thou so* far from helping me, *and from* the words of my roaring?"[144] About the ninth hour Jesus cried out in a loud voice, *"Eloi, Eloi, lama sabachthani?"*—which means, "My God, my God, why have you forsaken me?"[145]

At any time during this process, Jesus had the power to stop his suffering. If He had chosen not to complete His mission, for fear of pain, then all of mankind would be lost. His days of mortality ended; He died. Yet, three days after his death on the cross, Jesus rose from the grave. He had conquered death, and we have the same hope. Mortality will end for each of us, but the tests and trials are teaching us to yearn for something more. Suffering can show us the imperfections of this earth and promise the hope for a better life hereafter.

✒Conclusion✑

"IF THERE IS A MEANING IN LIFE AT ALL, THEN THERE MUST BE A MEANING IN SUFFERING. SUFFERING IS AN INERADICABLE PART OF LIFE, EVEN AS FATE AND DEATH. WITHOUT SUFFERING AND DEATH HUMAN LIFE CANNOT BE COMPLETE."

~VIKTOR FRANKL, MAN'S SEARCH FOR MEANING

The stories of Melodee, Joan, Beth, Craig, and Kimberly are only a small example of the spectrum of suffering. Storms will come to everyone, but there is sunshine to be seen as well. There is beauty to be found, even in the darkest nights.

"The most beautiful people are those who have known defeat, known suffering, known struggle, known loss, and have found their way out of the depths. These persons have an appreciation, sensitivity, and an understanding of life that fills them with compassion, gentleness, and a deep loving concern. Beautiful people do not just happen." [146]

Melodee is not convinced that she has become more beautiful through the process of beating cancer twice, but she has grown and changed and learned a few things along the way. She says, "Cancer is awful. It truly is like walking around with a dark cloud that never disperses, one you can never predict when and where or how strongly it will again strike. The treatment of cancer is even more ugly. How is it that with so much money and so many hours and brilliant minds dedicated to the study of cancer and of finding a cure, we have yet to discover a treatment that will eradicate cancer from a body without practically destroying and killing a patient in the process?

"Stage 4 cancer is terrifying in the fact that from the first diagnosis you are told, 'There is no cure.' Knowing a disease is terminal and will most likely kill you slowly is a true test of faith. Without a belief in something and in someone greater than yourself, it would become pointless to press forward, only to know your illness will one day take your life. This experience seems to come as closely as I can imagine to that most basic leap of faith it takes to initially believe without a doubt that God exists and that He knows you and loves you. In the same way that science has not been able to completely cure cancer, there is no way to scientifically prove the existence of God. The only way to prove His reality in your life is to suffer in a small way compared to how He has and feel the strength that can come by relying on that faith. Learning to press forward with a belief that everything will turn out, one way or another, is how you beat cancer (or anything with which you might struggle.)

"I am not sure how long I will be in remission, or how many times I will be able to keep fighting until I either have no more strength or until there are no other treatments to try. I do know, however, that I am alive today, and I know that it was through the hand of God and through His tender mercies that I continue to survive through my struggles. The fact that we found cancer so quickly was miraculous. My body responding to the first treatment is a blessing. I have also been blessed with strength through the suffering.

"I have come to believe that I will continue to survive as long as 1) There are lessons I still need to learn in mortality and 2) God has a purpose for me to fulfill on this earth. When my time is up, I will have gained the education I came here to receive and will have completed my earthly mission. If my time in mortality is cut short, that is not the end of my battle. I will continue to fight on the other side—to fight for those I love, to help them stay faithful and strong until we can be reunited once more. I will watch over them, help them to understand that it is through our suffering that we learn to truly survive, and remember always,

EVERYTHING WILL BE ALRIGHT IN THE END; IF IT'S NOT ALRIGHT, IT'S NOT THE END. [147]

"Jesus lost all his glory so that we could be clothed in it. He was shut out so we could get access. He was bound, nailed, so that we could be free. He was cast out so we could approach. And Jesus took away the only kind of suffering that can really destroy you: that is being cast away from God. He took it all so that all the suffering that comes into your life will only make you great. A lump of coal under pressure becomes a diamond. And the suffering of a person in Christ only turns you into somebody gorgeous.'"[148]

Acknowledgements

The authors acknowledge the infinite blessings of God in our lives. His love and blessings allow us to see the silver linings through each of our personal storms.

We also acknowledge those who shared their stories of suffering in order to help others learn from their struggles. They are the embodiment of love by sharing their story and being the means of helping others through their mortal suffering.

Thanks to Jefra Rees and Brandon Boulter who devoted precious time in editing the draft; to our loving spouses for their love and support; and to James Barrett, our photographer, whose keen photographic eye captured our vision of suffering.

The names of all the persons whose stories are told here have been changed to protect their privacy. The names of all the medical professionals have also been changed. Only the names of Melodee and her family members are true identities.

The Authors

ℭ𝒫Tom Baca℞

THE AUTHOR

Tom attended New Mexico State University, the University of New Mexico, and the University of Minnesota, where he graduated with a MPH in environmental science. He married Patricia Gibson of Quanah Texas and raised two children. They have five grandkids and two great grandkids. They have been married for 48 years. He is an author - *The Environmental Consequences of Nuclear Disarmament*, and *In The Beginning Did God Create Man or Did Man Create God?*

Melodee Cooper
THE CANCER SURVIVOR

Melodee is a Texan by birth, a Texas Aggie by choice, the wife of a fellow Aggie, and the mother of three boys, who joined her family through the help of both modern science and divine intervention. A former elementary math and science teacher, she is now working as a stay-at-home mom, an amateur decorator, a crafter, a blogger, and a holiday enthusiast. On May 27, 2014, Mel added, "breast cancer survivor" to her bio. However, on July 30, 2015, cancer came back with a vengeance. As Melodee continues to fight Stage 4 breast cancer, she believes in miracles and hopes to share her faith with others.

Rachel Gardner
The Editor

Rachel Gardner grew up in Friona, Texas. After high school, she began studying at Texas A&M University where she graduated with a degree in anthropology. She has been a member of the Church of Jesus Christ of Latter-day Saints her whole life and has seen the blessings of God on many occasions. She hopes that the testimonies shared in this book will help the readers have faith and strength. "Can a woman forget her sucking child, that she should not have compassion on the son of her womb? Yea, they may forget thee, yet will I not forget thee. Behold, I have graven thee upon the palms of my hands; thy walls are continually before me."[149]

End Notes

[1] The Holy Bible, Containing the Old and New Testaments. New York: American Bible Society, 1962, Genesis 3:17

[2] Yahoo Answers Source: old doc

[3] Bertha Spafford Vester *Our Jerusalem: An American Family in the Holy City*, 1881-1949. Jerusalem: American Colony, 364 pp.

[4] Library of Congress Exhibition Overview. See also Yaakov Ariel & Ruth Kark *Messianism, Holiness, Charisma, and Community: The American-Swedish Colony in Jerusalem*, 1881-1933, *Church History*, 65(4), 641-657.

[5] Callister, Tad R. *The Inevitable Apostasy and the Promised Restoration*. Deseret Book, 2006.

[6] C.S. Lewis Quote

[7] Rabbi Harold Kushner, *When Bad Things Happen to Good People*, August 24, 2004

[8] Mark Twain Quote, Samuel Langhorne Clemens, better known by his pen name Mark Twain, was an American author and humorist. He is noted for his novels *Adventures of Huckleberry Finn* (1885), called "the Great American Novel," and *The Adventures of Tom Sawyer* (1876).

[9] Jen Hatmaker, *Why Does God Allow Pain and Suffering?* September 17, 2013

[10] James F Faust, *The Refiners Fire*, Ensign Magazine, April 1979,

[11] Dallin H. Oaks, *Adversity*, Ensign Magazine, January 17, 1995,

[12] Gawande, Atul. *Being Mortal: Medicine and What Matters in the End*. Waterville, ME: CenterPoint Publishing, 2014.

[13] Cushman, Stephen. "Lincoln's Gettysburg Address and Second Inaugural Address." The Cambridge Companion to Abraham Lincoln: 59-71

[14] The Holy Bible, Containing the Old and New Testaments, Authorized King James Version, Isaiah 45:6-7

[15] The Holy Bible, Book of Job

[16] James E. Faust, *The Refiner's Fire*, Ensign Magazine April 1979

[17] KJB, Isaiah 53:3-6

[18] Smith, Joseph. The Book of Mormon: An Account Written by the Hand of Mormon upon Plates Taken from the Plates of Nephi. Salt

Lake City, UT: Church of Jesus Christ of Latter-day Saints, Alma 7:11
[19] Ibid, 1 Nephi 11
[20] Dr. Jensen, *Words of Wisdom*, Ensign Magazine, April 2, 2015
[21] Dieter F. Uchtdorf, *The Attributes of Jesus Christ: Long Suffering and Patience.* Ensign Magazine March 2015
[22] Sheri L. Dew, *This is a test. It is only a test*, Ensign July 2000
[23] Smith, Joseph, and Joseph Smith. The Doctrine and Covenants of the Church of Jesus Christ of Latter-Day Saints ; The Pearl of Great Price. Salt Lake City, UT: Church of Jesus Christ of Latter-day Saints, 1979, Moses 1:39
[24] Thomas S. Monson, *Living The Abundant Life*, Liahona, January 2012
[25] The Book of Mormon, Alma 7:11-12
[26] The New Testament, Corinthians 13:2-3, Book of Mormon, Moroni 7:44, 46
[27] Mother Teresa Biography: AmericanCatholic.org
[28] Ibid
[29] Ibid
[30] President Dieter F. Uchtdorf, Contributed By Jason Swensen, Church News staff writer 5 December 2015
[31] Einstein Quote, Goodread
[32] Richard Paul Evans is an American author, best known for writing *The Christmas Box* and, more recently, the Michael Vey series.
[33] KJB, James 2:17
[34] Quan, The Quintessential Man, 10 Key Lessons In The Art Of Being Self-Reliant, May 14, 2015
[35] Ibid
[36] Michael C. Anthony, *Becoming a Sculpture*, Posted on December 10th, 2014
[37] Book of Doctrine and Covenents, 18:10
[38] KJB, 1 Cor 3:16
[39] Ibid, Matthew 10:30
[40] Ibid, Matt 10:28
[41] Ibid, Psalm 139:14
[42] Pearl of Great Price, Moses 1:4-5

[43] Richard T. Ritenbaugh, Are You Living the Abundant Life?, July 2005

[44] Joan felt that any other word would not be true to the nature of things as they were. Her mother, grandparents, aunts, and uncles all felt the black population was beneath them and had to be held in their place. The town that she grew up in still does not have any blacks living within the city limits and only a couple in the surrounding areas. The little town just south of where she was born still has no blacks at all. It is a black free zone that they are still proud to proclaim.

[45] Stanford rape story that appeared in USA Today on June 22, 2016

[46] John Bytheway, *Five Scriptures That Will Help Get You Get through Almost Anything,* September 2008

[47] KJB, Philippians 4:13

[48] Spencer W. Kimball, *Faith Precedes the Miracle*, September, 2001

[49] Clark Spencer Larsen, Bioarchaeology: Interpreting behavior from the human skeleton

[50] Sheri L. Dew is an American author, publisher, and president and chief executive officer of the Deseret Book Company

[51] Pearl of Great Price, Moses 1:39

[52] KJB, 1 Corinthians 10:13

[53] KJB, Psalms 43:6

[54] KJB, 1 John 4:16

[55] Ibid, 1 John 4:8

[56] Ibid, 2 Corinthians 12:10

[57] Missouri Executive Order 44

[58] Jeffrey R. Holland, *Lessons from Liberty Jail, Ensign, September 2009*

[59] Ibid

[60] Ibid

[61] Ibid

[62] Ibid

[63] Jeffrey R. Holland, *Lessons from Liberty Jail,* from a CES Fireside given on September 7, 2008, at Brigham Young University.

[64] World Health Organization, WHO Department on Immunization, Vaccines and Biologicals

[65] Mayo Clinic, Diseases and Conditions: Hodgkin's lymphoma
[64] Elder David A. Bednar, *"Bear Up Their Burdens with Ease,"* *Ensign*, May 2014, 90.
[67] Sidney Rigdon, Joseph Smith, *Lectures on Faith*, 68–70
[68] KJB , Isaiah 62:5; Matthew 22:1–14
[69] Henry B. Eyring, Quote
[70] Book of Mormon, 1 Nephi: 8
[71] Book of Mormon, Mosiah 3:19
[72] Ibid, 1 Nephi 2:10
[73] Ibid, 1 Nephi 31:20
[74] Shanker Vedantan, *Haiti: Natural Disasters and Religious*, Jan 20, 2010
[75] Ibid
[76] KJB, Mark 9:23
[77] Delbert L Stapley, *Using Our Free Agency*, April 1975 General Conference
[78] Ibid
[79] Ibid
[80] http://www.stevenshope.org
[81] Jessica Bosari ,*The financial and emotional cost of addiction on families*, Jun 19, 2012
[82] D&C, 88:6
[83] Elder Holland, Quote
[84] William J. Mahe ,*How addiction affects the family*, Published: 4th October, 2013
[85] Marni Low, *Addiction Treatment Methods, Living with Addiction*, Posted May 6, 2015
[86] *Ibid*
[87] Luke Gilkerson, *Porn's Impact on Aggressive Behavior*, Friday, December 3, 2010
[88] KJB, Proverbs 6:27
[89] Steve Watters, *Resisting the Power of Pornography*
[90] Jeffrey R. Holland *Inconvenient Messiah*, BYU Speeches, Feb 15, 1982
[91] KJB, John 14: 25-27
[92] Ibid, John 14:26
[93] Ibid, John 16:13

[94] Ibid, John 15:26

[95] Elder Robert D Hales, October 1998 Healing Soul and Body

　　[96] Elder Quentin L. Cook Personal　Peace: The Reward of Righteousness

[97] Dallin H Oaks, *He Heals the Heavy Laden*, October General Conference, October 2006
eals the Heavy Laden, October General Conference

[98] Kent F. Richards, *The Atonement Covers All Pain*, April 2011

[99] Ibid

[100] Henry B. Eyring, *Adversity*, April 2009. General Conference

[101] Kent F. Richards, *The Atonement Covers All Pain*, April 2011,General Conference

[102] Kent F. Richards, *The Atonement Covers All Pain*, April 2011,General Conference

[103] Sermons and Writings of Ezra Taft Benson, 217

[104] KJB, Matthew 13:16

[105] KJB, Job 1:1

[106] KJB, Job 2:10

[107] Ibid, Job 6:10

[108] Ibid, Job10:1

[109] Ibid, Job 16:20

[110] Ibid, Job 17:15

[111] Ibid, Job 23:10

[112] D&C 105:40

[113] François Rabelais was a major French Renaissance writer, physician, Renaissance humanist, monk and Greek scholar. He has historically been regarded as a writer of fantasy, satire, the grotesque, bawdy jokes and songs.

[114] Alma 30:44

[115] John Funk, RaptureReady.com Omniscient, Omnipresent, Omnipotent

[116] Elder M. Russell Ballard, Be Still, And Know That I am God, May 4, 2014

[117] KJB, Genesis 1-2

[118] Journal of Discourses - Volumes 5-6 The King Follett Sermon

[119] KJB, Isaiah 40:21

[120] Michael Coren, *Why Do Bad Things Happen to Good People?*
Posted July 17, 2012

[121] Ibid, Psalms 91:5

[122] Jeffrey R. Holland, Lessons from Liberty Jail, From a CES Fireside given on September 7, 2008, at Brigham Young University.

[123] *From a devotional address given at Brigham Young University on July 12, 2011.*

[124] Book of Mormon, 2 Nephi 2:8

[125] Spencer W. Kimball, *Faith Precedes the Miracle*

[126] Book of Mormon, 2 Nephi 2:11

[127] KJB, Psalm 34:19

[128] "How Firm a Foundation," Hymns, no. 85, see also Isaiah 41:10

[129] KJB, Deuteronomy 31:6

[130] Ibid, Psalm 34:4

[131] Dallin H. Oaks, "*He Heals the Heavy Laden*," Ensign, Nov. 2006, 5–6

[132] KJB, Proverbs 3:5-6

[133] Ibid

[134] Ibid, Luke 22:44

[135] Marion G Romney, Ensign 12, May 1982

[136] KJB, 22:54

[137] Dan Corner The *Crucifixion of Jesus*, Our Precious Lord and Savior

[138] KJB, Isa 52:14

[139] KJB, Psa 22:7-8

[140] Ibid, Matthew 27:30

[141] Ibid, St. Matt 27:32

[142] Ibid, Matthew 27:33

[143] Ibid, Mat 27:28-32

[144] Ibid, Psa 22:1

[145] Ibid, Mat 27:46

[146] Tentmaker quotes

[147] John Lennon Quotes, Quotable Quote

[148] 20 Quote from Walking with God through Pain and Suffering, Article by Tony Reinke

[149] Isaiah 49:15-16

CPSIA information can be obtained
at www.ICGtesting.com
Printed in the USA
LVOW03s1214290317

528893LV00001B/40/P